Peter Fox

The players' coach

By Graham Williams and Peter Lush

London League Publications Ltd

Peter Fox
The players' coach

A CIP catalogue record for this book is available from the British Library.

Published in June 2008 by:
London League Publications Ltd, P.O. Box 10441, London E14 8WR

ISBN: 978-1903659-39-7

Cover design by: Stephen McCarthy Graphic Design
                   46, Clarence Road, London N15 5BB

Layout: Peter Lush

Printed & bound by: Biddles Ltd
                     King's Lynn, Great Britain

Foreword

For anyone with roots in rugby league the name Fox is synonymous with sporting success. Two of the three famous brothers from the West Riding village of Sharlston, near Wakefield, won the Lance Todd Trophy for man-of-the-match performances in Challenge Cup Finals at Wembley. Neil, the youngest of the three, was a scoring machine whose record 6,220 points in his playing career is unlikely ever to be beaten. Don had some of the finest rugby skills, with both hands and feet, that I have ever seen and was rated by Alex Murphy as the best scrum-half he ever played against.

Alongside what the media termed as the two 'Fabulous Foxes', older brother Peter had a more modest playing career. But it was after he had retired from playing that he was to emerge as a highly successful coach for club and country, developing and honing the rugby skills of some of Britain's finest players.

I have absolutely no memory of the first time I met Peter Fox over 40 years ago, because I was knocked out in the match we were involved in and was taken to hospital. He was then coaching the Black Horse amateur team in Wakefield's Sunday League which was playing my own team, the Flanshaw Hotel. Many years later I played my last ever competitive match for Wakefield's Walnut Warriors with Peter as our coach. Away to Rossington, near Doncaster, I again ended up in hospital with serious concussion!

I have much clearer memories of his achievements coaching Bramley, my own team Wakefield Trinity, Featherstone Rovers and Bradford Northern, and particularly, of course, of his success with a Great Britain side which had been given little chance against the Australians in 1978. Throughout a marvellous coaching career Peter had the remarkable ability to motivate his players and get the best out of his sides.

Peter epitomises everything you might expect in a great rugby league character. 'Northern' was his club for a long time and no-one would have tampered with that great Bradford name while he was there. He is 'northern' to his roots with the richest of West Riding accents which so enhanced his summaries during local and national radio match commentaries. The occasional mispronunciation of overseas players – Vagana was always a problem – genuinely endeared him to his army of radio fans.

His sometimes controversial views on developments within the game and the abilities of individual players or coaches were the stuff of phone-ins and letters columns. Whether you agreed with Foxy or not, he was great value. And as an after-dinner speaker of great renown he encapsulated audiences with a rich array of marvellous rugby league stories.

But aside from the public figure, there is also the Peter Fox who would give up endless amounts of his own time to support rugby league at grassroots level. There is the Peter Fox who, without reward or publicity, has given so much back to the wonderful game that has been his life. This excellent book is a fitting tribute to one of the great names of rugby league who has made a massive contribution to the game at all levels over very many years.

David Hinchliffe

David Hinchliffe is a life-long Wakefield Trinity supporter and former amateur rugby league player. He was the Labour MP for Wakefield from 1987 to 2005 and secretary of the All-Party Parliamentary Rugby League Group for 17 years. He has written and co-written several books on rugby league and is a trustee of the Rugby League Benevolent Fund.

Introduction

Peter was involved in professional rugby league from 1953 for just under 50 years. During that time, there were enormous changes in rugby league. One of these was the development of professional coaches, involved in the tactics and strategies of the game.

When Peter turned professional to play for Featherstone Rovers, the coach's role was mainly to keep the team fit and organise training. Team selection was done by the club directors or a selection committee. Sometimes the coach would have some say, sometimes very little or even none at all. It is remarkable today to recall that when Peter was Great Britain coach in 1978, he still did not select the team.

Rugby league has often been a progressive sport, introducing innovations and practices that were then adopted by other sports. But in this area league was well behind association football, which – on Sir Alf Ramsey's insistence – gave responsibility for selecting the England team to the manager in 1963.

Peter's frustrating experience of working with the England and Great Britain selection committees are well outlined in this book. It is interesting to compare his record there with his one for Yorkshire, where he did pick the team, and had eight wins from eight matches. Playing with a team which he had not chosen, but could only organise and prepare, Peter achieved a great victory against the Australians in 1978. It was Britain's last test match win against the Australians for a decade.

Another measure of Peter's success was his consistency. Despite often coaching clubs who had less resources than their competitors, or had financial problems, only three times in 22 seasons when he coached a team for a complete season did his side finish in the bottom half of the table. A team of his was never relegated.

To take over at Featherstone in January 1971, with no previous coaching experience in the professional game, and to win the Challenge Cup within two years was a remarkable achievement. To take Bramley to promotion in less than a season was also outstanding.

Apart from his triumphs with Featherstone, Peter is most associated as a coach with Bradford Northern. The club are one of the sport's great names. But they have not always been successful. It is easy to forget, when Bradford have won so much in the Super League era, that the club went out of business in 1963, and had to be rebuilt from scratch to rejoin the league in 1964.

Peter's achievement in bringing the First Division title to Odsal in 1980 and 1981 was a huge one. The last time Northern had finished top of the table was in 1952, when they lost the Championship Final to Wigan. The 1980 title win was the club's first. Even the great Bradford teams of the immediate post-war era, when the Challenge Cup was won twice, never finished top of the table or won the Championship. The last time Northern had won a league title was in 1974, but that was in the Second Division.

To retain the title was also – at that time – unprecedented in the two division rugby league structure, when all the teams in the First Division played each other, unlike the set up with one division. Hull KR, Widnes and Wigan matched the feat later, and Wigan surpassed it, but that Wigan team were mainly full-time players, when most of the other teams were part-time. In Peter's time at Odsal all the top teams' players were part-time, which made for a more even contest.

Peter would say himself that he was not a great player. But what he learnt battling for Batley in the lower reaches of the league he applied as a coach, and managed to bring the best out of his players. Often in sport the most naturally talented players do not make the best coaches. Maybe success has often come easily to them, and they cannot understand why less talented players cannot carry out their instructions.

It is impossible to say who is the 'best' coach in British rugby league over the last 30 years; the period when the role of the coach developed into the one familiar to the game today. However, it can be said with some certainty that Peter's achievements in 24 years of coaching, when the resources he had available to him are taken into account, are hard to match.

Graham Williams and Peter Lush

Acknowledgements

A book like this is always a team effort. However, the main work on Peter's playing career, and work and family life was written by Peter Lush. Graham Williams took the major responsibility of covering Peter's coaching career, including extensive interviews with him.

First of all, we would like to thank Peter and Joan for their hospitality, and Peter's patience in answering innumerable questions about his lifetime's involvement in rugby league. Joan's memories of their family life, and the scrapbooks she kept of Peter's career over the years, were also very helpful.

Thank you to everyone who was interviewed for the book, to David Hinchliffe for his support and writing the foreword, and to Robert Gate for his help with statistics.

Photographs form an important part of any biography. We would like to thank everyone who provided photos for this book, including Peter Barnes, Harry Edgar (on behalf of *Rugby League Journal*), Robert Gate, David Williams and Sig Kasatkin (RLphotos.com), Graham Chalkley and Sharlston ARLFC and Neil Fox. Any photos that are not credited are from Peter's collection. No copyright has been intentionally breached, please contact London League Publications Ltd if you believe this has been the case. Some photographs were very old, we have reproduced them as well as we can. We would also like to thank the RFL, Wakefield Trinity Wildcats RLFC and Batley Bulldogs RLFC for permission to reproduce match programmes and other documents.

It is rare for a rugby league biography to include poetry. We would like to thank Saxon White Kessinger for permission to reproduce *The Indispensable Man*.

Simon Howard wrote a project on Peter's coaching career, and this was a useful source of reference material. Graham Chalkley checked our work on Peter's early days in Sharlston and his time with Sharlston ARLFC. The staff at the University of Huddersfield, Pontefract, Batley and Dewsbury Libraries, were all helpful in making arrangements for us to carry out research.

Behind the scenes at London League Publications Ltd, Dave Farrar gave encouragement and guidance, Michael O'Hare carried out his usual thorough sub-editing, Stephen McCarthy designed the jacket, and the staff at Biddles Ltd printed the book. Our thanks to all of them, without them no book would appear. Needless to say, any mistakes in the book are our responsibility. We hope you enjoy our work.

Graham Williams and Peter Lush
May 2008

Sharlston Dam – a place for Peter and his friends to
visit in the summer when he was growing up in Sharlston.

Sharlston Primary School today. Peter's early school days were spent here.
(Photo: Peter Lush)

Contents

Early days in rugby league

1946-47 Wakefield Technical College rugby league team: Back: Mr Swan, Wilkinson, Peter Fox, Jack Greaves, Phil Shillito, not known, Alan Davies, Brian Rimmington, Mr Woodcock; front: Don Metcalf, Ray Hepworth, Joe Snowdon, Spike O'Grady, Terry Ketloe, Edward Jackson, Jimmy Wood.

1948 Yorkshire Schoolboys trial match.
Players include: Alec Dick (back, 6th from right), D. Jefferson (middle, 7th from right), Peter Fox (middle, 3rd from right), Edward Jackson (front 6th from right), Jimmy Wood (front, 2nd from right).

1. Growing up in Sharlston

Travel a few miles east of Wakefield towards Featherstone and Pontefract and you come to Sharlston. Today it is a quiet, well-kept commuter village. But until 1993, when the pit closed, it was one of many similar small mining villages in both West Yorkshire and the coal producing areas in the north of England. Today, the only sign of the colliery is a memorial on Sharlston Common.

But over the years Sharlston has not produced only coal. For a village of less than 3,000 people, it has produced a remarkable number of rugby league players for both the professional and amateur games. Many started their careers with the famous Sharlston Rovers amateur team, playing on their Back o' t' Wall ground in the centre of the village. The distinctive name derives from a wall that ran alongside the ground by the main road through the village for many years.

Families have always played a big part in the club. Three names appear in the teamsheets generation after generation, in alphabetical order: Chalkley, Dooler and Lingard. All contributed players to the professional game, including Challenge Cup Finalists and, in Carl Dooler, a Lance Todd Trophy Winner in 1967.

But arguably the most famous rugby league family from Sharlston is the Fox family. Tommy Fox played for Featherstone Rovers in the 1930s, and subsequently for Sharlston Rovers. But it is Tommy's sons who made a huge contribution to British rugby league. Peter, the oldest, played for Sharlston Rovers and had a solid 13-year professional playing career with Featherstone Rovers, Batley, Hull KR, Hunslet and Wakefield Trinity. However, his greatest successes came as a coach, with a victory over the Australians for Great Britain, Challenge Cup wins, First Division championships and much more. Tommy's middle son, Don, was one of the best scrum-halves of his generation, winning Great Britain honours, and playing for Featherstone Rovers and Wakefield Trinity. Neil, the youngest, won every honour in the game, and is the world-record points scorer - his feat unlikely ever to be beaten. But while their stories have been told elsewhere, this is Peter's story, and it started in Sharlston on 30 March 1933, when Tommy Fox and his wife Stella welcomed their first baby into the world.

Tommy Fox came from Featherstone. He played for Featherstone Rovers from 1931 to 1935, mainly at loose-forward, making 26 first team appearances, scoring three tries. He then played as an amateur for Normanton. Before the war he got a job at the pit in Sharlston after he had stopped playing rugby league professionally. Following the Second World War he came out of retirement to help relaunch Sharlston Rovers, playing in their most famous match, a 12-7 Challenge Cup first round first leg victory over Workington Town in 1946. Sharlston lost the second leg and the tie 23-14 on aggregate. Apparently Workington were interested in signing Tommy, but at the age of 37 he decided against returning to the professional game and the upheaval of a move to Cumbria.

Peter remembers the Workington match and the crowd packed into the tiny Sharlston ground. He recalls Workington star Billy Ivison playing under an assumed name because he was on leave from the army. Ivison was injured early in the match, and sent Peter to buy cigarettes for him at a local shop. Ivison went on to be one of Workington's greatest players, with 385 appearances for the Cumbrians, and caps for Great Britain and England.

Workington lost in the second round at Wakefield Trinity. Peter recalls: "I went to Belle Vue with some pals to see the match because Herbert Goodfellow, our local hero in

Sharlston, was scrum-half for Trinity. They went all the way to Wembley, beating Wigan in the Final 13-12. A commentary on the Final was on the radio, and I listened to it with Barry Chalkley and Dennis Brown. When Billy Stott, Trinity's centre, kicked the winning goal, we ran into the street jumping for joy."

Peter did not know Tommy's father, who died young. He recalls: "My grandmother was on her own, I went to live with her for about a month when I was working in Wakefield, but I returned home because the travelling to and from work was too difficult. I had thought my dad would let me have a motor bike, but no way! She had a big family, and my dad had brothers and sisters. I used to go to Featherstone to visit relations regularly."

On his mother's side, the Schofield family, he remembers his grandfather who lived in Ellen Terrace, well: "My granddad would always be in his flat cap, white scarf, neat and tidy with a big grey moustache. He had an allotment opposite his house, and I used to help him with the vegetables. He used to come to the Working Mens' Club every Saturday morning. He would ask if I had any pocket money. I used to give him 1/- [5p] of my money and he used to bet on Templegate's double, from the *Daily Herald* for me. Years later I discovered what Templegate's double was. The bookie was in the ground behind the club. It was my granddad who first introduced me to gambling – he was a smashing fellow. He was not involved in rugby, but was a mate of Luke Nixon, who he said was the best scrum half from Sharlston, who played for York for a while." Stella Schofield was from Sharlston, and a rugby family. Her brother, Tom Schofield, played for Sharlston Rovers before the war.

Peter remembers growing up in the village: "I was born in Westfield Terrace – 'short street' as it was known. During the war we moved just across the way to 6, Albert Terrace, which was twice as long as 'short street'. Peter (who was my age), Ken and Dennis Chalkley lived at number 5. Dennis played at Wembley for Halifax in 1949. Joe Mullaney, who was our Don's pal, lived at number 4, and we had several other friends in the street.

"There was a patch of ground of around 40 square yards between the streets. We played both cricket and rugby there, picking teams from all the local kids. We were always very competitive.

"Don was born on 15 October 1935 and Neil on 4 May 1939. As they grew up, rugby soon became part of their lives. When we moved to the Working Mens' Club in 1945, I was 12, Don nine and Neil six. There was a patch of grass just behind our backyard where we would play rugby, two against one. I made them tackle me round the lower legs so they learnt good rugby techniques at an early age.

"As they grew older, they became more difficult to contain - they would run my tail off at times. So we would go to play on the rugby club field next to the club, for me to practice my goalkicking. I wouldn't let them place-kick the ball back to me, it took too long, so they would drop-kick it back over the posts. I think it stood them in good stead for their kicking skills later in life."

The local school was also a short walk away. Many of the rugby league players from Sharlston started their education there. "I went to school at five. I walked to school and started in the infants. Then it was Standard 1, 2, 3, 4 and 5, which was just below scholarship age, 10 or 11." Peter remembers Miss Bell who taught in Standard 2, and Miss Dennison, who taught Standard 5. "The latter was a disciplinarian. That influenced my approach to rugby – discipline, it governed everything I did. Sometimes there were fights with the other lads at school, everyone would make a circle with two in the middle fighting. One lad was a bit of a bully, but I stood up to him. Another was always in trouble, but his younger brother took me under his wing and helped me stand up for myself. The older brother and some other older boys used to make the little ones fight each other just for their fun. I wasn't 'cock of the school', but I could look after myself. I remember Joby Musgrave looked after Don and Neil at school. He used to help my mum and dad with stocktaking at the club.

"Mr Musgrave and Mr Lindop were teachers, who had come out of the forces: the RAF. Mr Lindop would come up and clip your lugs from behind if you misbehaved, but didn't use the cane. Mr Musgrave would jab you in the back with the knuckle of his finger, it made you gasp for breath. The head was Mr Day, followed by Mr Butterfield. You had to report to them for the cane – it was one or three on the hand. It wasn't used very much, all the boys respected the masters. It was a good school. At 11, the best three or four in the class would go for a scholarship for the grammar school. I took the scholarship test, but I didn't get into grammar school."

There was no organised sport at Sharlston School when Peter was there, mainly due to the war. However, village life offered many opportunities for sport and entertainment: "The cricket field was off Grime Lane. Then there was Sharlston dam, a big lake. In the hot summers we used to sit on the wall, and used to swim in the dam, diving off the wall. Sharlston Wood was at the back of the dam. The men had a gambling ring there, and we used to look out for the police for them.

"Every Sunday afternoon we played rugby on Sharlston village green. The men would come out of the WMC and play. That was where I first learnt to play in a team.

"In the wartime summers, when the clocks were all put forward by two hours to save daylight, we would camp on Sharlston common. Everyone knew everyone in the village, and it was safe. Peter Chalkley's dad was secretary of the rugby club, so he always had a rugby ball. We used to get onto the rugby field and play there. We had to make sure Peter was happy, or he would take his ball home. Later we bought a ball ourselves."

From 1939 to 1945, Peter was aware of the war, but it did not have a major effect on village life, unlike some of the cities in the north which were bombed. "Tommy Chalkley, our next-door neighbour, had built bunk beds in his cellar – if the siren went we would go in there. Occasionally a bomb would fall – but not in our area. The nearest one was at Featherstone. I remember that I had a gas mask. Miners didn't go into the forces because mining was a reserved occupation. My uncle Ken, dad's younger brother, was captured at Arnhem. Another uncle was in the RAF. But the war didn't have a great effect on me. We had evacuees from London in Sharlston during the war. I remember we couldn't buy bananas until the end of the war. There were ration books for sweets too and for sometime afterwards."

Tommy Fox became steward of the Working Mens' Club (WMC) on VE Day [8 May] in 1945. The club is still there and is at the far end of the ground from the Sharlston pub which is now the team's clubhouse. Peter has mixed memories of living at the WMC: "I was 12 when we moved to the WMC. I hated it! I was good at maths, so I used to end up working behind the bar because I could work out the change. I used to lean over the bar and listen to the players talking about rugby. Also, I had to be in by 10.30 on a Friday and Saturday for cleaning up. On the other hand, we had the only billiards table in the village. On Sunday afternoons we used to play billiards and snooker, although I wasn't any good because I am blind in one eye. My mates loved it though. We lived at the club – our lounge was at the back of the bar. Every Thursday, my mum together with Aunt Kate and Aunt Hilda scrubbed the concert room, on their hands and knees. It was hard work.

"My dad used to say to me 'never work for a committee', which was useful advice for me later when I became a rugby coach. You were under pressure from everyone, and had to be careful what you said all the time."

Peter had lost the sight of his eye in an accident when he was six years old. The day before war broke out an older boy threw a dart and hit Peter in the eye. He remembers travelling on the bus with his mother to hospital for treatment for a number of weeks, but the doctors could not restore his sight. He says: "She took me to Leeds Infirmary once a week for months in the first year of the war. We walked to Cock and Crown, about one mile, every Thursday throughout the winter to catch the bus to Leeds. I was in short trousers and my legs were chapped with the rain and snow."

Peter says that his mother worked hard all her life. "She worked for a lady at Shelling Mill as a cleaner, at the Working Mens' Club, then at Pinderfields Hospital as a cleaner. People said it was never cleaner than when my mother worked there."

In 1946, Peter left Sharlston School and went to Wakefield Technical College: "At 13, you could go to Whitwood Tech or Wakefield Tech. My friend Barry Chalkley had gone to Whitwood and I passed the exam for both. But my other friends were going to Wakefield Tech, so I decided to go there to do engineering. It was a good job I did, as Whitwood did commercial studies, and I probably wouldn't have been any good at that." He went to Wakefield Tech for two years.

As well as developing his education, the school offered Peter the first chance to play organised rugby: "Mr Sykes was the woodwork teacher and my form teacher. I almost cut my thumb off with a chisel in one of his classes – I still have the scar. Mr Woodcock, the metalwork teacher, took me to one side. He said 'You're from Sharlston, so you must play rugby. Can we start a team and enter the Wakefield Schools League?' He went on 'You coach and train the boys, and I'll enter the team in the league'. It was the first time Wakefield Tech had a rugby team. This was 1946-47. In 1947-48 we won the Jackson Cup. All the schools in Wakefield competed for it. There were five other schools in the league: Marygates, Snapethorpe, St Austins, Cathedral and Ings Road."

Some of the early players from that team were Roy Luck, A. Howell, D. G. Leith, Edward Jackson, G. Gill, Goodchild, B. Flowers and Roy Hepworth. Phil Shillito went on to play for Leeds, Don Metcalfe played for Featherstone and Wakefield Trinity, Edward Jackson, Jimmy Wood, Jack Greaves, Roy Hepworth and Peter all played for Sharlston Rovers.

On 20 December 1947 as a curtain raiser to the Wakefield Trinity versus Oldham match at Belle Vue, the Wakefield Schools team played Oldham Schools. This was the first appearance of school teams at Belle Vue for many years. Spike O'Grady, Crabtree, Wood and Peter were in the team from Wakefield Tech.

Peter was then invited to a county trial at Snapethorpe. He remembers that "Don played too; he was 11 years old. Jackie Fennell played. But Don didn't get picked from the trial." Given that Don was three years younger than some of the boys playing, maybe that was not surprising. But his time would come. Peter also played for Wakefield Schools at Oldham, Leeds and Hunslet.

Peter's first major rugby league honour came with selection for the Yorkshire Schools under-15 team to play Lancashire at St Helens on 24 April 1948. Yorkshire lost 24-3, but Peter scored Yorkshire's only try. It was the first county schools match after the war: "We travelled to St Helens by bus from Leeds. Our teacher came as there were four players from our school. First we caught the bus from the Bull Ring in Wakefield to Leeds. He asked the conductor to squeeze another two onto the bus so we could get to Leeds. Of course we didn't have cars in those days. We had lunch with the Lancashire players – some had stubble on their chins, they seemed older than us. It was an under-15 match, but they were bigger and harder. It was a tough, hard match. The FA Cup Final was going on at Wembley – Manchester United versus Blackpool, and they gave the score over the tannoy." From that Yorkshire Boys team, Jack Lendill went on to play for Leeds, and Jackie Fennell for Featherstone.

Peter worked hard at the school: "I studied mechanical engineering. We got jobs as engineering apprentices. All my mates were at the Tech, but it wasn't easy, we had lots of homework. We also did practical work, joinery, metalwork, as well as maths and science."

This led to an apprenticeship in Wakefield: "I was an apprentice engineer at British Jeffrey Diamond [BJD]. I was in the machine shop, then the fitting shop. At 19 I moved into the drawing office for the last year of my apprenticeship. A few lads had applied for the drawing office. The boss was Archie Rawding. He was in the Sharlston Church Choir, as was I, so maybe that gave me a bit of leverage. He knew I was a bright lad. So I served my time in the drawing office, working on mining machinery and designing coal cutters and conveyor belts. I was a draughtsman for one of the senior design engineers.

I enjoyed my time with BJD. It was a big company, on Chantry Bridge in Wakefield. The drawing office was at the far end behind the church, with the factory behind it. They also had a factory at Thornes, where they made crushing machines. It was a separate division of the company.

BJD didn't have a rugby league team, but there was a workshop competition, held at Belle Vue. Each team was allowed to have a professional player, and Don Froggett played for us."

Peter's rugby league continued to develop when he left Wakefield Tech: "I played a couple of games for Sharlston Rovers when I was 15, but at that age men's rugby was too tough for me. So I played for Streethouse Intermediates at under–18 level. We won the Leeds & District League championship in a match at Buslingthorpe Vale. Wilf Adams and Frank Mortimer, two of the Streethouse players, were selected for the Leeds & District League to play Wigan. The team lost at Wigan, they weren't picked for the return match, but I was. We beat Wigan at Buslingthorpe Vale. Our coach was Bill Duffy, who later became coach at Wakefield Trinity. He signed both Frank Mortimer and Wilf Adams. He later tried to get me to Wakefield through Wilf Adams, but at the time I was having trials with Featherstone Rovers."

Peter returned to play for Sharlston Rovers for the 1951-52 season. The club was briefly suspended during this season, following a match when two players were sent off and gave false names to the referee, but still reached two finals. Peter appeared in both, a 15-3 defeat against Eastmoor in the Wakefield & District Open-Age League Cup Final and an 8-5 defeat against Middleton Old Boys in the Yorkshire Junior Cup Final at Featherstone Rovers' Post Office Road. The latter was – and still is – one of the most prestigious tournaments for amateur clubs. Peter played full-back, and was "outstanding" according to the *Wakefield Express* report:

Middleton Old Boys 8 Sharlston Rovers 5
Yorkshire Junior Cup Final

"If Sharlston Rovers had made use of three overlaps during the final with Middleton OB at Featherstone, they would have won the Yorkshire Junior Cup. However, in each case the player concerned ignored his unmarked colleagues and was brought down yards from the line. The game opened quietly with Middleton getting possession more than Sharlston, who were without their regular hooker. After 10 minutes Sharlston lost Nightingale with a broken ankle and Middleton looked even more menacing. Rovers' forwards held on and kept the ball tight, but their policy starved their wingers, Wynn and Hobbs of possession. Just before the interval Joyce scored a try to put Rovers ahead, Fox converted. Middleton ran in eight points soon after the interval. Sharlston's outstanding players were Booth at scrum-half and Peter Fox at full-back."

The next season, Peter continued to play for Rovers. In the Challenge Cup, the team fought through the qualifying competition to face Hull National Dock Labour Board in the final round. Rovers drew 9-9, with the Hull side equalising near the end, and Peter narrowly missing with two attempted drop-goals. The match report said: "Peter Fox was the pick of the Rovers' backs. His fielding of the ball was almost faultless, he linked up intelligently with his backs and he kicked all the important goals." Sadly, Rovers lost the replay 8-7, and the chance to play a professional club in the first round proper. This was Peter's last season in the amateur game. Don had already signed for Featherstone Rovers, and soon Featherstone were returning to Sharlston to offer Peter a trial.

Inevitably, various professional clubs were interested in signing Peter: "I had three trial matches for Dewsbury. I played at full-back against Keighley in an 'A' team match and kicked six goals. Stan Moyser and George Withington were playing for Dewsbury that day. But they had a goalkicking full-back, so they didn't sign me. So I continued playing for Sharlston Rovers. I played there for a couple of years, sometimes at full-back, then as loose-forward. At school I had played scrum-half, so I could control the game." Peter also remembers an approach from the chairman of Doncaster just before the club joined the Rugby League, but his father felt he was too young to sign for them.

However, rugby league was not Peter's only sporting interest: "From 1950 to 1952 I also played football, for the Sharlston Church Choir team. On Saturday morning I would play football, and in the afternoon play rugby. In football I usually played left-half, but sometimes went in goal. We were in the Horbury & District League, and were runners-up in two cup finals. I also had trials for the Normanton Minor League team to play in the English Shield. My wife Joan's dad, Arthur Nicholson, was the football team's coach. In the trial I played left half, and was moved into the Probables team at half-time. I was picked to play for the Normanton Minor League team in goal. We played Whitwood and lost 1-0, and then drew 0-0 with Goole & Thorner from near Hull. I saved a penalty. Norman Gittins – a friend of mine - was in that team. I'm still in contact with him. He should have played professionally."

Boxing was another sporting interest for Peter before his professional rugby league career: "After leaving school in the early 1950s, until 1952, I joined White Rose Boxing Club. It was run by Albert Rayner, who was an amateur rugby league touch judge from Eastmoor. He used to skip for hours and was very fit. We used to box against other clubs, but I couldn't get an ABA licence as I was blind in one eye, so I couldn't box in the championships, only for the club. You had to have an ABA licence to box after becoming 18, so I had to stop. Cricket was another sport I enjoyed. I played for Sharlston in the West Riding League, mainly played in the second team, and was an opening bowler. My pal Ted Dix was a great sportsman and played in the first team, but never played professionally."

Sharlston Choir outing to Robin Hood Bay: from left: Reg Musgrave,
John Alack, Norman Gittins, Peter Swann, Peter Fox, Eric Parkin, Rev. R. Dawes.

Cricket did not play a major part in Peter's sporting life, but he does remember an outing to Headingley to watch the 1948 Australian tourists against England: "The vicar took me, Ted Dix, Eric Parkin and Ken Spires to watch the Monday of the match [the fourth day]. It was one of the finest day's cricket ever: Hutton, Washbrook and Hammond batting for England; Lindwall and Miller bowling for the Australians. We were going on holiday to Robin Hood Bay with the vicar and other members of the church choir, and had just finished school. But rugby was always my main sport. It was always there in Sharlston. It was my ambition to play for the blue and whites – Sharlston Rovers. All the kids in Sharlston had that aim."

Another youthful activity was the army cadets: "I was in the army cadets at Sharlston, with Barry Chalkley and Ronnie Ramsden. We went on a two week camp near Seahouses, with the Kings Own Yorkshire Light Infantry. It was very hard, but we enjoyed it. Peter Chalkley, my neighbour, and I tried to join the army full-time, but they wouldn't accept me because of my eye. I was exempted from National Service as well. I even tried to join the police, but they wouldn't take me. So I concentrated on night school and getting through my apprenticeship." Peter went to night school four nights a week as part of his apprenticeship, and passed his HNC in mechanical engineering.

As well as playing football for the church choir team, Peter was a member of the choir: "I was a server at morning communion in the church, then in the evening was in the choir. I did that for a few years, that was when Joan and I first met. She was in the church choir at this time. She was two and a half years younger than me. She was 15 at the time. She had professional singing lessons, and was guest soprano for the Sharlston male voice choir for a couple of years. We started courting around this time. She was in the same class as Don at school. Joan worked for a hairdresser after leaving school, and used to work on Saturday afternoons while I was playing for Sharlston. She wasn't interested in rugby then, but started going to matches when I was coaching."

So by the summer of 1953, aged 20, Peter was established in amateur rugby league, had completed his apprenticeship at BJD, was starting work as a detail draughtsman and courting Joan. But an invitation to training and trials with Featherstone Rovers was soon to come, and launch his career in professional rugby league.

Left: Playing for Yorkshire Schoolboys against Lancashire at St Helens in April 1948.
Right: Peter with his parents, Tommy and Stella, on holiday in Blackpool.

Sharlston Rovers 1951-52.
Back: J. Clark, M. Haigh, P. Chalkley, F. Simpson, C. Richardson, J. Lapish, A. Oldroyd;
Front: F. Wynn, P. Fox, B. Flowers, J. Fisher (captain), E. Booth, M. Wood, R. Hobbs.
(Courtesy Sharlston Rovers ARLFC)

2. Signing for Featherstone Rovers

Peter was not the first member of the Fox family to play rugby league at Featherstone's Post Office Road ground. Tommy had played there in the 1930s, and younger brother Don, after playing association football in Sharlston, and then rugby league for Streethouse Intermediates, had joined Featherstone Rovers Intermediates in 1952. Don signed a professional contract for the club at the end of the 1952-53 season. He then made his first team debut in the Yorkshire Cup in September against Leeds - Featherstone lost 32-7 - for a 53-14 defeat over two legs.

Peter recalls his early days at Featherstone: "I played for Sharlston at full-back, and loose forward. Don had joined Featherstone Rovers, so I went training with them, and then played in the 'A' team at Huddersfield. In the Huddersfield team were Dave Valentine and Mick Sullivan. I tackled Dave Valentine into the ground and he dislocated his collarbone. Then from a scrum I made a break on the short side, and Mick Sullivan tackled me. He cracked me on the nose. Years later, when he was with St Helens and I was with Hull KR, he said 'You've never caught me for that crack on the nose, Foxy'. I thought Mick Sullivan and Billy Boston were the best wingers to play for Great Britain. Dave Valentine was a tough player. Tackling was my main strength. I could tackle anyone."

Peter was joining a team that had played at Wembley in 1952, and were looking to improve on a poor league performance in 1952-53 when they finished 24th: "At Featherstone, apart from Don, we had some pretty fair players. Don Metcalfe became the captain – he could win tackles and was a quality player. Cliff Lambert was good and Ken Welburn, Willis Fawley and Fred Hulme were all regulars in the first team. Jackie Fennell was a fine full-back, and Ray Cording was effective on the wing. Alan Tennant had played in the 1952 Challenge Cup Final, as had Eric Batten. I didn't go to the 1952 Final, but watched it on television in the WMC. It was the first Final on television and Featherstone lost 18-10 to Workington."

A week after Don's first team debut, Peter travelled to Fartown to play for the 'A' team. *The Pontefract & Castleford Express* reported that in Rovers' 16-15 victory, the team had been "well served by three trialists". One of these was Peter at loose-forward.

Peter's first team debut came the next week, on 19 September at Rochdale. *The Express* said that "The loose-forward position goes to a young trialist who had an outstanding game with the 'A' team at Huddersfield." As well as Peter's debut - under the 'A.N. Other' label as he was still an amateur - the match saw debuts for new recruits Bill Shreeve from Bradford Northern and Derek Howes from Wakefield Trinity. Don was at scrum-half, and kicked three goals. Featherstone won 9-6, to end a run of four defeats. *The Express* said that "the trialist loose-forward again did well."

Peter retained his place for the visit of Hull FC the following week. Rovers beat their illustrious visitors 29-7, their **first victory over Hull FC in a league match for 20 years**. The following Wednesday, Peter signed professionally for Rovers, and kept his place for the visit of Keighley, again at loose-forward.

Peter got £250 to sign for Featherstone, a good amount when he was earning around £600 a year: "Don got £400 to sign and my dad said I should ask for more, but I said no, let me sign. We got £7 for a win and £3 for a loss in the first team. In the 'A' team it was £3 for a win and £1/10/0d for a loss."

Keighley came away from Post Office Road with a 13-13 draw, with Don scoring all Rovers' points, including a long-range penalty near the end of the match to secure the draw. Rovers then went down 23-7 at lowly Batley, but on 17 October beat Hull KR 36-16 at Post Office Road. Another victory followed at Doncaster, 21-10, to leave Featherstone ninth in the table, with 15 points from 12 matches. It was only October, but they were within two points of the previous season at the end of December. But on 31 October, Rovers rested Peter, with Cliff Lambert taking his place at loose-forward. This was a sign of what was to come for much of Peter's time at Featherstone – spells in the first team with Cliff Lambert often being preferred at loose-forward. Peter remembers Lambert as "a good player, but not an international". However, given the competition for the loose-forward position at international level at this time, many capable aspiring Great Britain or England players never won caps.

Peter was recalled to the first team for the trip to Barrow on 14 November, with Lambert moving into the second row. He remembers the match well: "At training during the week, our coach Eric Batten said: 'Listen, Foxy, you're going to be instrumental in us winning the game.'

"'What's the plan?' I asked Eric. 'Don't worry', he said, 'I'll let you know'.

"Now, Barrow was a seven hour bus ride in those days, and on the way up, every half hour, I asked Eric to tell me his plan, so I could get it into my head. 'There's plenty of time' he said.

"Two minutes before we went out onto the pitch, Eric came over to me and said, 'Listen, they have a stand-off half called Willie Horne who went on the '46 tour with me. He mesmerised the Aussies with his sidestep, swerve, drop-kicking, goalkicking, handling skills and touch finding.' I was thinking 'not a bad player this Willie Horne'.

"'Now', said Eric, 'first scrum go round the blind side and crack Willie Horne'. Then he smashed his fist into the palm of his hand. Well, I was a coach's dream. At the first scrum, round the blind side, I flew at Willie, my feet left the ground and I missed him by a fraction. Over his shoulder I went, crashing to the ground. I got a grazed hip and a bruised shoulder. To cut a long story short, I tried three more times to get Willie and on the fourth time I crawled to the touchline and said to Eric: 'I think you'd better change this plan or we're going to get beat.' We lost 15-8 on a quagmire, but I did kick a goal – my first points for the first team.

"I wasn't the only man who lost out to Willie Horne, who I later played golf with in the Rugby League Golf Tournament. Bill Wookey, a great friend of Willie's, who now runs the rugby league golf days, always asks me to repeat this story when saying a few words at the golf day dinner."

Peter was back in the 'A' team the next week, scoring a try in an 18-8 win at Hunslet. His next match was also in the 'A' team, in a 15-11 win at Hull on 16 January. *The Express* reported that: "The path to victory in the second half was found largely through the judicious kicking of Fennell and Peter Fox, who extracted every atom of help from the wind ...Fox completed the scoring with a drop goal."

The next week, Peter was back in the first team for a trip to Widnes, with Lambert moving to the second-row. Poor play by Rovers' backs resulted in a 13-0 defeat.

For the rest of the season, Peter played regularly for the 'A' team, usually at loose-forward. He "did well" in a 38-18 defeat at Wakefield in February and scored a couple of tries at Hull KR and against Batley on Easter Monday. The 'A' team also reached the semi-final of the Yorkshire Senior Cup, losing 10-2 at Huddersfield at the end of the season. Peter had shown he could hold his own in the first team, but his chance of a regular place was blocked by either Cliff Lambert or Derek Howes.

Featherstone's first team finished 14th in the league, a considerable improvement on 24th the season before. And Peter managed the move from amateur rugby league well: "I was fitter and stronger when I played for Featherstone, ready for action. Eric Batten was our trainer and he used to run us to death. I was an office worker, and I thought this was great. No one was my mentor though. When I signed for Featherstone, Derek Howes had joined them from Wakefield. He said he would help me, but he never played there long enough.

"The amateur game had been tough, but I was with a good team. Later, when I was at Batley, we often struggled and we had to tackle all the time. There it was very tough. Featherstone were quite good at this time. They had been to Wembley in 1952. Only a couple of the team were miners, others had building jobs or worked at the colliery in other jobs. It was hard, we worked all day, then trained at night. We trained twice a week, physical exercises, and running and passing, we never really did tactics in those days. The players had more about them on how to play. We played off each other. Our Don was the creator at scrum-half. He was only 17. Tommy Smales was at Featherstone at this time, and I remember playing with him." Don was the first team's regular scrum-half this season, with Tommy Smales often in the 'A' team.

At the start of the 1954-55 season, Rovers announced that Eric Batten had signed on for another season as player-coach, although *The Express* pointed out that he was approaching 40, and that his playing days were drawing to a close.

Peter remembers this season as one when he was hit by injuries. He started it in the 'A' team, kicking four goals in a 26-0 victory over Dewsbury. He kept his place for the next four 'A' team games, with three victories, playing twice in the second-row, and kicking another seven goals, then he scored a try and a goal at Batley in a 22-8 defeat. Peter was back in the first team at loose-forward for a 20-11 loss at Widnes. Featherstone were continually penalised by the referee, and had winger Ray Cording injured early in the first half.

Further 'A' team action followed, including a 24-15 defeat of Leeds 'A', despite losing their centre Kelly, who was sent off. Peter had been selected at loose-forward, but moved to centre and "it was his sturdy example, particularly in attack, that led Featherstone to victory," according to *The Express*. Peter missed most of November through a pulled muscle, and returned to action on 20 November on the 'A' team's right wing, kicking three goals in an 8-0 win over Bradford Northern.

A recall to the first team came on New Year's Day, for the local derby trip to Castleford. Featherstone won 19-8, in front of 6,100 fans. Peter gave "adequate service" from loose-forward according to *The Express*, and kept his place for Bramley's visit to Post Office Road on 8 January. Rovers won 23-16, with Peter's "supporting good work" setting up the first try for Featherstone.

Another first team appearance, a 22-10 defeat at a snow-covered Headingley followed the next week. But Peter was unable to break into the first team again, and played on-and-off for the 'A' team throughout the rest of the season, the muscle injury he had suffered earlier reoccurring, which restricted his appearances. The first team finished ninth, with 47 points from 36 matches.

Peter was now aged 22, and the 1955-56 season was an important one for him at Featherstone. He had shown in his first two seasons at the club that he could play at first team level, but his opportunities for a regular place had been blocked by Cliff Lambert, and at times in his second season, injuries. Peter had accumulated experience in the professional game, but now needed to play more regularly in the first team to develop his playing career further.

Peter started the season in the 'A' team. Playing at loose-forward, he scored a try in a 34-14 win at Post Office Road against Hull KR. Another 'A' team game followed, a 38-14 win at Hunslet. Peter kicked seven goals from eight attempts, with the other one hitting the post which "seemed to go over, but was disallowed", according to the match report.

On 10 September, Peter and Mal Kirk were recalled to the first team, who were missing six players through injury, and rested Joe Mullaney because of his selection for England the following Monday. Featherstone had played "ineptly" against Wakefield and Hull, while Dewsbury had beaten champions Warrington and Rochdale, but Rovers "cantered home" 27-12. Peter kicked a second-half penalty, and with Mal Kirk "improved the pack immensely" according to *The Express*.

Four days later, Featherstone travelled to Bramley, and Peter's display won headlines in the local paper. "Match winner Fox: Peter this time" said *The Express*, with the report saying: "The role of Featherstone match-winner, which has been played on many occasions by scrum-half Donald Fox, was filled at Bramley on Wednesday by his brother Peter." Featherstone were already below full strength, and after 20 minutes lost winger Cording through injury. Metcalfe scored a try for Rovers, but Peter missed the conversion. Two penalties put Bramley 6-3 up, but in the second half, Peter kicked two penalties to win the match. *The Express* said "…with three minutes to go, Bramley were penalised again. In the gathering gloom, Fox prepared carefully for the vital kick, and it won the game."

Peter stayed in the first team for one of the season's most memorable matches, a victory over Wigan at Post Office Road. In those days of a single division of 31 clubs, most fixtures were arranged between teams of the same county, and this was Wigan's first visit to Featherstone in the league since 1933-34. A crowd of 7,900 saw a memorable Featherstone triumph, 13-6, with Peter kicking five goals. Don was out injured with a bruised heel, so Peter took over the kicking duties. It was a tense match, and Peter's fifth goal, which put Rovers seven points clear, was greeted with "jubilation". Peter remembers being congratulated for his goalkicking performance by Wigan's Jackie Cunliffe after this game.

Rovers' fine form continued with a 25-18 triumph over Huddersfield at Fartown, **their first win there for 27 years**. Peter kicked an early penalty, and Rovers managed to fight back from 13-10 down at half-time to win. Peter's brother Neil was playing for Rovers' under-18 side in a curtain raiser, and kicked a penalty from near half-way. Don and Peter were told about this, and "confidently accepted the challenge to emulate their younger brother, but failed from positions quite near to where Neil had succeeded."

But the next week the wheels fell off at The Watersheddings, against an Oldham team that had only won once all season. *The Express* said that "Rovers reached rock bottom", and lost 25-6. The report added that Rovers' tackling was deplorable, and the team seemed to be thinking about an after-match trip to Blackpool. Peter "had one lively spell", which was "such a notable achievement in the Featherstone pack as a whole that he was cheered by Oldham followers".

Peter was one of the casualties of this display, being left out of the next couple of matches. Meanwhile, Neil had signed for Wakefield Trinity, much to the surprise of Rovers who expected him to join his brothers at Post Office Road. It would be over 10 years before the three brothers played together – at Wakefield!

Featherstone Rovers 1953-54, relaxing after the match.

Peter returned to the 'A' team in a 20-10 win at Batley, kicking three goals, but was sent off in the last minute. This was his first dismissal in the professional game. A first team return came against Keighley on 26 November. Rovers won 22-16. Once again a return to the 'A' team followed, and on 10 December, Peter and Marchant "were the best players".

Peter was back in the first team at loose-forward against Hunslet on 31 December. Rovers won 23-9, with Peter dropping a goal towards the end of the game. The next week, Peter made a try for Peter Johnson in a 13-9 victory against Hull at Post Office Road; Rovers' display was "their finest victory of the season" and kept them in sixth place in the table. Peter retained his place for a comfortable victory over Castleford on 21 January, revenge for an 18-9 defeat at Christmas, and he remembers this match: "Cas beat Featherstone at Christmas and Don got a hammering. My dad went to see the committee, as he was worried about Don. He said I should play to give him some protection. So I was picked for the return match and we beat Cas. Kenny Pye played scrum-half for them and Colin Anderson – a tough player, was in the pack. He later signed for Featherstone. Fred Ward was second-row for Cas. He had said to Colin Anderson – you take Fox, I'll take Lambert. Colin had told him to get lost! Fred later took Hunslet to Wembley as a coach." Peter kicked a long range penalty, and his kick was missed by Smart for Johnson to score.

Rovers' good run ended at Workington the next week, with a 23-9 defeat. Cliff Lambert then resumed at loose-forward until Peter returned to first team action on 25 February for a 14-4 home win over Oldham. Don Metcalfe put Peter in under the posts for a rare first team try, and *The Express* said that "Featherstone's forwards were in much better fettle than at Wigan [in the Challenge Cup] and for that the inclusion of Peter Fox counted greatly. He and his brother Donald, at scrum-half, were always in the thick of things and the kicking of both was so useful in the second half that one wondered why they had not employed such tactics before, so inviting were the conditions."

Peter kept his place for a crucial 11-7 victory over Halifax the next week, which put Rovers into the top four in the league table. But a 12-5 defeat at Keighley undermined Rovers' hopes of a championship play-off place. A 5-5 draw at Doncaster, when Rovers finished with 11 fit players, was a further setback. Peter played in all three first team games over Easter. A 26-12 victory over Bradford Northern was followed by a 15-4 win at

Wakefield on Easter Monday. But a 7-7 draw with Huddersfield, when Peter played on the wing against Lionel Cooper, and stopped the great Australian from scoring, left Rovers sixth in the table, with a 68.75 per cent record, compared to fourth-placed Hull's 69.11 per cent. The league was decided on percentage records that season because Belle Vue Rangers withdrew from the league just before the season started, and new fixtures could not be drawn up in time to ensure all the teams played the same number of matches.

But Peter then lost the loose-forward spot again to Cliff Lambert, although he returned to the first team for the midweek trip to Wigan on 18 April. By now, the chance of a play-off place had gone, but Rovers' pack played well, and *The Express* said "If the forwards can find form like this next August, they will make a lot of people happy". The paper's end-of-season review said that it had been the club's second-best season in the league [since their championship winning season in 1928], with 48 points from 36 matches, and the team scoring 579 points on the field. Peter finished fifth in the clubs' leading points scorers with 31 points from 14 goals and one try in 18 appearances.

Peter made more appearances that season than in the previous two combined. He was still not certain of a first team place, but had never let the team down, and had contributed match-winning performances on occasion, memorably against Wigan in the famous Rovers' victory. But events off the pitch were to change his plans for a future at Post Office Road.

A few weeks into the 1956-57 season saw the end of Peter's time at Featherstone as a player. It was a change made by the club committee at Featherstone that caused this. The club had advertised Eric Batten's job as coach, and he declined to take the post of trainer he had been offered instead and he left the club. Peter recalls: "In 1956 Eric left Featherstone to join Batley. Bill Hudson became coach at Featherstone. I used to think the world of him as a player he had been at Batley, then joined Wigan and played for Great Britain. But I didn't get on with him at Featherstone. We won at Hull in a cup match, but then I left to join Eric at Batley." Of course, in those days the club committee picked the team. Peter outlines: "In those days the selection committee, not the coach, picked the team. Eric would have had a say. It was like that still when I coached Great Britain."

Peter had been selected for the first team in the pre-season trial match, and scored a try as they won 33-12. He played in the second-row in a 23-14 defeat at Barrow, and then in a 14-11 home defeat by Hull in the next match, when Woolford sent Peter in for his second first-team try for Rovers. *The Express* said after the Hull defeat that "Peter Fox tackled two men at the same time while some of his forward colleagues were showing nothing like his enthusiasm for their defensive tasks."

Colin Anderson had signed for Rovers, and he played in the second-row at Hull in Rovers' 7-6 win. Peter returned to the first team on 8 September in a 22-9 home win over Halifax, once again in the second-row. Cliff Lambert was again first choice at loose-forward. This was Rovers' first league win of the season, but they could not continue this form on the following Wednesday, losing 12-8 at York in the Yorkshire Cup. A crowd of 11,000 saw Peter's last first team game for Rovers. Peter played for the 'A' team on 29 September in a 27-12 defeat against Halifax. Then, on 5 October, *The Express* announced that Peter and Tony Storey had gone on the transfer list. The club wanted £750 for Storey and £500 for Peter. The local paper said that Peter "is one of the toughest men in the game, with a natural ability". Another 'A' team appearance followed, a 13-2 win over Dewsbury 'A', with Peter contributing a try and a goal. Then it was announced that he had been transferred to Batley, rejoining Eric Batten who was trying to revitalise a club who had finished bottom of the league the previous season. A new period in Peter's playing career was about to begin.

Featherstone Rovers RLFC – the team that won 27-12 at Dewsbury on 10 September 1955.
Back: W. Bradshaw, J. Barraclough, W. Shreeve, F. Hulme, K. Elford, P. Fox, M. Kirk;
front: P. Johnson, D. Metcalfe, T. Smales, J. Fennell, R. Cording, M. Clamp.

BATLEY

Full Back :
1—TAYLOR or
TALBOT

Threequarters :
2—IRELAND
3—SUTCLIFFE
4—LAWTON (J.)
5—FIELD

Half Backs :
6—GELDARD
7—PRATT (W.)

Forwards :
8—HARRISON
9—MOYSER
10—FOX
11—KELLY
12—ARMSTEAD or
PRIESTLEY
14—PLATT

BATLEY
like so many
other clubs wear

LITESOME

SUPPORTERS &
SPORTS WEAR

Obtainable from all good
Sports shops. Enquiries
invited from club secretaries.

LITESOME

FRED HURTLEY & SON
LTD.,
Dept. 170, KEIGHLEY,
YORKSHIRE.

WAKEFIELD TRINITY

Full Back :
1—ROUND

Threequarters :
2—SMITH (F.)
3—SKENE
4—FOX
5—ETTY

Half Backs :
6—POYNTON
7—HOLLIDAY

Forwards :
8—WILKINSON
9—OAKES
10—SAMPSON (M.)
11—VINES
12—FIRTH
14—LAMMING

Referee
Mr. E. CLAY (Rothwell).

Touch Judges
Mr. J. W. JOWETT and Mr. H. CRAVEN

Fox against Fox – Peter for Batley against Neil for Wakefield on 16 January 1960
(Courtesy Batley RLFC)

Peter (on right) looks on as a brawl breaks out between Batley and Wakefield at Belle Vue.

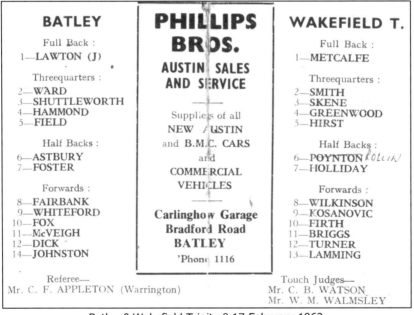

BATLEY	PHILLIPS BROS. AUSTIN SALES AND SERVICE	WAKEFIELD T.
Full Back :		Full Back :
1—LAWTON (J)		1—METCALFE
Threequarters :	Supplies of all NEW AUSTIN and B.M.C. CARS and COMMERCIAL VEHICLES	Threequarters :
2—WARD		2—SMITH
3—SHUTTLEWORTH		3—SKENE
4—HAMMOND		4—GREENWOOD
5—FIELD		5—HIRST
Half Backs :		Half Backs :
6—ASTBURY		6—POYNTON
7—FOSTER		7—HOLLIDAY
Forwards :	Carlinghow Garage Bradford Road BATLEY 'Phone 1116	Forwards :
8—FAIRBANK		8—WILKINSON
9—WHITEFORD		9—KOSANOVIC
10—FOX		10—FIRTH
11—McVEIGH		11—BRIGGS
12—DICK		12—TURNER
14—JOHNSTON		13—LAMMING

Referee—
Mr. C. F. APPLETON (Warrington)

Touch Judges—
Mr. C. B. WATSON
Mr. W. M. WALMSLEY

Batley 0 Wakefield Trinity 0 17 February 1962
(Courtesy Batley RLFC)

3. A new start at Batley

In moving from Featherstone Rovers to Batley, Peter was going from a club who had been in the top half of the table and challenging for the Championship play-offs on occasions to one who had finished rock bottom of the League in 1955-56, with 15 points from 34 matches.

Batley's history dates back to 1880, and they were one of the clubs that broke away from the Rugby Union to establish the Northern Union in 1895. Known as the Gallant Youths, they won the prestigious Yorkshire Cup in 1884, and then won the first Challenge Cup competition in 1897, beating St Helens 10-3 in the Final. They retained the cup in 1898, and won it again in 1901. But, as true professionalism developed in the game, moving it away from the original 'broken time' payments for missing work, Batley found it more difficult to compete with their bigger local rivals. The Yorkshire Cup was won in 1912-13, and the Championship in 1923-24, but that was their last major trophy win. In 1952-53 they had reached the Yorkshire Cup Final, losing 18-8 to Huddersfield, but that was a rare bright spot for their supporters, as was finishing sixth in the league in 1950-51, but then they gradually slipped down the table, although their last place in 1955-56 was the first time they had suffered that indignity.

The club had suffered a big blow in January 1955, when popular local winger and team captain John Etty was sold to Oldham for £2,650. Attendances dropped at Mount Pleasant, and the club had come close to collapse. The directors had to organise fundraising events to ensure the club's survival.

So there was much for new coach Eric Batten to do when he arrived at the club, and Peter was happy to join him at Mount Pleasant to try to help Batley climb the table. This was an opportunity for him to establish himself as a regular first team player. It was also an important time for his future development in the game.

Looking back to his move to Batley, Peter says that "During my first season at Batley we found it hard to progress. We were unable to recruit ready-made players, and this made it difficult for Eric Batten to motivate the team. Eric was more of a trainer than a coach, and his emphasis was on fitness. Batley had few notable players, but George Palmer, a former Hull player was captain of the side, with Eric Battersby at hooker, Peter Anson and a young Jackie Briggs in the second-row, me at loose-forward, Bill Riley at stand-off with Philip Walshaw at full-back, we had the nucleus of a sound team. John Etty's brother Jim was also signed during the season."

Peter made his debut for Batley at loose-forward against high-flying Huddersfield on 20 October. The *Batley News* reporter Peter Hinchliffe said that "Peter Fox was very impressive. He handled well and made a number of openings for his half-backs. I hope his try will be the first of many that he will score for the Mount Pleasant club. Considering his performance on Saturday I see no reason why this hope should not be realised. Another notable feature about Fox's play is that he provides cover for his half-backs. It was very noticeable that stand off Hart, who has been somewhat in the background during recent weeks featured in a number of good attacking moves. I am sure that this was due to the cover provided by Fox. Batley's try came in the 33rd minute when Fox forced his way over the line after a play-the ball." Peter also kicked a goal in a 17-7 defeat.

However, this was Batley's 11th consecutive defeat, and they were the only team in the League yet to win a competition point. Peter Hinchliffe wrote in his *Spotlight on Sport* column: "A further sign that the Batley directors are intent once again on bringing their club into the limelight was provided last week with the news of the signing of loose-forward Peter Fox and the veteran campaigner Ernest Ward... Fox showed himself to be a forceful young player and a real asset to Batley's forwards."

A 17-11 win at fellow strugglers Doncaster bought to an end one of the longest runs of defeats in the club's history. Hinchliffe wrote that "Loose forward Peter Fox in his second game for Batley did not fulfil the promise he showed in the match against Huddersfield. All the same, he seems to have bought added life and vigour to the pack."

Further defeats followed. Peter remembers his time at Batley as frequently involving a lot of tackling, and the match report for the 15-5 defeat at York said that Palmer, Anson and Fox "tackled hard and defended dourly". The next week, Salford won 29-23 at Mount Pleasant, but the match report said that Batley "put up a second half fight that must have bought a glow to the heart of every man between Birstall and Batley Cave. Palmer, Anson, Fox and the unnamed trialist all threatened the Salford line."

The next week, Batley had a rare win at Huddersfield's Fartown ground, 13-9. Their good form against Salford had continued, with Peter making an important contribution: "Batley were magnificent. This was their finest hour. Loose-forward Fox also had a good game. His strong, robust play provided just that punch that the Batley pack has been crying out for. He also provided excellent cover for his half-backs."

At this time, clubs mainly played teams from their own side of the Pennines. But Batley's next two fixtures were against Lancashire teams. In a 14-9 victory at lowly Liverpool City, "Anson and Briggs worked well in the second-row, and so did loose-forward Fox, though his passing was a little wild at times." Then came the first home win of the season, a narrow 14-12 win over Widnes: "Fox, in particular, showed that a forward can attack as well as defend... Fox, Riley and Smith were prominent in raids on the visitors' line."

However, the club was unable to sign veteran Ernest Ward, despite a 'very reasonable' offer to Castleford for his services. Peter remembers trying to learn from the Great Britain veteran: "Going to a match in Lancashire I sat with Ernest on the bus, and was quizzing him about the game, but he only answered 'Yes' or 'No'. He must have got fed up with me. He was a very quiet man, and a great player, but was a veteran by then."

On 15 December, Peter returned to his former club, but Batley's successful run ended with a 13-7 defeat: "Anson, Briggs and Fox gave competent but uninspiring performances," said the local paper. Unfortunately the team's early season form returned, with a run of seven defeats. The first was three days before Christmas, when Liverpool City won 10-6 at Mount Pleasant. The game was abandoned after 60 minutes due to fog, so the result stood. The pitch was in a "shocking" condition, less than 500 fans were present and, after 25 minutes, the fog meant it was impossible to see across the ground. Peter's Christmas was not improved with a 37-6 defeat at Leeds.

Peter was not the regular goalkicker, but kicked one at Hull, and another against Hunslet in a 30-4 home defeat: "In the second half loose-forward Fox took over at full-back and played an extremely good game... A goal by Fox was some encouragement."

Peter continued at full-back the next week at Castleford, replacing Philip Walshaw who was injured. He kicked four goals in a 19-14 defeat, including a 35-yard penalty.

The directors offered the team £18/10/0d a man as an incentive for the Challenge Cup first round tie at Hunslet. This was £11 more than the usual winning money of £7/10/0d. Peter Hinchliffe said that the club needed to strengthen the pack: "Batley lose games because forwards are not giving backs adequate supply of ball. In Eric Batten Batley have one of the most capable managers in the league, but he will not be able to put the club higher unless there is money to buy players. The team put up a "splendid fight against the finest pack of forwards in rugby league" at Hunslet, but lost 14-7.

A win came at last against Blackpool. Jim Etty, Peter Anson and Peter all played well. Hinchliffe said that "They produced a little of the tough style of play usually associated with Halifax or Hunslet." However, he also wrote that "Since Eric Batten's appointment as team manager last October a marked improvement has been seen in the play. There is still a lot to be done however before Batley are once again a really powerful side."

Two more defeats followed, but Peter was praised by Hinchliffe for both his performances. Against Keighley he "showed more enterprise than he has been doing in recent weeks" and put Batley on the offensive at start of second half with a good touch-finding kick. A 16-5 defeat at Salford was the team's 24th league defeat of the season. However, Hinchliffe said that he "would single out Fox as the outstanding Batley forward. He was obviously trying to put a little thought and anticipation into his play." He also reminded his readers that before they judged Eric Batten to remember that before he arrived Batley had not won a game this season.

Peter scored his first try since his debut for the team in a 12-7 victory over Bramley, when the Batley pack created an opening for him. Against Hull, in a magnificent performance which resulted in a narrow three-point defeat, "Anson and Fox both worked hard, Fox in particular showing that he knows more ways than one of beating a defence. His intelligent kicking and occasional long overhead passes caught the visitors wrong footed."

The next week, Batley beat Rochdale 8-4, in a dull game with no tries. But the season ended with four defeats, including a 31-4 rout at the hands of Wakefield Trinity at Mount Pleasant. Against Dewsbury, Peter played in the second-row for the first time, and later scored another try in the final match of the season against Bradford Northern, but Batley lost 22-12 after leading at half-time.

Batley finished 28th, with eight wins in 38 matches, scoring 399 points, but conceding a massive 700. Peter had established himself in the first team, making 27 appearances, scoring three tries and six goals. For both Peter and the team, it was something to build on for the future.

1957-58

Batley continued to improve this season – but only marginally – finishing 26th in the league with 10 wins from 38 matches. Peter played fairly regularly in the first team until early December, then returned for a couple of games in April. He remembers it was "not a good season". Mick Hirst had signed from Featherstone, with Norman Field joining the Post Office Road side in part-exchange.

Peter scored a try in the first home match, a 22-12 defeat against Bramley: "Hainsworth, Fox and Palmer were often prominent... Near the end Fox kicked over and touched down," reported the local paper.

In the Yorkshire Cup, Batley faced a daunting first-round trip to eventual winners Huddersfield. The local paper described the 68-19 defeat as a "massacre". Huddersfield were 25-2 up at one stage and eased off temporarily. Batley took full advantage of this, and scored "three good opportunist tries. Peter scored the first two, the first a scrambled affair and the second after a good forceful run. The half-time score was a respectable 25-19, but then the home team's domination returned, with Dyson and Sullivan scoring 50 points between them."

The first win of the season came on 21 September in the local derby with Dewsbury. Despite losing loose-forward Barry Whitaker after three minutes with a dislocated shoulder, Batley won 21-12, with Peter playing in the second row. The next week at Blackpool, Peter "worked hard and... used his weight to crash over for his second-half try."

A struggling Castleford side were the next visitors to Mount Pleasant. Peter returned to loose-forward, and was part of a memorable 24-8 win. Peter Hinchliffe said that "In the past two seasons I have never seen Batley play as well for the full 80 minutes as they did on Saturday ... [the] forwards completely dominated the Castleford six."

But there was a return to losing ways at Widnes the following week, although "Fox showed up well in the forwards. His intelligent touch finding kicks saved his colleagues a considerable amount of work and gained yards on numerous occasions." Batley's cause was not helped when Battersby broke his leg.

Along with his colleagues, Peter played poorly in a 12-9 defeat at bottom-of-the-table Doncaster, giving the home team their first win since March. His next game was at Huddersfield in November in a narrow 16-12 defeat, playing at loose-forward, where he had replaced Briggs.

Three weeks later, Peter came into the team at full-back in a narrow 13-8 defeat in the return match against Huddersfield. The scores were level until a couple of minutes from the end. Peter Hinchliffe wrote: "Peter Fox was brought back into the full-back berth in place of the trialist rugby union man, the first team choice for the past three weeks who was the victim of flu. Although this was only the second time that Fox has appeared at full-back for Batley he is no newcomer to the position. He was sound on defence and although he was a little slow in swinging his side onto the offensive, he rarely made a mistake.

Peter next played in two matches in April. The last match report said it had been a "dismal season" for the Mount Pleasant club, although one highlight was that Philip Walshaw broke the club's goalkicking record for a season with 113 goals.

1958-59

Peter missed most of this season due to studying four nights a week at night school for his Higher National Certificate. Batley dropped one place in the league, to 27th, with 11 points from 38 matches. Frank Watson was appointed first team coach, taking over from Eric Batten, with Arthur Staniland running the second team. Watson had been signed the previous season from Leeds. Peter says that "he had been a good half-back, but when he joined us had got slower – and he wasn't fast to start with. He was quiet, but not bad as a coach."

In the close season, Stan Thompson was signed from Workington, Albert Fearnley and Stan Moyser from Featherstone and Arthur Talbot from Hunslet. During the season, Norman Field rejoined the club from Featherstone, and half-back Ian Geldard was recruited from Leeds. Mick Hirst left for Keighley and Philip Walshaw to Bradford Northern.

There was something for the supporters to cheer in the early part of the season, with a run to the Yorkshire Cup semi-final. Victories at Mount Pleasant over Featherstone and Hull KR were followed by a 21-13 defeat at Belle Vue to Wakefield Trinity. In the Challenge Cup, Batley lost 19-2 at Leigh in the first round.

Peter returned to action on 7 March, with a "quiet game" in a 15-12 defeat at Bramley. It was Batley's ninth consecutive defeat, and they had yet to win in 1959. The next week, mighty Wakefield Trinity came to Mount Pleasant. Although Batley lost 28-16, Donald Warters reported in the *Batley News* that "improved Batley gave an entertaining display and held a powerful, but sleepy Wakefield Trinity until the last 10 minutes. Then Batley faded and Trinity scored 10 points." The fearsome Derek Turner was making his debut for Trinity, and must have been surprised when Batley led at half-time as Batley's forwards "held the strong Wakefield six". Peter's brother Neil scored 19 points for Trinity with a try and eight goals, watched by a 6,000 crowd, mainly from Wakefield.

Peter's final game of the season was in the local derby with Dewsbury. Batley lost 10-5 at Crown Flatt. He also played once for the 'A' team before the end of the season, beating Bradford Northern 20-15. Four days later, the first team won their first game since Boxing Day with a notable 10-5 win over Halifax. Interestingly, despite the poor season, one highlight for the club was that Stan Thompson set a new club goalkicking record, with 120.

1959-60

His studies completed, Peter returned to playing regularly the following season, and made 30 appearances in Batley's best campaign for many years. The club finished 16th in the league, with 18 wins and three draws from 38 matches. This was the first time they had managed more wins than defeats since 1951-52, and was their best position in the table since 1950-51. Sadly, this was not reflected in the cups, with a narrow 5-2 defeat against Keighley in the Challenge Cup, and a 46-8 loss at Hunslet in the Yorkshire Cup.

Batley started the season badly, with some first team players missing, while others had problems playing because they were undertaking national service and a couple had left the club or retired. The shareholders meeting was told that Mr J. Oldroyd was the new secretary-manager, that there had been a 33 per cent increase in gates in 1958-59, £4,000 had been spent on new players, and the loss on the season had been less than £300.

Peter started the season in the 'A' team, kicking five goals against Dewsbury. The first team lost their first five matches, and then beat struggling Liverpool City on 5 September. Peter won back his first team place on 19 September, playing in the front-row against Blackpool in a 19-9 win. The local paper said that: "There was a greater determination in a pack that had a better service of the ball... The introduction of Derek Harrison and Peter Fox as prop forwards with Whitford as hooker and Kelly and Armstead renewing their Wakefield Trinity days, infused plenty of enthusiasm."

Peter says that Derek Harrison "was not a giant, but a solid player. He did not make many mistakes, but was not a ball handler like a front-row forward today, but a ball carrier. Bob Kelly became the pack leader. Our pack was stronger this season. In the backs, Norman Field was a very strong winger, and scored quite a few tries, although he wasn't that fast. He went on to play for Great Britain. At half back, Ian Geldard was quick."

Batley then enjoyed a period of fairly regular victories – certainly at Mount Pleasant, where only Hull managed a win before Wakefield won 8-2 on 16 January. In the *Batley News*, Harry Beevers regularly commented on how the pack had improved with Harrison and Fox in the front-row. Peter missed the defeat against Hull, and the match report said that "reserve forward Helliwell tried hard, but he has not the ability of Fox". The next week, on 14 November, Batley won 10-5 at Bramley, and Beevers wrote that "Harrison, playing his best game for the club, and Fox in addition to their grand work as prop forwards, were again always to the fore in open play…" The next week, Peter gave "an inspiring display" in a 23-13 win over Salford, including scoring a try.

Although playing at prop forward, Peter could also play a creative role in the team. Although criticised on occasions for trying over ambitious passes, on 12 December at York "Fox… threw out a long pass to Field who was able to gather and touch down." However, Batley lost 17-10.

On Christmas Day, mighty Leeds were beaten 8-6 at Mount Pleasant, in front of 5,000 fans, the biggest crowd of the season, despite wet weather. Harrison and Fox gave "wonderful support" in the open. In the next home match, on 2 January, Barrow were beaten 28-2. But then the team hit a bad run, with two draws and seven defeats in the next nine matches. This included the defeat against Wakefield, when reports said that Batley deserved a draw.

Bob Kelly returned to the team on 12 March, and the local paper headline said "A Victory at Last" – a 21-6 win over Rochdale Hornets. It commented: "In the open play Harrison and Fox played on sound lines in supporting the work of those forwards already mentioned."

Towards the end of the season, Peter took on the goalkicking duties, with two at Liverpool City in a 7-7 draw, but then only one from seven attempts in an 8-2 win at Doncaster, and two against Hunslet in a 12-3 win.

On 23 April, "Batley ran riot at Huddersfield's expense", according to the *Batley News*, with a tremendous 37-18 win over their illustrious visitors from Fartown. Peter scored a try and kicked five goals for 13 points in a memorable victory, which with a 16-2 victory over Keighley the next week finished a successful season for a club of their size.

1960-61

In August, prior to the start of the season, the club announced that they had made a loss of £2,319 in 1959-60, despite saying that "playing strength was better than for many seasons". This meant that there were few resources available to strengthen the team, who dropped three places to 19th in the table, with 16 wins and a draw. Huddersfield finished any hopes of progress in the Yorkshire Cup, while in the Challenge Cup a 9-0 win over struggling Bradford Northern was followed by an 11-2 defeat at Swinton.

Peter again was a regular member of the first team, having consolidated his place in the front-row, and continued his partnership with Derek Harrison. Although Jim Lawton was the regular goalkicker, Peter had some opportunities, and kicked 26, his best performance with the boot. Added to two tries, he scored 58 points, the second-highest after Lawton's 130.

The season started with a disappointing home defeat against Whitehaven. Peter missed a midweek 26-2 loss at Halifax, but returned the following Saturday at Odsal against Bradford Northern. In a 14-7 win, the *Batley News* said that "Fox, Harrison and Harwood were often in the picture with some good forward play". Three days later, Batley beat Castleford 12-6 at Mount Pleasant, and Fox and Lawton gained much ground through kicks to touch. The local reporter was also "impressed with the bursts of Fox and Langhorn".

However, the home loss to Huddersfield in the Yorkshire Cup, and a 10-4 defeat to mid-table Widnes had the local paper saying that "something needs to be done to strengthen the side". A 17-12 win at Keighley drew the comment that "to say that a Batley win created a surprise is merely an understatement".

Batley and Wakefield are just seven miles apart. While Batley's traditional local rivals are neighbouring Dewsbury – to an outsider it is hard to tell where one finishes and the other starts – matches against Wakefield were also a local clash, and a chance for Batley to challenge a club that was one of the leading forces in the game at this time.

Trinity came to Mount Pleasant on 17 September, including Neil, and went away having lost 5-2; Batley maintaining their unbeaten Yorkshire League record. Harry Beevers wrote that "Not one of the 8,000 spectators would begrudge Batley the fruits of victory. The win was no fluke" he said that Batley showed "splendid team work. Harrison... along with Peter Fox (brother of Wakefield's centre) was always in the thick of the fray." The paper said that Batley had a thrilling win and that "slow moving Trinity were shocked."

Alfred Drewry in the *Yorkshire Post* pointed out that Batley were the first team for a year to prevent Trinity from scoring a try. He said that "This was no backs-to-the-wall effort. Batley did just as much attacking as Trinity and they did it with just as much skill and resolution, and they made no mistakes in defence. Batley made shrewd use of tactics. Peter Fox, so cool that he gave the impression of strolling through the game, and Lawton kicked accurately to touch..."

Peter looked forward to facing Trinity: "I always liked playing against them. We often played well against them at Mount Pleasant. I would go through the opposition players and identify their strengths and weaknesses, and go through this with our team. I always admired Derek Turner, he was always tough to play against. When Neil was playing, I always told our players to stay close to him, and stop him getting the ball on the run. If he had the ball, he was a powerhouse, no one could stop him. He had a strong hand-off and you couldn't touch him. For me, the games against Trinity were more important than Batley's matches with Dewsbury. Trinity were my local team, where I'd gone as a youngster to watch Herbert Goodfellow play."

The next week, Batley lost 2-0 at Hull KR, but then only lost once in the next seven games, at home to lowly Bradford Northern on 22 October. At Salford the week before, "Batley's measure of superiority at Salford was far greater than the two points that separated the sides when the final whistle sounded."

Peter missed the three games after the Bradford defeat, but returned for the derby match with Dewsbury, a hard fought 4-4 draw at Crown Flatt. But then the team hit a bad patch, with nine consecutive defeats, including failing to score on three consecutive occasions over Christmas and on New Year's Eve. It must have been a gloomy holiday season for Batley's fans.

In the 15-7 defeat to Hunslet in January, the local paper said that "Fox and McVeigh have rarely played better", and the next week, after an 8-0 defeat at Widnes, said that "McVeigh, Fox and Kelly [were] tireless workers in the loose."

The run ended with a 17-7 home win over Keighley on 4 February, with Peter kicking four goals. This was followed by the Challenge Cup win over Bradford, and a 22-9 loss at Leeds, when "Kelly, Dick, Fox and McVeigh were always in the thick of the fight".

But on 25 February, there was "a most disappointing exit" at Swinton in the Challenge Cup. Peter's drop-goal had given Batley the lead, and "Kelly and Fox with Harrison and Dick were often in the thick of the fray."

Things looked up after this, with four consecutive wins, including a 14-8 triumph over Halifax which the *Batley News* said was "another grand win, one which could rate among the best of the season." Peter kicked three goals in the first half. But after a 12-8 win over Huddersfield, the wheels fell off again, and the season ended in an anticlimax, with four defeats and then two wins in the last two matches. Peter was "outstanding" in the 15-10 loss at Featherstone, and the team were "magnificent" in a 12-6 win at Fartown on 26 April.

On 29 April, Peter captained the side against Bramley in a 13-7 win, and "sealed a good display by scoring Batley's third try."

The *Batley News* concluded that it had been a season of "ups and downs," but that "there is a good deal of hope for the future." But that would depend on the club's financial position, and whether resources could be found to strengthen the team. Peter felt that this season "gave the club renewed hope for the future."

1961-62

Brian Cartwright's history of Batley, *A 'Ton' full of Memories*, says of the 1960s that "more dismal than happy times were experienced on the field", and this season was one of them. Despite a promising start, Batley failed to build on their mid-table positions of the past two seasons, and sank back to 26th, with nine wins and two draws from 36 matches.

In June, the RFL had decided that from 1962-63, the league would be split into two divisions. The top 16 would form the First Division, and the bottom 14 the Second Division. Had Batley maintained their form of the previous two seasons they would have been challenging for a place in the top flight. As it was, a shocking run of form after Christmas made it clear that Second Division rugby would be on offer at Mount Pleasant in 1962-63.

Peter again played regularly for Batley, with 29 appearances. The season started against Featherstone, with Don playing for the visitors and going home with winning money after a 15-4 win. Peter remembers Don as a player "who could do anything on a rugby pitch. He was strong, a good ball-handler, good tactical and drop-kicker. The 40-20 rule would have been great for him. Harry Street wanted Wigan to sign him, but Featherstone wouldn't let him go."

Two narrow wins, 9-8 each time, against Castleford and Keighley followed, but a portent of the future came with a 41-2 defeat at Hull. Three days later, the team recovered with an enjoyable 15-0 win at Dewsbury in the Yorkshire Cup. Against Bradford Northern, Batley won 10-0, despite hooker Whitford losing the scrums 26-25 – at a rate of more than a scrum every two minutes, very different to the game today. The next week, Batley beat Leigh 17-7, but then seven consecutive defeats followed, including a 21-11 loss at Featherstone in the Yorkshire Cup.

When league leaders Workington Town came to Mount Pleasant on 4 November, Batley's fans must have had little cause for optimism. But the home side won 10-0, and "shocked the rugby league world" according to the local paper. Peter had not played since the defeat at Featherstone on 19 September, but the report said "Fox, reintroduced at prop, and McVeigh in the second row brought a new enthusiasm which seemed infectious." The win must have had a mixed reaction from the Batley directors – the gate was fewer than 3,000 and the paper said that they would "have to dig deep to provide winning pay".

Batley then beat Doncaster 24-10, with Peter kicking two goals, but the crowd was smaller than 1,300. The team's confidence was not helped with a 37-4 defeat at Leeds. Batley conceded nine tries, and Lewis Jones intercepted a pass from Peter for one of them.

The next week, Batley visited Belle Vue to face a Wakefield team in the middle of an unbeaten run that started on 2 September and would last until 17 March, a record 28 matches. Batley lost 24-13, a considerable improvement on the previous week's display at Headingley. The *Batley News* said that "Batley's best forward, undoubtedly, was Peter Fox. He always seems to be at his best against brother Neil's side, and his bursts and touch finding kicks helped no end on Saturday. And the robust Trinity forwards held no terrors for Fox – he can look after himself and did."

On 9 December, Batley beat Keighley 8-0, although the crowd was again disappointing. A 29-0 defeat at Hull KR followed, after which all the Christmas matches were postponed because of frozen grounds - another blow for the club's finances. On 6 January, the weather had improved enough for the team to come out of hibernation to beat York 7-5, but that was their last win of the season, except for a 9-0 win on 21 April against Dewsbury. Some of the defeats were close, a point at Doncaster, two at Hunslet and four at home to Huddersfield, but this run made Second Division rugby a certainty for the following season.

In the Challenge Cup, a 21-14 defeat at Featherstone was a respectable result, and Batley came close to providing a shock. Peter had missed the previous two games, and his return "strengthened the pack" although he also had a pass intercepted by Don for one of Featherstone's tries.

In the middle of this run of defeats were two draws. One was 7-7 with Halifax on 3 March. The other was two weeks before, on 17 February, when Challenge Cup holders Wakefield Trinity came to Mount Pleasant.

As mentioned previously, Wakefield were in the middle of a remarkable unbeaten run, a post-war record at the time. Before the match, Trinity had won 23 games, and the Batley players earned every penny of the special bonus they were offered to stop their mighty neighbours. Trinity expected to win easily, but as the *Batley News* said a "pushover became a hard fight".

Trinity were missing some players through international call-ups and injuries, but still should have been too strong for Batley. However, Harry Beevers wrote in the *Batley News* that "Batley are far from being a Second Division side. Their football at times has been delightful... with just a little luck they would have pulled off another surprise win." He also recognised that Batley stood firm against the Trinity attacks, especially in the first half when Trinity had the slope and the wind on their side. However, he concluded that Wakefield were not superior to Batley in "any department of the game". He said that Peter "gained useful ground with grubber kicks", and was one of Batley's "virile forwards" who laid the foundations of an excellent display. With McVeigh he contributed some telling work." Peter recalls that the newspaper coverage concentrated on Trinity's unbeaten run "and did not give us any credit." But Batley could not build on this result. The 7-7 draw with Halifax was memorable for Peter giving the team a tip for the Grand National, Mr What, which won at Aintree. At half time Batley were losing and then found they had backed the racing winner. Peter remembers telling the players that they should go out and beat Halifax as well, but in the end an away draw meant the players got winning money.

This moral victory was followed by one win in the last 11 matches, a 9-0 derby victory over Dewsbury which Peter missed. Peter did take on some of the goalkicking duties towards the end of the season, landing another six, and was also praised in match reports for his efforts in the pack.

The final straw in a miserable period was an 18-11 defeat in front of 700 lost souls at Odsal on 28 April. Bradford Northern were on the verge of collapse, and finished bottom of the table. Batley finished 17 points behind Hull, who had 37 to finish in the crucial 16th place. Second division rugby was on the horizon for Mount Pleasant.

Training night at Batley. Back: Jimmy Lawton, unknown, Derek Harrison, unknown, unknown, Peter Fox, Brian Ward. Front: Stan Moyser, Nobby Clark, Bob Kelly, Alan Pratt, Ian Geldard, Peter Armistead.

1962-63

To make up for the reduction in the number of fixtures brought about by two divisions, the RFL introduced an Eastern Competition and Western Competition for the first seven weeks of the season. So instead of starting with Second Division matches, Batley faced Wakefield, Leeds, Featherstone and Huddersfield. The campaign started well with a 5-4 win at Dewsbury in the Lazenby Cup, with Peter kicking a goal.

The club had announced that they had lost £2,296 the previous season, and had an accumulated deficit of £8,827. Despite there being few funds for new players, most of the previous season's squad stayed at Mount Pleasant, including star winger Norman Field.

The season proper started at Belle Vue, with an 18-9 defeat, including a try from Peter. The details of that score are clear in Peter's mind: "It came about through a move started by Kenny Rollin, Trinity's scrum-half, a Sharlston lad and our Neil's best mate at the time. Batley were defending in our own 25 when Kenny broke through in the centre with his full-back supporting him. I was in the right centre for Batley, having been covering the Trinity left wing. Kenny came straight at me. Now, Kenny knew I would not take a dummy, but I knew that Kenny knew that, so as he got nearer I bowed my head. As I went for Kenny my right hand went out and Kenny's pass stuck. I set off over our 25 yard line, crossed the halfway line and only then did I look over my shoulder to see who was chasing me. It was Trinity's South African centre Alan Skene. I crossed Trinity's 25 yard line with him still chasing me. I cut in towards the posts and with 10 yards to go I steadied, knowing what

Skene would do. And he did. He dived in an effort to tackle me, but it was too late and I scored under the posts. Skene unfortunately dislocated his shoulder. It was a try I will never forget and neither will Kenny. Kenny and I use the same gym these days and I always remind him and our mutual friends of just how I scored that day."

However, Trinity scored twice in the last 10 minutes to secure their win. Two days later, a 9-9 draw with Leeds at Mount Pleasant, with three goals from Peter, was a very respectable result.

Three further defeats followed, all by reasonable margins. Then Wakefield came to Mount Pleasant, including Neil, and went away having lost 13-11, by three tries to one. Once again Batley had shocked their neighbours, and Peter "played a grand game" according to the *Batley News*.

The Yorkshire Cup, however, offered no comfort for Batley, with a 28-2 defeat at Castleford. On 5 October, the *Batley News* said that "Second Division games to start tomorrow," and commented that "Dewsbury and Batley must begin well if they are to draw support and finish well in the promotion fringe. There are not going to be overworked turnstiles for the clubs at the lower end of the Second Division." Unfortunately, Batley's cause was not helped by Len Boustead breaking his leg in the final Eastern Competition match against Huddersfield.

The Second Division campaign opened at Salford, against a home team who had not won since March. Batley returned to Yorkshire after a 16-8 defeat. The next week, Keighley won 18-10 at Mount Pleasant. Peter kicked two goals and the local paper said that "Transfer listed Fox was the only Batley forward to show any initiative and though I am not a lover of those long passes he throws out there were some times on Saturday when some of them could have been turned to advantage. But why didn't Fox turn first-half penalty awards into goal points instead of the 'up and under' move?"

The next week, after a 31-3 defeat at Rochdale, the paper quoted one supporter saying that the team was the "worst he could remember. They never gave up, but were too slow." A 5-5 draw with York, and 7-5 defeat at Liverpool saw Batley bottom of the table.

But then their supporters in a 792 crowd were encouraged with a nine try 43-0 win over Salford. It was the club's biggest victory for some seasons, and Peter contributed six goals. But a 14-5 defeat at Keighley followed, although things improved with a 9-0 home win over Rochdale in front of 2,000 fans.

Peter's final game for Batley in this spell at the club was at York on 1 December 1962. He was acting captain, and played his part in a 15-12 win. But Batley were short of funds, and when First Division Hull KR offered to buy Peter, they could not turn the offer down. The local paper believed that the fee was £1,750, not the £2,500 that Batley wanted. The reported commented: "But it is most unhappy that, when Batley are doing well, a player of note has to be sold."

So at the age of 29, Peter headed off to Humberside. His new club had finished eighth in 1961-62, and had just appeared in the Yorkshire Cup Final, losing 12-2 to Hunslet. A fresh challenge awaited him.

1961-62: Batley versus Leigh at Mount Pleasant. Back: J. Ireland, P. Fox, C. Sutcliffe, D. Harrison, J. Westbury, A. Dick, N. Field; front: B. Whiteford, M. Shuttleworth, B. Pratt, J. Lawton, R. Astbury, I. Geldard.

Peter (on left) in action for Hull Kingston Rovers

4. Frustration at Hull Kingston Rovers

In moving to First Division Hull KR, Peter was taking a considerable step up from Batley. The Humberside club were one of the game's major clubs, and had just won the Eastern Division Championship and been runners up in the Yorkshire Cup. Rovers had been founded in 1883, and joined the Northern Union's Yorkshire Senior Competition in 1899-1900. The club had won the Championship twice in the 1920s, and been runners up in the Challenge Cup, but their last trophy when Peter joined had been a Yorkshire Cup win in the 1929-30 season.

In November, Rovers had been hit by the sudden retirement of Ken Grice, one of their prop forwards who had been with the club since 1950, although he came back into action in April. Peter recalls: "Jim Drake retired, and I was signed to strengthen the pack and to play at prop, although [a few months] later he made a comeback. He was coach Colin Hutton's first choice at prop."

The *Hull Daily Mail* reported that Rovers' scouts had watched Peter play for Batley at York, and no doubt aware of Batley's ongoing financial problems, moved in with an offer. Peter was on the transfer list at £2,500, but Rovers paid a fee reported as £1,750. Peter met Rovers officials in Leeds, and terms were quickly agreed with Batley, allowing him to make his debut for Rovers at Swinton on 8 December. He recalls: "Batley always needed money, and Hull KR came in for me. It was not easy, working in Leeds and finishing at 5pm, to get to Hull for training at 6.30pm. I'd bought a mini in 1962, and use to take Cyril Kellett, Arthur Bunting and Les Chamberlain with me to training. I used to slip away five minutes early from work to try to miss the traffic. Of course there was no motorway in those days, so we used to go on the old road through Knottingley. There were always a lot of lorries going to Hull, and I used to try to overtake them. The club had said I could train at Batley, but I preferred to try to go to Hull."

Alan Lockwood and Peter 'Flash' Flanagan were competing for the hooker spot at Craven Park when Peter arrived: "The hooker when I went there was Alan Lockwood. He always wanted to slip his arm, so I was left with no attachment to the scrum. Later he left the club and Flash was the regular hooker. He went on to do remarkably well for Rovers, and we got on fine. I acted as his protector in the scrums. Two other players I got on very well with were John Taylor and Davy Elliot. Davy lost his place at stand-off to Alan Burwell, who only wanted to play in that position, usually leaving no place for Davy."

Rovers lost at Swinton 27-5, with the *Hull Daily Mail* saying that "new signing Peter Fox distributed some astute passes... it was hardly a game on which to judge him." Peter kept his place in a shock 17-8 win at Warrington the next week, Rovers' first at Wilderspool for 34 years. The *Mail's* preview said that "There still remains the problem of bringing Rovers' pack to the solidity and strength of the earlier months. The acquisition of Peter Fox from Batley may partly solve it." The match report from a 'Special Reporter' said that "Coverdale and Fox were to the fore in some grand foraging."

Peter kept his place for a 3-0 win over Huddersfield in his debut at Craven Park, with the *Mail* reporting that "Fox sold a smart dummy as a result of which Flanagan was nearly there... Fox had a sound home debut."

Then came the great freeze of 1963, as Arctic conditions wiped out over two months of fixtures with snow and ice making matches impossible. It would have been difficult for players and supporters to travel to matches anyway, even if clubs had undersoil heating

29

that could have thawed the pitches. On 23 February, Rovers played a full scale practice game on Bridlington's south beach, which ensured them of a surface fit for training. The players got changed in the Bridlington Spa building, and several hundred spectators, many of them regular supporters who had travelled from Hull, watched the game.

On 2 March, Peter played against Keighley in a narrow 6-5 win in the Challenge Cup at Craven Park. It was their first game for 10 weeks. The team's Challenge Cup run was to end with a semi-final defeat against Wigan, but the next time Peter featured in the first team was on 4 May in a 19-15 defeat at Wigan. John Taylor, Les Chamberlain and Jim Drake were all injured, so Peter was recalled to the front row. Rovers were 15-5 up at half-time, and 15-14 ahead with the clock showing full-time before Wigan clinched the points in injury time. The *Mail* reported that "Peter Fox worked tirelessly and it was his readiness to send the ball on its way that won Rovers the position for their first scoring strike."

At a time when usually there would have been a couple of fixtures to play, and the players would have been preparing to play cricket or plan for their summer holidays, there was a third of the league programme still outstanding. The Challenge Cup Final had been put back, and as Cup fixtures had taken priority, the league season was extended to 1 June. For the only time in his 18 months at Craven Park, Peter got a regular place in the side. Two days after the Wigan match, John Grosse in the *Hull Daily Mail* said that Peter "played so well at blindside prop [and] is again included." He "played a big role" in the next match, two days later, a 32-18 home win over Castleford. Rovers were 22-2 ahead at half-time. Two days later, Rovers won the Hull derby at The Boulevard 19-5. Two Hull FC players broke their arms, and Rovers' "makeshift pack dominated Hull's forwards." Peter remembers the match well: "The Hull players were second-row Sykes who I thought tried to stiff arm me, I ducked slightly when I saw it coming and his forearm hit my forehead. Then winger Terry Hollindrake, the former Keighley player, tried the same ploy and suffered the same break. In later years, every time I met up with Terry he laughed about the incident. I don't think he will ever forget it."

Then came a five-day break, and on 13 May Rovers lost 13-3 at Leeds. Cyril Kellett hit the post with three consecutive kicks, which could have put Rovers 9-8 up. Two days later, Rovers went down again, at home to Wigan 34-12. The match preview said that "Peter Fox retains the blind-side prop berth," with the other two front-row positions being between four players. At this time Peter had become first choice at prop.

On 18 May, Rovers made the long trip to Workington, and lost 39-3, Peter scoring Rovers' try, his first points for the first team, with the *Mail* saying that "Fox forced his way over for a consolation try." The match preview had said that "Only blind side prop Peter Fox keeps his place in the front row." The Rovers coach left Hull at lunchtime on Friday, and Peter met it at Boroughbridge. The half-time score was 19-0, and the final result was Rovers' heaviest defeat of the season. Only six Rovers fans made the long trip. The *Mail's* report said that "Elliott and Fox making big efforts to find a gap in this competent Cumberland defence."

The season finished with defeats at Oldham and St Helens, and victories at home over Leeds, Workington and Warrington. At Oldham, John Gosse said in the *Mail* that the "pitch was in the worst condition I have ever seen rugby league football played on." On Rovers' performance, he said that "Too often Brain Tyson, their outstanding mud-hopper and Peter Fox were left to plough a lone course". This 11-5 defeat was followed by a 34-11 win over Leeds, with Bob Harris scoring five tries for Rovers. Vernon Rowe wrote in the *Mail* that "Peter Fox consolidated his position in the front row with a strong, hard-working performance." Three days later, Rovers went down by a point at St Helens, but were winning until seven minutes from time. Two days later, Rovers got revenge over Workington, with a 29-2 win at Craven Park. John Gosse said that "The raiding of Tyson, Fox and Coverdale obliterated Workington's resistance." The season finished, to everyone's relief, on 1 June, with an 18-13 home win over Warrington.

Peter finished the season with 15 first team appearances, 11 of which had been between 4 May and 1 June. He showed that when given a decent run in the first team, he was well worth his place. Rovers finished 10th in the First Division, with 27 points from 30 matches.

1963-64

Peter's first appearance in the new season came on 21 August against Leeds at Craven Park. He scored a try in Rovers' comfortable 22-3 win. The *Hull Daily Mail* said that "Peter Fox returned to the side with a workmanlike display which he finished off with a late try."

The preview of the next match, at Workington, said that "With plenty of experienced forwards to call on, including Harry Poole, [Rovers] have reason to be optimistic." Peter kept his place for the trip to Cumberland three days later, the home team winning 19-9, which was an improvement on the previous season's debacle. His next appearance, however, was at St Helens on 14 September. Rovers were 25-3 down at half-time, and lost 40-5, which the local paper described as their "biggest defeat". The *Mail* said that "Peter Fox replaced Jim Drake who was injured." In the second half: "Rovers continued to press and after Bunting had almost stumbled over under the posts, front-row forward Fox had to be hurled back by three St Helens defenders."

Three days later, Peter continued in the Rovers' team to visit Dewsbury in the Yorkshire Cup. A 6,000 crowd saw the home team win 17-13. They had been 10-8 up at half-time, and Rovers' only score in the second half was a converted try in the final moments of the match.

The following Saturday, Rovers lost at Wigan 20-16 but the pack, including Peter, took a beating in the scrums according to the *Mail*. On 28 September, Neil's Wakefield team came to Craven Park. With Batley, Peter had often enjoyed victories over Trinity, and did it again with Rovers. Neil scored all Trinity's points, but Rovers won 22-7, with the *Mail* calling it a "copybook-football win". The report also said that "Peter Fox and Flanagan tested the [Wakefield] defence with some forthright football."

John Gosse said on the day of the Wakefield match: "The only West Riding player who might feel that he has been somewhat overlooked is Batley's former skipper Peter Fox, who was some time finding favour after his signing in December 1962. He had a long spell in the reserve side, but has still made 20 first team appearances and is playing strongly enough just now to make one of the prop positions his own."

The Eastern Division fixtures were now played throughout the season, interspersed with the league matches. Peter played in Rovers' home match with Keighley, when three tries from Alan Burwell helped Rovers to win 28-7. The *Mail's* report said that "Peter Fox had a huge slice of luck when a pass he had knocked on bounced straight off Alf Barron back into Fox's hands and a quick transfer sent David Elliott chasing under the posts."

The next week, a combined Hull XIII faced the Australians who were touring that autumn. Peter played in the front-row. After holding the tourists to 5-5 at halftime, the home side went down 23-10 in front of 10,481 fans. The Australians went on to retain the

Ashes, winning the first two tests before Great Britain won the final game at Headingley. It was to be Peter's only appearance against a touring side.

Peter kept his place for Rovers' next match on 19 October, a great 19-6 win for Rovers at Fartown. Rovers scored five tries against a Huddersfield team who lost full-back Brian Curry through injury in the first half. The *Mail* said it was "A match to remember for the Robins – for a second-half display in which they laid on great football to swamp Huddersfield and sweep to a well-deserved win, and for a tough first half which left the crowd furious after full-back Curry was carried off."

Rovers' next two matches were against Keighley. On 26 October, they went down 12-11 in the return Eastern Division fixture. The *Mail's* report said that Rovers' lead just slipped away... desperate fight back fails." Rovers were 11-0 up at half-time and in the first half Rovers dictated the game, with Fox especially prominent. John Gosse said that "Fox... distinguished himself".

The next week, Peter scored a try in a 22-10 win in the league at Craven Park. John Gosse wrote in the *Hull Daily Mail*: "Rovers, however, winning the first three scrums, piled on the pressure with Tyson, Flanagan and Fox dangerous..." He described their second try: "Three minutes later [after 29 minutes] Rovers went further ahead. Again Bunting made the running, with Luffman backing up well, and as Keighley fell back Clark seized on the ball to send an inside pass to Fox who made a ragshop of the visitors' defence and finished with a try under the posts, easily goaled by Kellett."

On 5 November, Rovers announced the signing of John Bath, the Hull and East Riding rugby union prop forward. Also, in the next first team game, Les Chamberlain took a new role at blindside prop. This left Peter demoted to the 'A' team, and three days after playing in a 9-5 defeat at Featherstone on 16 November, he put in a written transfer request. The *Mail* reported that the request would be considered by the board. It said that Fox joined the club from Batley last December and had made 25 first team appearances, scoring three tries. He had also played in seven 'A' team games, in which he kicked one goal.

Peter returned to the first team the following week, a visit to Featherstone, facing Don, who was their captain, and needed six points to equal Jim Denton's club points scoring record, Hull KR lost 8-3, with Don contributing five points, but missing six penalties. The record remained intact for a few more days. John Gosse wrote that Peter Fox was playing up strongly in the Rovers pack in the first half.

But Peter's prospects of regular first team rugby were given another blow when, on 6 December, Rovers signed Frank Fox, Halifax's 23-year-old Yorkshire prop forward. However, at the same time Les Chamberlain joined Leeds. He couldn't train with Rovers because of work and wanted a club nearer home.

On 11 January, Peter played for the 'A' team against Doncaster. The team included Cyril Kellett, who had asked for a transfer in December, and Arthur Bunting. Peter returned to the first team at Castleford on 25 January. Rovers lost 14-6, and were below form. Castleford only had 12 men in the second half, with Keith Hepworth leaving the field injured. A couple of weeks later Cyril Kellett resolved his differences with the club and came off the transfer list.

Rovers now started on a run in the Challenge Cup that would take them to their first Wembley appearance and first Final since 1925. However, Peter by now was consigned to the 'A' team, where he scored a try against Wakefield on 7 March, and on Easter Monday was in the team that beat Hull 'A' 15-5.

Peter was not in the 16-man squad for the Challenge Cup semi-final against Oldham, but neither was his rival for a place as prop, Frank Fox, who subsequently asked for a transfer. The semi-final was a draw, and the replay was abandoned in extra time due to bad light, much to Oldham's frustration as they were winning 17-14. Hull KR won the restaged replay.

Peter made a brief return to the first team – as captain - for an Eastern Division match at Bramley on 22 April. He played in a token first team without a single member of the Cup side. At first the game was fairly even according to the *Mail*: "In this period [first half], Frank Fox, Peter Fox and Brian Mennell got through a lot of work up front for Rovers.." Peter kicked a penalty in second half, the only goal he scored for Rovers' first team.

By now Peter had clearly despaired of getting any first team action at Craven Park, and joined Hunslet on loan towards the end of the season, playing a couple of first team matches. The move had been initiated by Rovers. Peter recollects that "[Hunslet] chairman Harold Inman and secretary Harry Jepson came to my home to tell me that Hull KR had offered to loan me to Hunslet. I took up the offer, and played a few games, but in the summer they didn't sign me and then went on to reach the Challenge Cup Final in 1965. It seemed to be my luck never to play at Wembley."

Peter's chances of a first team place at prop had been further reduced by John Taylor moving into that position. Rovers announced a 16-man squad for the Challenge Cup Final against Widnes. But they then had a crisis at prop forward. Taylor had been sent off at Huddersfield, and was given a one-match ban – the Wembley final. John Bath and Frank Fox were both injured, and Jim Drake failed a fitness test the day before the match. So Brian Mennell was summoned to London, and played at prop, after only three first team games and 19 'A' team matches. Mennell was fifth choice for the position and, according to reports of the match did not let the team down. Peter remembers that the match was lost in the forwards to Widnes's powerful pack, and says that "I could have done something for them."

If Peter had still been at the club, and not taken the chance of a few games with Hunslet on loan, even though he was out of favour with the first team selectors, surely he would have been considered for the Challenge Cup Final place, as an experienced prop forward, compared to a 21 year old with minimal first team experience.

On 13 May, Peter played for Hunslet at Craven Park, his new team going down 25-10. The *Mail's* report said that "The forward exchanges were always lively, and sometimes became a bit overheated with former Rovers forward Peter Fox collecting more than one caution."

In his second season at Craven Park, he played 13 games, scoring two tries and kicking a goal. Rovers finished ninth in the First Division, with 30 points from 30 matches. Again, when Peter was given a run in the first team he had shown that he could play at First Division level, but the competition for places in the front row meant he had few opportunities in the second half of the season, and missed out on a Wembley appearance. Disappointment also came when Hunslet decided not to sign him for the 1964-65 season, and as Peter recalls, they also reached Wembley in 1965. So in the summer he returned to Batley to continue his playing career. A famous match at Craven Park was on the horizon…

SCORE SHEET	WAKEFIELD TRINITY (White jerseys with circlet of Red & Blue White shorts)	LITESOME KICK-OFF 3-00 40 minutes each way	BATLEY (Cherry and White jerseys White shorts)	SCORE SHEET
Goals :	Full back 1 Metcalfe		Full back 1 Warner	Goals :
	Three-quarter backs 2 Jones 3 Davies 4 Fox N. 5 Coetzer		Three-quarter backs 2 Pratt 3 Abed 4 Ward 5 Raynor	
Tries :	Half backs 6 Poynton/A. N. Other 7 Holliday		Half backs 6 Geldard 7 Doyle	Tries :
	Front row forwards 8 Dolton 9 Shepherd 10 Campbell		Front row forwards 8 Fox P. 9 Fryer 10 Hinchliffe	
Points :	Second row forwards 11 Haigh 12 Bell		Second row forwards 11 Sharrett 12 Johnston	Points :
	Loose forward 13 Fox D.		Loose forward 13 Foster	
	Substitutes : 14 .... 15 Plumstead		Substitutes : 14 Pearman 15 Kennedy	
	Referee : J. T. Dixon (Barrow)		TOUCH JUDGES : G. T. L. Smithson (Pink Flag) / M. Marsh (Yellow Flag)	

Three brothers in action: Neil and Don for Wakefield Trinity against Peter for Batley.
(Courtesy Wakefield Trinity Wildcats RLFC)

Peter, Don and Neil – before training at Wakefield Trinity in 1966.
(Courtesy Neil Fox)

5. Back to Batley

After 18 months on Humberside, Peter returned to Batley. Now aged 31, and a player of considerable experience, he still had much to offer to one of rugby league's smaller professional clubs.

Although often in the lower reaches of the league table, Batley had always had the capacity to defeat or upset the game's giants. In February 1964, Batley won 3-0 at Halifax in the Challenge Cup, a memorable giant-killing feat. A similar triumph, 7-5 at Craven Park over Peter's former club, Hull KR, on 6 February 1965, was the highlight of his second spell at Batley.

Few rugby league pundits gave Batley much chance at Craven Park. Rovers had been runners-up at Wembley the previous May and were in the top half of the league table, whereas Batley were struggling near the bottom. For Peter, it was a chance to remind the Humberside club of what he could do – one newspaper preview said that "Rovers' forwards... may not have matters all their own way against Batley's pack led by Peter Fox, who thought he had something of a raw deal after joining Rovers...and getting very little first team play."

Rovers' pack included two new forwards, Frank Foster and Bill Holliday, who had cost £13,000 and they dominated the game early on in front of a 10,000 crowd. However, it was Peter who gave Batley the lead on 26 minutes, with a drop-goal. Rovers replied with a try from Arthur Bunting, with Cyril Kellett's conversion making the score 5-2. But just before half-time, Batley were awarded a penalty on the touchline, when Bath fouled Peter. Full-back Alan Warner was moving the ball back to improve his angle, when Peter told him to kick it from as far near the tryline as possible, reasoning that if it missed or fell short, Batley would have a chance of winning possession.

That was exactly what happened. The ball dropped under the cross bar, Rovers' experienced full-back Cyril Kellett hesitated, and Malcolm Shuttleworth gathered the ball to score under the posts. Warner kicked the goal to give Batley a two-point half-time lead.

The *Batley News* gave much of the credit for the victory to the pack, saying that they "completely subdued the star-studded combination which the Rovers were able to field. Sharp, Hinchliffe, Foster, Johnston and Fox were always on the move, and in the open play Fryer was never far behind." For the backs, scrum-half Butterfield stood out. Another newspaper report, headed "Peter Fox kicks out old pals" said that it was a "tactical triumph" for Batley, and that their handling was "superior, indeed it was flawless, otherwise Rovers would not have been denied possession for such long periods".

Near the end of the game, Rovers had their best chance to win the game, when stand off Alan Burwell broke through. Peter recalls: "Burwell had two men outside him, and only me to beat. He only had to pass, and they would have scored. But I knew he would try to dummy, so I smothered him. At the end of the game, Jackie Briggs ran onto the pitch and congratulated me, saying that tackle won the game for us."

One of the national newspapers had a photo of Peter back at work sitting at a drawing board, with a headline of "Peter knows how to fox 'em", saying that he had helped his club to the shock result of the first round of the Challenge Cup. The *Hull Daily Mail* sports headline for 6 February said that said that "Rovers get Cup KO from battling Batley". The match report commented: "Batley's grim determination, their magnificent cover defence which rarely gave Rovers a scoring chance, plus the possession advantage which they maintained for much of the match, all combined to flatten the Robins' hopes of a second trip to Wembley." Peter Fox's drop-goal "was no more than they deserved" The paper said about Batley's try: "Then came disaster. Out on Batley's left, Warner took a difficult penalty shot. The ball hung in the wind and dropped just under the bar, but as Kellett hesitated in gathering it, Shuttleworth came racing up to grasp the ball and score an astonishing try under the posts, where Warner converted to give Batley their lead back." The teams were:

Hull K R: Kellett, Harris, Major, Moore, Blackmore, A. Burwell, Bunting, Bath, Flanagan, Drake, Tyson, Foster, Holliday.

Batley: Warner, Ward, Smith, Shuttleworth, Fearman, Geldard, Butterfield, Fox, Fryer, Sharp, Hinchliffe, Johnston, Foster.

Sadly, the Cup run ended against Hunslet three weeks later, as it had the previous season, although this time Batley travelled to Parkside. Special Sunday training sessions to prepare for the big match did not help Batley, who lost 24-4. The half-time score was 2-2, with Peter having kicked one goal from five attempts, but Hunslet ended the game easy winners, and went on to Wembley, losing 20-16 to Wigan in one of the best Challenge Cup Finals of that era.

Peter had returned to Batley at the end of August. The previous season, they had finished ninth in a 13 team Second Division, Bradford Northern having dropped out of the league just before Christmas when the club went out of business. The team had won eight out of 24 games. But for 1964-65, the RFL had prematurely abandoned their idea of two divisions, and returned to one league of 30 teams, with each team playing 34 matches.

Prior to this arrival, Batley had made a poor start to the season, conceding 86 points in the first three matches, including the pre-season Lazenby Cup match. The *Batley News* reported that the club was in contact with Hull KR about Peter returning to strengthen the pack, saying "Batley has not been too fortunate for prop forwards since Fox was transferred to the Craven Park club and the intention now is to re-sign him in order that he can take over the position of pack leader. If this rather surprising move comes off, it will help Batley's forward troubles – and Fox is also a goalkicker."

Peter was signed in time to play against Blackpool on 29 August. It was not a great start – a 13-12 home defeat against the team that would finish bottom of the table. Ian Geldard also returned to the team, following a broken ankle, but star winger Norman Field had retired to concentrate on developing his business interests, after becoming the club's third player to win full international honours the previous season, when he played for Great Britain at Wembley against Australia.

The local paper reported that Peter "assumed the role of pack leader and covered a good deal of ground in his efforts to infuse life into the other forwards, who responded well in the early stages." The next week, Batley won 4-2 at Liverpool, when Peter "had a good game", but then a midweek 35-9 defeat at Hull followed in the Yorkshire Cup.

The first victory of the season at Mount Pleasant followed, 15-13 over Salford, who had a man sent off after 19 minutes. The match report said the pack was "well led by Fox", and the next week, in an 18-5 defeat at Odsal to the newly revived Bradford Northern, "most deserving of praise was skipper and prop forward Peter Fox. Nobody did more than he to hamper Northern's progress in the first hour. He did an enormous amount of tackling and drilled the pack so well that the Northern six were well and truly held in the loose." Northern won the game in the last quarter, scoring 13 points in that period.

Leeds won 38-5 at Mount Pleasant the next week. The crowd was fewer than 3,000, poor for a match against one of the game's glamour sides. One factor affecting Batley's gates at this time was the rise of Leeds United Football Club. Their Elland Road ground was an easy journey from Batley, and they had not only won promotion to football's First Division, but under manager Don Revie were challenging for the title and other honours. With rugby league still playing only on Saturdays at the weekend at this time, clearly some fans transferred their allegiance to Elland Road. The difference between rich and poor clubs in rugby league was also shown in this match – Leeds' new signing Rod Morgan, at £4,500 had cost more than the entire Batley team.

Peter missed the next match, a 41-13 defeat at Hull KR, through badly bruised ribs and shoulder and a ricked ankle. However, he was fit enough to return against Wakefield Trinity on 10 October. Once again, Batley raised their game against their glamorous neighbours. Neil was not playing for Trinity, and each side scored two penalties in a 4-4 draw. Bill Bowes wrote that "Had [Batley's] trialist full-back been on form with his goalkicking…Batley would have won… Fox was a tower of strength in the Batley pack."

Peter played in defeats against Hull and Halifax, then did not play for more than a month. One of these matches was a 10-4 home defeat against Doncaster, with only 650 fans present, a very poor crowd for these times. Peter returned to the team for a 7-3 home win over Bramley on 12 December, kicking two goals, but this was followed by a miserable 31-4 defeat at Castleford, the home team scoring nine tries.

Both the Christmas matches against Dewsbury were postponed. Both clubs were at such a low ebb that there was discussion in the *Batley News* about whether they should amalgamate. Nothing came of this proposal, or one from a "keen supporter", John Whitfield, who suggested that they would fare better playing rugby union.

A defeat at York opened the new year, but then Batley beat Hull 4-2 at Mount Pleasant, Peter kicking both goals, but in front of only 500 supporters. He also made "a useful contribution" to a 9-7 win at Blackpool the next week.

Then came that great win at Craven Park, although reality bit back the next week, with Bradford Northern winning 25-2 at Mount Pleasant in front of 2,824 fans, mainly from Bradford. Only 400 saw a 15-3 home win over York the next week, with Peter kicking three goals.

The ongoing problems facing the club, which lasted throughout the rest of the 1960s, were shown with a 7-3 defeat at home to Liverpool City. The Merseyside club were perennial strugglers, and probably bought few supporters with them. Around 200 fans were present, and only £23 was raised from gate receipts. It was the smallest crowd in the club's history at the time.

Peter missed a couple of games, including the home match against Hull KR, and returned to the team when Featherstone came to Mount Pleasant. The *Batley News* said that his return was "important" to the team, and that his work was "first class". The report continued: "He led the forwards, he rallied the side, and he took over with success as goalkicker when Warner was off target."

April was a busy month for Peter, with seven first team appearances, including matches over the Easter holiday. He kicked a further 12 goals in this period and scored a try against Keighley from a 40-yard run, the only game Batley won. To add some extra fixtures for the teams in the bottom half of the league, the RFL had introduced the remarkably named "Bottom 14 Cup" for teams who were not in the newly expanded 16-team end of season Championship play-offs. Batley beat York 9-8 in the first round, with Peter kicking three goals, but then lost 24-9 at Doncaster, despite Peter again finding the target three times with the boot.

Batley finished 26th, with 19 points from nine wins and a draw. Peter had played 28 first team games, scoring 32 goals, his best season total as a professional player. But Batley faced the dilemma they had faced since Peter first joined them in 1956: low gates meant they could not afford to compete in the transfer market, but the resultant struggling team could not attract bigger crowds to bring more resources into the club.

1965-66

The Batley directors attempted to find the resources to rebuild the team, and made a record number of signings. Whereas the previous season most recruits had been from amateur sides, now most of the new players came from other professional clubs, including Jack Pycroft from Oldham for a club record £1,760. Pycroft made his debut for Batley in November, and never played alongside Peter. An appeal fund, including contributions from the Supporters Club and the directors helped raise the fee.

The season started with two home wins, against Whitehaven and Doncaster. Peter played his first game on 4 September, a 37-9 defeat to Halifax at Mount Pleasant. The next week, Wakefield Trinity came to Mount Pleasant. The match was shown on television, but this time Batley could not surprise their illustrious neighbours, and lost 23-7. Neil missed the match – he was recovering from an appendix operation. Don was also playing for Trinity this season, but only moved to Belle Vue five days after this match.

Peter missed the next two games, but returned for the next match, at Wakefield on 2 October. For the first time in a professional game, all three Fox brothers played in the same match. Peter captained Batley and Neil led Trinity. Fortunately, this game was not shown on television, because it was abandoned in the last minute due to violent play.

Trinity were 5-2 ahead at half-time, and winning 13-2 when the match finished, officially abandoned by the referee, J.T. Dixon from Barrow, although he claimed that "It was an utter brawl, I couldn't do anything about it". Batley had been penned on their line, and defending grimly. The *Batley News* report felt that Trinity were the instigators, and named Campbell and Haigh, saying that Trinity had "mixed it" in the second half. What was certain is that there was a fight between the packs, and police officers and coaching staff intervened to try to stop it. There was a photograph in the national papers of a Wakefield coach with a stranglehold on Johnston, the Batley forward.

Many supporters felt that the referee should have taken action earlier. The result stood, fortunately, although some players received warning letters from the RFL.

The next week, Peter played his final game for Batley, a 26-0 home defeat against Bramley. It was a sad end to eight seasons' service to the club. Without Peter the investment in new players did not pay off. Batley's next win came on 11 December against Hull KR, and the team finally finished 28th in the league, with only 14 points.

Two of Peter's team mates at Batley were Jackie Briggs and Malcolm Shuttleworth. Both still live in the town, and are active members of the Batley Past Players' Association.

Jackie Briggs was becoming established in the Batley first team when Peter joined from Featherstone in 1956. He first played rugby league for Dewsbury YMCA under-16s, then played as an amateur for Dewsbury, as well as working with Harry Street on the groundstaff, but turned professional for Batley. Apart from a short spell at Dewsbury, he played for Batley for the rest of his career "always as a forward – I was never fast enough to be a back."

He remembers Peter as "a good thinker about the game, he helped quite a few of us and we helped him. Peter always knew about the opposing players, and pointed out where they could be dangerous to us." Playing for Batley at that time "was hard going. We lost more than we won, but we enjoyed our rugby."

Although Batley's local rivals were Dewsbury, matches with Wakefield Trinity were always a highlight: "With Peter being from Sharlston, Don playing at Featherstone and Neil at Wakefield there was always some local rivalry. Wakefield were a good team, we always looked forward to playing them. They had great players such as Derek Turner and Don Vines as well as Neil. I played in the 0-0 draw in 1962, and the match at Belle Vue that was abandoned a couple of minutes from the end."

One of Jackie's best memories of his time at Batley was when Peter was playing for Hull KR – their great Challenge Cup win at Halifax in 1964. He did not play in the win at Craven Park in 1965. He recalls that: "Peter always thought about the particular game he was involved in. In those days we trained twice a week, mainly physical training. Then the forwards would work on their own. Peter would often take charge, coming up with different moves the forwards could make. To me, this showed he was a natural coach, which he eventually became."

Jackie coached local amateur teams after retiring from the professional games. He still goes to watch Batley occasionally, especially when there is a past players reunion, and watches the local amateur teams.

Malcolm Shuttleworth first played rugby league with Batley Boys. He joined the Royal Navy aged 17, and served until he was 24, playing rugby union for service teams, local club sides and the Hampshire under-21 team. There was no rugby league in the armed forces at that time. "When I got out of the navy I had trials for Leeds, but played as a centre and they had Lewis Jones, so they didn't need me! So I joined Batley in December 1958 and never regretted it. Peter was already with Batley when I joined. Often players from the bigger clubs, such as Halifax or Leeds, would join us at the end of their careers. And if we did get a talented young player, they would try to tempt them away – Batley always needed the money."

He recalls that "Peter was different from other players. He was a great lad – he had joined us from Featherstone, but was not a miner. He was a draughtsman – a good office job. He was a great talker and a bit ahead of his time. I remember we were playing against Wakefield, with the South African Ivor Dorrington in their pack. Peter would talk the opposition to death in the scrum. A scrum broke up and Dorrington said 'Foxy, if you want to fight now, we'll fight, or go off and fight, but stop talking!' Peter was a bit more diplomatic for the rest of the game.

Peter could see an opening and would try long passes, but they didn't always go where they were supposed to. It was always someone else's fault if they were intercepted. The ball was heavier then, and it was more difficult to do long passes."

He also remembers Peter "as a thinker about the game. He did his homework and would talk about the other team's players. He knew about the other teams." He also recalls Peter's racing tips: "One game, he found out at half-time that his horse had won, and was saying to everyone 'I told you to back it'. For away games, we would stop and have a meal, a drink and a singsong on the way home. Peter's song was *Grandfather's Clock*."

Times could be hard at Batley: "We had signed Jackie Pycroft, and were asked by the board if the players could contribute. So we agreed to play the next game, at Odsal, for free. We played against Bradford. I was the captain by then. After the game, I was called into the Bradford directors' room, and was asked if it was true if we had played for free to help the club. I said it was, and Trevor Foster gave me a cheque on behalf of Bradford Northern that covered the team's losing pay. He said he had never heard of such a gesture from the players at a club before."

Malcolm remembers the 0-0 draw with Wakefield: "We often did well against Wakefield Trinity. There was always a good crowd for those games. We were an average team with a lot of local players." However, the highlights of his career were two tries in famous cup victories: "At Halifax in 1964, I did a fantastic run, the length of the field, to score. At Hull KR the next year, I remember Peter moving the penalty kick on the wing back. It was unusual for Cyril Kellett to make a mistake, but he did and I scored. I think I played better games, but people remember the tries. Hull KR had just signed two new forwards, and our win was a shock."

When Malcolm retired from playing, he coached the Batley Boys teams, and remembers going round pubs in Batley to collect money to buy them a decent playing kit. His wife helped repair the shirts so they looked good as a team. His team developed into an open age side, and one of the players, Carl Gibson, went on to play for Leeds and Great Britain. He also coached the 'A' team at Batley for a while. Now, he has a season ticket for Batley, and also watches Batley Boys matches. He worked for Fox's Biscuits in the town, and remembers the supporters on a Monday morning commenting about the team's performance at the weekend, at times one of the disadvantages of playing for your home town side.

1966-67: Wakefield Trinity

Peter was tempted out of retirement to join Wakefield Trinity at the end of August 1966, initially to assist the 'A' team as pack leader. He played two games, after which he was selected for the first team at Swinton on 17 September. This short period was the first time that the three Fox brothers had been at the same club as players.

However, neither Neil nor Don played in this match, and so the three Fox brothers would never play together on the same side in a professional rugby league match.

Trinity lost 27-13 at Station Road, and Peter went off injured at half-time. This injury bought to an end his 13-year professional career, which encompassed 245 matches, 17 tries and 119 goals.

Now, aged 33, new challenges in rugby league lay ahead for Peter Fox.

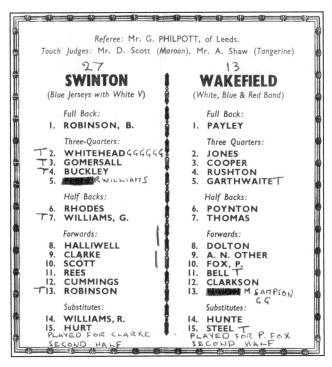

27   13

SWINTON
(Blue Jerseys with White V)

Referee: Mr. G. PHILPOTT, of Leeds.
Touch Judges: Mr. D. Scott *(Maroon)*, Mr. A. Shaw *(Tangerine)*

WAKEFIELD
(White, Blue & Red Band)

Full Back:
1. ROBINSON, B.

Three-Quarters:
T 2. WHITEHEAD GGGGGG
T 3. GOMERSALL
T 4. BUCKLEY
5. ~~PETER~~ R WILLIAMS

Half Backs:
6. RHODES
T 7. WILLIAMS, G.

Forwards:
8. HALLIWELL
9. CLARKE
10. SCOTT
11. REES
12. CUMMINGS
T 13. ROBINSON

Substitutes:
14. WILLIAMS, R.
15. HURT
PLAYED FOR CLARKE
SECOND HALF

Full Back:
1. PAYLEY

Three Quarters:
2. JONES
3. COOPER
4. RUSHTON
5. GARTHWAITE T

Half Backs:
6. POYNTON
7. THOMAS

Forwards:
8. DOLTON
9. A. N. OTHER
10. FOX, P.
11. BELL T
12. CLARKSON
13. ~~EVANS~~ M SAMPSON G G

Substitutes:
14. HUNTE
15. STEEL T
PLAYED FOR P. FOX
SECOND HALF

The teams from the match programme for Peter's last game as a professional rugby league player – for Wakefield at Swinton on 17 September 1966.

Doing a turn at a Batley RLFC reunion in 1978, with the other players joining in the chorus.

Playing the other code: 1970 Works tournament Development department football team.
Peter's side reached the final, but lost 2-0.

Left: The 1979 IMI apprentices: back: J. Dobson, Michael Carter, Kevin Jewison, Anthony Skellington, Paul Chilton, Mark Walker, Peter Wynn, Peter Fox, Ian Marshall, Michael Lynch, Jonathan Harpin, Mohammed Ajub, Christopher Dickinson.

Below: Retiring from work at IMI in 1993.

6. Work and family life

Peter's working life was spent in the engineering industry. After finishing his apprenticeship, he stayed with the company with which he had served it: British Jeffrey Diamond (BJD), who manufactured mining equipment, and then moved to Yorkshire Copper Works in Leeds where he worked as a design draughtsman. Subsequently, this company became part of a new holding company, Imperial Metal Industries (IMI), in 1962.

After his time in the drawing office, he became the training and safety officer for the engineering division, being responsible for about 950 of the 6,000 employees. Part of his role was as manager of the apprentice training centre, guiding the young apprentices into the world of work in their first two years in the company. Peter trained around 400 engineering apprentices at IMI.

Peter recalls: "I liked my work. I was well known in the company, and used to go round the factory. I knew the supervisors and the managers both through work and rugby league. The apprentices weren't always easy, but I had two very good supervisors, and I only had to sack one apprentice in the time I was there. Of course, rugby training was in the evening in those days, so I never had a problem with my rugby activities and work, although occasionally I had to take a day's leave for an away match."

Peter was not the only professional rugby league player at the Copper Works. A feature in the company magazine in the early 1960s lists John Wilson, Philip Walshaw, Peter, Harry Street, Don Robinson, Terry Clawson, Cliff Lambert, Roy Bell and Brian Shaw as professional players working for the company, along with George Philpott, a grade one referee. Had the company fielded a works teams at this time, they could have held their own in the professional game. However, the company never used Peter for any publicity connected with his rugby league role.

Peter was also an active trade unionist: "I started the union at BJD, and then recruited the drawing office staff at the Copper Works. Draughtsmen were 'group 2' employees. Then when I was promoted to 'group 1', which was the senior staff, they wanted me to be their union rep as well. I used to negotiate with Ken Hamill, who was the boss at the head office, who was a Castleford supporter."

Occasionally it was difficult to fit in work and rugby commitments: "When I was training officer, the company sent me on some courses at Portsmouth Polytechnic. I was coaching Bradford Northern at the time, and they flew me back up north for a match at Castleford. A friend of the directors had a small plane that we used."

Peter worked for IMI until he retired to become a full-time coach at Bradford Northern in 1993.

Another activity that Peter developed while still coaching was after-dinner speaking. At first this was mainly to support players at their testimonial dinners, or to raise funds for cricket clubs: "I just used to ask for my petrol money, but then I used to get offered a fee, although I would never charge amateur rugby league clubs. I did some dinners with Freddie Trueman, while another good speaker was Peter Parfitt, the former Middlesex and England cricketer. He lived in the Dales near Trueman. I also did a dinner with Emlyn Hughes, the former England and Liverpool footballer. I told him I had seen his father playing for Workington against Sharlston, and he didn't know about the matches."

Family life

Peter and Joan celebrated their golden wedding in 2007. They were married on 30 November 1957 at St Luke's Church in Sharlston. Don was Peter's best man, and Neil was a groomsman, so, as Joan recalls: "On that Saturday the three Fox brothers were missing from their rugby teams". Peter was aged 24 and Joan was 22. They bought a house in East Ardsley, and Peter remembers that "Joan's uncle Albert helped negotiate to buy it, and got £20 off the asking price." Peter and Joan lived in that house for 20 years, then moved to their present home, still in East Ardsley. The couple have two daughters, Karen and Susan. Both girls did well at school, passed the 11 plus exam and went to Morley Grammar School.

Karen went on to Keele University to read English and French. She met her husband, Viji, at university, and they now live in Tenterden in Kent, where she works at Cranbrook School teaching English and French. They have a teenage daughter, Ellie.

Susan read German at Hull University, and then did a postgraduate diploma in international marketing at the University of Staffordshire. She has worked for Royal Doulton, Elizabeth Arden and Revlon in sales management. She married Andrew, and they have one daughter, Olivia. They live in Harpenden in Hertfordshire.

Joan says that "Having come from an all-boys family, Peter now has all girls, but we wouldn't have it any different, and we are truly blessed with our children and grandchildren." When the children had settled at school, Joan started work in 1967 at Blackgates Infant School in Tingley as a non-teaching assistant, and stayed there for 26 years until she retired in 1993: "I loved that job. I missed the children so much when I finished. I used to listen to their reading, and did sewing and art with them." Another great interest of Joan's is flowers, and she is now chairman of East Ardsley Flower Club after being a member for over 30 years.

Joan rarely saw Peter play rugby league: "Before we got married I was always working on a Saturday, so I never went to see him play. Then when we got married, we had two children and I couldn't drive, so I didn't go to the matches. I do remember going to Featherstone Rovers once with my father to see Peter play.

"When Peter started coaching the girls were older, and we all went together to the matches as a family. I would always keep quiet, but the girls always stood up for Peter, especially Susan. It was funny the things people would say. Once we were playing the Australians, and I was with Peter's dad, and an RFL official was being critical of Neil. So I said to the official 'this is Neil and Peter's dad'. Another time, Susan and I were walking up the hill at Odsal, and one fan said to another: 'I don't know why he plays Austin', and his mate replied 'Peter Fox and Austin are drinking partners.' But Peter didn't drink.

At Bradford Northern we had seats with our names on, so everyone knew who we were. I always felt for Peter if the team lost, but I didn't get involved in arguments about the game. As the coach's wife you're a bit on your own; you're not a player's wife, or a committee member's. All the clubs Peter coached at were friendly towards us, except Leeds, where I thought there was a funny atmosphere."

Peter and Joan now enjoy their retirement, including regular visits from their children and grandchildren.

Peter and Joan cutting the cake on their wedding day: 30 November 1957.

Golden Wedding

Peter and Joan (Photo: Peter Barnes)

Family group: Viji, Karen, Ellie, Joan, Peter, Olivia, Susan, Andrew.
(Photo: Peter Barnes)

7. Moving on

His playing days over, Peter looked for new ways to stay involved in the game that had occupied his leisure hours for so many years. The first opportunity to present itself was that of commentator for Batley and Dewsbury Hospitals' Radio. Over the next few years nearly every winter Saturday would be spent either at Crown Flatt or Mount Pleasant describing the action. He was fortunate because at Crown Flatt, Dewsbury had a young progressive team among whom the Bates brothers, Alan and John, Nigel Stephenson and Jeff Grayshon. The latter would go on to play a big part in Peter's future career.

Another way of keeping active was through golf, which provided a way for him to keep fit and mentally active. "I started by taking lessons at Temple Newsam with colleagues from IMI. A friend of mine Joe Poulter, a supervisor in the mechanical maintenance department invited me to join South Leeds Golf Club. South Leeds soon became my second home.

"I joined in 1966 and the following year was my first year of competition. I was given a handicap of 20 and that summer I won the Captain's Prize, which was for the best gross score of the day. My 77 was unbeaten, a quite unique score in my first year of competition. That evening the prizes were presented by the Leeds United manager, Don Revie, who was a friend of South Leeds captain, Alan Calvert. It was a great start in my new sport."

Peter's game quickly improved and his handicap fell sharply. By 1970 Peter had a handicap of 12 and that year won the South Leeds Second Division Championship. That same year he went on to win the Leeds and District Second Division Championship over 36 holes at Garforth with a score of 161, to become the inaugural winner of the Bill Darby trophy.

Peter subsequently enjoyed winning other events such as the Leeds and District Spring four-ball competition of 1979 representing South Leeds off a handicap of nine with friend and colleague Brian Lumley, handicap 20, the pair posting a score of 61 at Selby golf course.

Over his long time at South Leeds, where he is still a member, Peter won several other prestigious trophies. The first in 1971 was the South Leeds Highfield Trophy with his friend Ted Revis. Also that year Peter won the S.L. Boulby Cup. Peter was proud of that win "because it was a difficult trophy to win. You had to qualify to enter and then the top-16 played off in match play. I was fortunate to win it a second time in 1976."

Peter's last major trophy at South Leeds came in 1986, when his handicap was rising again to 12 after attaining his lowest mark of five. That year he won the Second Division Championship again, some 16 years after his first victory.

Peter served South Leeds as handicap secretary for four captains – Arnold Skinner in 1983, Dennis Sidebottom in 1984, John Armistead in 1985 and Jeff Bennett in 1986. Peter remembers them well: "Arnold Skinner was originally from Oldham, so being a rugby league man he took me under his wing straight away. He and John Armistead are no longer with us, but Dennis Sidebottom and Jeff Bennett are long-time friends that I cherish along with several other long term members of South Leeds Golf Club."

There was also a golf society at IMI that ran its own competitions. Peter was society captain for quite a period in the 1970s and 1980s. Peter recollects "one competition particularly and that was the Tigers trophy which I won in 1975 and 1976. The latter of those victories, when we played over 36 holes at Lindrick, the former Ryder Cup venue, particularly stands out. That year I won with a score of 158, with our secretary, Geoff Parker, an old friend of mine, in second place on 161".

The Rugby League Golf Society

The rugby league golf tournaments were originally organised by the secretary of the Rugby League, Bill Fallowfield. Two tournaments were held each year – one in Lancashire in the spring, for the Major C.W. Robinson trophy, and one in Yorkshire in the autumn, for the A.B. Sharman trophy.

Thinking back Peter remembers that "those tournaments provided a very necessary challenge for me. They also provided a means through which I could keep in touch with many rugby league colleagues. Among the former players I had the chance to meet on the fairways were Willie Horne, Gus Risman and Andrew Turnbull, as well as officials such as Bill Fallowfield."

In 1969 Peter won the Major C.W. Robinson trophy for the first time, a big achievement for someone who had only taken up the game three years earlier. Then in 1971 he won the A.B. Sharman golf trophy at Ilkley and retained it the following year. Peter won his last rugby league golf trophy – the Major C.W. Robinson trophy again – in 2001. As this was to be the last competition for that trophy Peter was allowed to keep it. First competed for in 1953, the Robinson trophy has many famous names engraved upon it – Lionel Cooper 1954, 1955 and 1956, A.B. Sharman 1962, Bill Fallowfield 1964, Jim Lewthwaite 1966, Alex Givvons 1968, Ron Rylance 1974, Andrew Turnbull 1988 and Frankie Jones 1991. No wonder the old trophy is one that Peter treasures.

The A.B. Sharman trophy has not been put up for competition for the last 15 years. Since 2002 the trophy offered for competition is the Willie Horne Trophy, in celebration of the great Barrow stand off. It is Horne's friends based in the north west who are the major supporters of this tournament. The 2007 tournament provided Peter with an unforgettable moment. "In what will probably be my last tournament I was presented with a trophy to mark my 40 years involvement with the Rugby League Golf Society and a rugby ball autographed by all the current society members. Among the names on the ball are particular friends I will never forget such as Ian Ellis, Ronnie Nelson, Percy Yates, little Tony and a long time playing colleague of Willie Horne, Bill Wookey, who is the main organiser of this wonderful golf tournament."

Coaching

Interesting though they were, commentating and golf tournaments were no substitute for a closer involvement with rugby league. Coaching was the obvious route to take, but Peter did not initially make any moves in that direction. Yet when he describes his role as a player he stresses that he always thought as a coach: "I used to coach the teams I played with anyway, on the pitch during the match, so I knew that I had the know-how. At Batley I used to dictate the team's play each week. I used to analyse the opposition, tell my team-mates all about their opposite numbers, tell them what their opponents could and couldn't do because I knew all the players in the league that I'd played against".

Unexpectedly an opportunity presented itself in 1967 when a friend, Dave Jackson, asked Peter "if I would be prepared to coach a new amateur team, based at the Black Horse public house. The team had been formed to take part in the new Wakefield and

District Sunday League. I initially refused, but Dave was persistent and quite soon got the answer he wanted."

Having overcome his initial reservations Peter had accepted his first coaching appointment and in characteristic fashion he got down to work. He recalls: "Amateur clubs are bedevilled by low commitment and poor discipline, but I was determined that no matter how few turned up to training I would always run the session. Unless I did there was no way I could get the team fit and that was the top priority. Once the fitness was improving there was time to work on their on-field organisation."

The Black Horse's organisers had hoped that Peter would operate as player-coach, but his appearances on the field were few and far between. His last was in the semi-final of one of the local cup competitions. Victory in that game took the new club into its first final, but there was to be no fairytale ending to the season. Peter refused to play in that match, held at the Brookhouse Rugby League club's ground, where Hemsworth Miners Welfare got the better of Black Horse.

Peter continued with Black Horse for the next two or three years, combining this new role with his hospital broadcasts. However, Peter was enjoying coaching and looking to move beyond the amateur game. At that time when professional clubs went looking for a new coach they were far more interested in his on-field experience, preferably at the highest level. As far as club directors and committee men were concerned international honours were a better indication of a man's potential than his coaching qualifications. For a man like Peter, with a keen interest in the theory of the game, the road ahead hardly appeared smooth. All he could do was carry on broadcasting and hope that a suitable opportunity would soon present itself.

Fortunately chances to break into professional coaching with a local club regularly presented themselves. Peter made the shortlist at Wakefield Trinity in May 1970, but his brother Neil, who hadn't even applied, was offered the job. He also made the shortlist at Dewsbury, but another Sharlston lad, Tommy Smales, beat him to that one. However, another local opportunity would soon arise.

The spectator

With commentating taking up so much of his time Peter was not able to get to watch many other matches. However, always found time to go to Wembley for the Challenge Cup Final. A bitter memory from this period is the 1968 Challenge Cup Final, when Peter's brother Don missed a last minute conversion in front of the posts that would have won the game for Wakefield Trinity. The game is known as the 'watersplash final' as the pitch was flooded following torrential ran, and most people believe it should not have been played. Neil was injured and missed the game, and Don was only kicking because of Neil's absence. Peter remembers: "Don picked the ball up, and I knew what was going through his mind. He was going to wipe the ball, but he was wet through. Also, there was no solid ground for him to place the ball. He needed a towel to dry the ball. Someone should have come on and dried the ball. And then he was putting the ball in the water and mud. He'd kicked goals earlier in the match, but the conditions made this one difficult. Neil and I were heartbroken when he missed it. Don was also heartbroken, not so much for himself, but because he had lost a winners medal for his team mates. He was one of the great players of his era, winning many honours in the game. It is sad that many people only remember him because of that missed kick."

National coaching course at Lilleshall in 1971. Peter is in the back row, 4th from right. Also in the group are Tommy Trelore (middle, 4th from left), Paul Charlton (back, 3rd from left), Alec Givvons (back, 3rd from right), Mike Stephenson (middle, one from right), Joe Chamberlain (front, 2nd from left), Dave Elliott (front 2nd from right). The two head coaches are Albert Fearnley and Laurie Gant.

Left: Peter with the Bill Darby Trophy, presented by the Leeds & District Union of Golf Clubs

Below: The signed ball Peter was presented with by the Rugby League Golf Society in 2007, to mark 40 years participation in their tournaments. (Photo: Peter Lush)

8. Winning the Cup with Featherstone

Then with little or no warning Laurie Gant resigned from his job as coach at Featherstone Rovers, after losing the 13th match of the season. Rovers advertised the coaching job and Peter decided to apply. A shortlist of three was drawn up – Peter, Tommy Smales and Harry Poole – and interviews with the Rovers committee were scheduled in December 1970. Up against two former British internationals Peter was hardly considered favourite. After he completed his interview Peter went off to his golf club while the committee deliberated.

There was still no news when he arrived home. Peter clearly remembers when he knew the job was his: "Shortly after 11 o'clock a car parked up in front of our house and two Rovers' representatives – the chairman, John Jepson, and the president, Reg Rugg – got out. Obviously the committee had liked what I'd said about changing the culture of the club and had decided to give me a chance." Excited and very happy, Peter jumped into his car and drove over to Sharlston to tell his father.

It was January 1971 and Peter was about to embark on a new coaching career. Recognising the scale of the task he was facing, Peter stepped down as commentator on hospital radio. Not wishing to leave Black Horse in the lurch Peter invited Don Robinson to take over his coaching position. He accepted, but Peter was always surprised that Don, after such a great playing career, never aspired to coach in the professional game.

Circumstances were hardly ideal; it was the middle of the season and Rovers were fourth from the bottom of the league. Fortunately there was some talent in the squad Peter had inherited from Laurie Gant. The challenge would be to find and release it.

Like most professional clubs in those days, the Rovers' team was not chosen by the coach alone, but by a selection committee. Peter, as coach, and Brian Wrigglesworth, the assistant coach, were just two of the seven members of that committee, the other five being John Jepson, vice chairman Ralph Asquith, Eddie Lee, Bill Farrington and Arthur Street. Peter realised it was never going to be easy to win them round: "While John Jepson would back everything I proposed, Ralph Asquith dominated the rest of the committee. Asquith's hold over those committee members was very surprising because he never ever attended away matches." Unless he could win the selection battle Peter knew that the changes he wanted to make to the team could not be made permanent.

Being relatively unknown meant Peter had a lot to prove as a coach. The players were somewhat sceptical of his appointment because he had not reached the very top as a player, and had not previously coached a professional side, and even held their own meeting to discuss what they should do. Les Tonks, who had already returned from his loan spell at Hull KR, was at that meeting and spoke just as it drew to a close. Most of the players were still unsure, until Les spoke. For him it was simple: "I don't know what you're going to do about it, but I'm going to do everything he tells me because I know he knows his rugby." With those few words Les Tonks had bought Peter the time he needed to get acclimatised.

For Peter, the priority was to win over the players and get some victories under his belt. And to do that "I had to get the team better organised. My first priority as always was the pack. Les Tonks took over the open-side prop position and his return caused a pack reshuffle – a young Keith Bridges was given a run at hooker; Vince Farrar, previously used primarily as a utility forward, was made first choice blind-side prop, and

Jimmy Thompson and Steve Lyons were paired as the new second-row. I also wanted to sign Tony Halmshaw, a loose-forward, from Halifax, but no money was available."

A couple of talented players were staying away from the club. One of them was Charlie Stone, who after signing for Rovers from Old Pomfretians RUFC in October 1970 had returned his signing-on fee and ceased playing. The other was the experienced John Newlove who, at 26, was considering retirement. Peter sought them out: "I convinced both of them to give the game another go. Under my tutelage both players rediscovered their appetite for the game and, as a result, I had successfully filled the loose forward and left centre positions in my team."

Peter's first match in charge was a first round Challenge Cup tie at Thrum Hall on 23 January. Rovers might have been the underdogs, but they didn't play like it and went through to the next round 18-13. Peter had his first victory. Although Rovers managed to hold Hull to a draw at Post Office Road in the next round, dreams of cup glory ended in the replay at the Boulevard.

Results improved and so did Peter's relationship with the players: "By then the players had got used to my methods: how I would train them for each game and prepare them individually to meet their opponents. And how, despite my vehemence, there would be no swearing and no verbal abuse, just a firm demand that they, as players, carry out the game plan I had set for them."

Following impressive home wins against Workington Town and arch rivals Castleford, Rovers recorded their highest ever score with a crushing 65-5 victory over Whitehaven. At the season's end Rovers had climbed from 26th to 20th in the league table.

A coach in Peter's position was limited by the committee when it came to planning for his first full season in charge, as he quickly discovered. Once all the fixtures were complete the committee had a meeting and without consulting Peter decided to transfer Peter Harrison, a promising young forward, to Wakefield Trinity.

Peter was well aware that "as a coach you only have a limited time to prove that you have the ability to bring the best out of your team. To do that you have to rely on what you'd picked up from your playing days. Fortunately I'd had the chance to play under two coaches I greatly respected – Eric Batten at Batley and Ken Traill at Wakefield Trinity. Batten's disciplined training regime impressed me and I was determined that my teams would attain the same levels of fitness. During my time at Belle Vue, Traill had shown himself a master of the art of finding and putting the right player into the right position in his team. It was a lesson in the art of team-building that I would not forget. From my own playing career I also brought an understanding of tactical plans and the importance of on-field leadership to team performance."

Keen to progress in his new profession, Peter enrolled on the National Coaching Scheme. The aim of the scheme in those days was to develop coaches who could efficiently teach the principles of the game, primarily to young people. Passing an examination at the end of the course gave a new coach some standing, but the course material was totally focused on practical organisation and teaching technique. Although a growing number of professional clubs were looking for those with qualifications, the scheme had no pretensions about preparing coaches to work at that level, as its detractors were only too willing to point out. Undeterred, Peter attended the three-week-long residential course at Lilleshall, a former stately home in Shropshire, in July 1971. At the end of the course Peter had gained a Grade 1 certificate and three great friends in Tommy Trelore of Dalton, Paul Charlton, then playing with Salford, and Rochdale's Joe Chamberlain.

1971-72

The single division structure of 30 clubs that operated in professional rugby league at that time had many critics. For many clubs there was nothing to play for after Christmas because they were already too far down the table, but for a new coach it offered breathing space to get a team in shape. Benefiting from the fixture formula in place at the time, Rovers' fixtures were mostly against those clubs that had also finished in the bottom half of the previous season's league table.

For the new campaign, Peter decided to make the man at the heart of his team, scrum-half Steve Nash, captain. However, under Nash Rovers' season began indifferently – a 9-2 defeat at the Boulevard ending their interest in the Yorkshire Cup immediately.

The league season also started falteringly with only one win from the first four matches. It took a victory in Blackpool to get the league campaign moving. That victory was the first of five from six matches that pushed Rovers up the table.

Rovers were also briefly active in the transfer market. First team appearances for scrum-half Terry Hudson were severely limited by Steve Nash's consistent form so he was sold to Hull KR in October. In return Rovers received a club record £7,500 fee. A young winger, David Dyas, was also recruited from Rovers juniors in December.

Rovers' travelled over the Pennines for the first round of the inaugural Player's No.6 Trophy in mid-November. Their interest was short-lived as St Helens inflicted an emphatic 37-7 defeat. That season, those clubs defeated at the first round stage could enter a one-off competition, the Player's No.6 Top Tries Competition. So two weeks later Rovers met Batley, during which they ran in 12 tries in an emphatic 54-0 victory. Unfortunately, Swinton went one try better to leave Rovers as runners up – the competition being decided purely on the number of tries a team scored in their one additional match.

After that it was back to the league where another five wins put the club into the top 10 by the end of the year. The start of 1972 saw Rovers hit a passage of inconsistent form. Having gained a surprising win against Widnes at Naughton Park, Rovers then allowed Widnes to come to Post Office Road and beat them. Oldham also gained a surprise victory at Post Office Road.

Amateurs Dewsbury Celtic provided Rovers with an easy passage into the second round of the Challenge Cup. Next up in that competition was a trip to Halifax, where the home side proved too strong, winning 11-5. It was a result that meant Rovers could focus solely on the league as winter drew to a close.

One week later a defeat at Wilderspool made it look like Rovers would slip out of the top 10 in the league, but playing a new brand of exciting, attacking rugby they won all their remaining seven fixtures to secure seventh place in the final league table. This earned Rovers a home play-off tie against Castleford, three places below them, on Sunday 22 April. Reversing the respective league positions the visitors won narrowly, 18-14, to end Rovers' season. But Peter was pleased with his side's progress, especially as the club had the youngest playing staff in its history.

Forays into the transfer market were few and far between because Rovers, being a small town club, just did not have the cash available. It also rarely needed to buy players because the club had an abundance of talent on its doorstep. The credit for that success owed much to the active under-16 youth set-up in the town. Although it was an independent organisation, Featherstone Juniors, run by Kenny Everson, was provided with all the help and facilities it needed by the professional club. In return Rovers received a steady stream of well-coached young players eager to play for their home-town team. For Peter it meant there was an 'A' team, strong enough to win the Yorkshire Senior Competition Championship in 1971-72, that could back up his first team with talented young players like Keith Bell, Micky Gibbons, and Loggie Wood.

Once the season was over Peter modestly summed up the progress made: "We have at Featherstone one of the youngest playing staffs in the history of the club and maybe one of the youngest in the league at the moment.

"While we have disappointed at home on odd occasions this term, our away record is one of the best for many years, if not our best ever. We have concentrated on playing fast, open football and without making too many promises I feel sure that our standard will continue to rise having regard to the abilities of our playing staff."

1972-73

From the start of the new season there was an important change to the laws of the game. The number of consecutive tackles permitted before a scrum was called was increased from four to six, which gave an advantage to a team like Rovers that wanted to play constructive, attacking football. A new fixture format for the league was also brought in. Rovers would play all the other clubs in Yorkshire, with the exception of Dewsbury, and only three clubs from west of the Pennines – St Helens, Salford and Wigan. Hopes were high in the Rovers camp that this could be a great season. There was also a change of captain, Peter appointing John Newlove to give Steve Nash more opportunities to develop his own game.

Under Newlove there was a mixed start to the season. If victory over Batley raised any hopes of Yorkshire Cup success they were ended in the quarter-final by Leeds at the start of September. Rovers bounced back and gave a clearer indication of their potential with a 19-14 defeat of the challenge cup holders, St Helens. Seven consecutive victories followed, one of them a Player's No.6 Trophy first round tie at Whitehaven, before Rovers had to visit St Helens for the second round tie in October. Without Nash, Farrar, Tonks and Thompson, Rovers were inevitably knocked out, 24-8.

There was also disappointment around the turn of the year when three away defeats – at Leeds, Castleford and Salford – struck a blow at hopes of coming top of the league.

Two weeks after losing in the league at The Willows, the Challenge Cup draw paired Rovers and Salford in a first round tie in January 1973. Salford's chairman, Brian Snape, a man Peter admired, had made a number of captures from rugby union: Maurice Richards, Keith Fielding and ace goal-kicker David Watkins. Salford also included Barry Kear, a £4,500 pre-cup deadline signing from Featherstone. Peter and his team revelled in the role of underdog: "Highly rated Salford were many critics' choice to win the Cup, but Keith Bridges and his props, Les Tonks and Vince Farrar, took the ball from all 12 first-half scrums. There was a packed crowd of over 9,000, the majority of them cheering us on, as Rovers outscored the visitors by four tries to one, to claim a famous 18-11 victory."

Two league wins over Bradford Northern and Bramley paved the way for the visit of Rochdale Hornets in the second round of the cup. Hornets provided stiff opposition in the first half and turned round only 4-3 down. It was a different story after the break as Rovers ran in five tries in 23 minutes to make sure of progress to the next round. Following two further league victories Rovers prepared to travel to Warrington for the cup quarter-final. League leaders Warrington, with big names like player-coach Alex

Murphy, international forwards Dave Chisnall and Kevin Ashcroft and former rugby union stars John Bevan, Mike Nicholas and Frank Reynolds, were made clear favourites to beat a Rovers' side missing Vince Farrar. Rovers belied all the pundits' predictions to thrill the 16,000 spectators with a stunning 18-14 success.

Featherstone equalled a club record 11 successive victories when completing a league double over Hull, which they then extended to 12 with a victory over Halifax. A surprise home defeat by Wakefield, which was the only match lost at Post Office Road all season, undermined Rovers bid for the league title. But with the league losing its importance Rovers were able to fully focus on the Cup and their semi-final date against Castleford at Headingley.

In preparation for the semi-final, Rovers went for training in Bridlington, using it as a bonding session for the players, on the day before the match. At the end of the session Jimmy Thompson waited for everyone but Peter to leave the bath. Then in an emotional moment Jimmy took the opportunity to say "Listen Foxy, when thy came to Featherstone I wasn't sure of thee and when Steve Lyons left I blamed thee, now I realise what tha's done for us and I want to tell thee I'd chop off my right arm for thee, for everything tha's done for us at Rovers." Peter realised then that the bond between players and coach was secured.

It was predicted to be a classic derby, but the Rovers' forwards led by Thompson took control, subduing the Castleford attack and giving the Tigers no chance to get into the match. Steve Nash was in brilliant form scoring one try and a drop goal as Rovers stormed to Wembley with a convincing 17-3 victory.

So the greatest moment for Peter had arrived – Wembley – not as a player, but the next best thing as a coach: "I was grateful to the Rovers' committee – John Jepson, Ralph Asquith, Mr Fawley, Mr Blackburn, Bill Farrington, Mr Guy, Mr Harrison, Eddie Lee, Mr Fawley and Charlie Raybould – for giving me the chance and the sole responsibility to take the team to Wembley. I was also very appreciative of the support I had received from Jim Reed and Derek Hobbs, the financial and general secretaries; from Jimmy Williams, the physiotherapist, and his father Billy who was still helping out; from the groundsman, Fred Lavine, who kept the field and the playing tackle in top condition with his assistant bagman Trevor Walker and last, but not least Annie Jepson, the chairman's wife, who was in charge of the players' tea room and all the spare equipment. With their support we were off to Wembley."

The thrill of reaching Wembley was awe-inspiring, but the league competition was still running. Rovers having finished second in the League, their highest ever position, were drawn to meet Dewsbury in the Championship quarter-final on the Saturday before Wembley. Unfortunately, but understandably, Rovers had their minds focused on the Challenge Cup and Dewsbury won convincingly.

Peter selected his team for Wembley as early as possible and when all the players were passed fit, he told the lads who had made the team and also who the unlucky ones were going to be. Undoubtedly the most disappointed was Keith Cotton, a great servant to the club, who just missed out on a substitute spot. Rovers' team, which is regarded as one of the club's finest, was:

C. Kellett, P. Coventry, M. Smith, J. Newlove, K. Kellett, N. Mason, S. Nash, L. Tonks, J. Bridges, V. Farrar, A. Rhodes, J. Thompson, R. Stone. *Substitutes:* D. Hartley, B. Hollis.

The squad went to Crystal Palace on the Wednesday before the Final to prepare for the game. Peter ensured the preparation was intense: "My game plan was as thorough as any match ever was and as always I insisted that my players' discipline should be faultless. As ever I also reminded all the team that they should 'tackle, tackle and tackle' and when they had done that they should 'tackle again'."

Peter remembers thinking that the attitude of the two teams as they walked out at Wembley said a lot about their preparation: "Bradford Northern's players were waving their arms in the air to their supporters and wives; looking totally at ease. In contrast Rovers' players came out quite reserved, eyes down and concentrating on the game plan, or so I hoped."

The game as a contest was effectively over in 20 minutes. Cyril Kellett kicked an early penalty, then within seven minutes, after the forwards had laid the foundation, skipper John Newlove scored the first try, converted by Cyril Kellett. A try to Vince Farrar, again converted by Kellett made the score 12-0. A second try to John Newlove, once again converted by Kellett made it 17-0 in as many minutes. Just before the interval Eddie Tees kicked the third of his three penalties to give Northern some hope. Peter's only major concern during the interval was to make sure his team were not complacent about winning.

Ten minutes into the second half Kellett kicked his fifth goal to make the score 19-6. A Dave Redfearn try reduced the deficit, but then Mick Smith beat half-a-dozen Northern players to score under the posts to restore the gap. Although Northern again struck back with a converted try to make the score 24-14, that was as close as it would get. Rovers' Lance Todd Trophy winner, Steve Nash, dropped a goal in the 70th minute before substitute Dave Hartley scored a try, converted by Kellett to make the score 31-14.

In the final minute of the match Rovers were awarded a penalty on the halfway line. Kellett took the ball and Peter was convinced he would put it into touch and end the match, but instead he placed the ball, took aim and kicked a goal. That was a record eight goals from eight attempts, which meant he beat the previous record of seven held by Peter's brother, Neil. It was one more great moment to savour on a great day as Peter remembers: "No player was more deserving of entering the record books than Cyril. After that came the final whistle and a chance to enjoy the moment. Rovers had won the cup – the greatest moment and achievement so far in my coaching career."

The bond Peter had built up with the players in just two years was clearly phenomenal. John Robinson of the *Sunday People* captured the mood when he wrote: "Take a bow Peter Fox team builder extraordinary, the likely lads of Featherstone took Wembley by storm and nobody can be prouder than coach Fox, the man who put the team together from nothing."

Rovers were given a civic reception by the Featherstone Urban District Council. Peter remembers that when Cyril Kellett was introduced "all those present burst into song, one which was appropriate for the time: *Nice One Cyril*. A little later a private function to celebrate our victory, given by the Earl and Countess of Swinton, our patrons, marked the pinnacle of a wonderful year."

One of the main reasons for the club's success was due to Peter finally being able to convince the Rovers committee in October that team selection should be his sole responsibility. While it might have reduced the number of arguments it was not a degree of independence that most professional clubs conferred on their coaches at that time.

After such a successful season Peter might have expected to have things largely his own way at the club, but he soon found out that was not to be: "When Brian Wrigglesworth resigned as assistant coach I proposed that Keith Cotton, the former first team centre should replace him. However, the committee were of a different mind and appointed the former Castleford and Great Britain tourist, Peter Small, to the position. Keith Cotton decided to leave the club."

1973-74

With his new assistant Peter had to prepare for a season that was to be the most cup-focused in the game's long history. The re-introduction of two divisions meant there would be no easy league fixtures. Rovers were also to enter four knock out competitions – the Yorkshire Cup, the Player's No.6 Trophy, the Captain Morgan Trophy and the Challenge Cup – that were spread throughout the season. A lack of floodlights always prevented Rovers from entering the BBC2 Floodlit Trophy, but it was the only knock-out competition they missed. It was a schedule that badly disrupted the nine-month long league programme and was only tried for this one season. Peter remembers: "It meant that the coach and the team had to treat every game as if it was the most important if it wanted to be successful."

As he welcomed the challenges the new season presented, Peter took the chance to reflect on what the club had achieved so far: "Anyone who saw Featherstone Rovers last season will realise that we always put the accent on open football. We also have tremendous forwards who take things as they come. But it's always been my policy to play the game as much as possible in the threequarters. It's paid off. We scored more points last season than ever before."

With the team largely unchanged it was expected that Rovers would build on the previous season's success. Things did not turn out that way. Rovers suffered five defeats in their opening seven matches, including early exits from both the Yorkshire Cup and the Player's No.6 Trophy. Contributing to - and in many ways overshadowing - this poor start was an injury crisis that had already sidelined Mick Smith, Jimmy Thompson and Vince Farrar. Rovers had to respond to their problems with grit and determination, the reward for which was six successive victories, including a nail biting win at Wigan, 14-13, and an impressive victory at Wakefield.

It was fortunate that Featherstone had already signed several young players from the amateur ranks, such as Graham Bray from Rossington and David Busfield from Earlsheaton Youth Club in Dewsbury, because they had to be drafted into the first team almost immediately. Peter had also been able to recruit Keith Toohey from Batley, a player that he had long admired.

Next up for Featherstone, in mid-November, was a meeting with the touring Australians. Although it was only six days before the second test, which they had to win, the Kangaroos fielded a strong team. In a full blooded encounter that thrilled a crowd of 5,659, Rovers took the tourists all the way, before being defeated 18-13.

After that, Rovers completed a quick double over Wakefield to book a place in the semi-final of the Captain Morgan Trophy. Workington Town were overcome 37-18 to book Rovers a place in the final against Warrington at the Willows on 26 January 1974. Unfortunately, there was a poor build-up to the final as Rovers only won three of their next seven league matches. There was, however, some good news for the future in the successful debut of a local youngster, Peter Smith.

In cold, wet conditions, the final at the Willows turned into a no-frills, rugged contest. Rovers were missing several key players from the previous year's Wembley team – John Newlove, Steve Nash, Vince Farrar and Jimmy Thompson – as well as new signing Keith

The 1973-74 Featherstone squad: Back: C. Wood, K. Bell, D. Busfield, S. Sayer, R. Stone, J. Bridges, W. Harris, J. Thompson, R. Wilson, P. Smith, M. Gibbins, D. Hartley. Front: C. Kellett, M. Smith, S. Nash, G. Bray, J. Newlove (captain), P. Coventry, H. Box, M. Mason, D. Dyas, P. Metcalfe (mascot).

Toohey. A new look Rovers team put up a very brave fight, but it was not to be their day. A dour match, which Warrington won 4-0 through two first-half penalty goals, proved to be the first and last Captain Morgan Trophy final.

One week later, Rovers were back in cup action, this time to defend the Challenge Cup. Rovers' opponents were Barrow, finalists when Featherstone first lifted the famous silver trophy in 1967. Featherstone scored three tries to one in an 11-3 success that led to a meeting with Hull KR in the second round. In a tense, gruelling encounter, Featherstone won 12-9. Their reward was a quarter-final meeting with Bradford Northern, the previous year's defeated finalists. The match was in stark contrast to the 1973 Final with points being at a premium. A try by David Hartley, converted by Harold Box was enough to give Rovers a 5-0 win at Odsal and a second consecutive Challenge Cup semi-final.

Leigh provided the opposition in the semi-final at Headingley. Preparation was not straightforward as Peter remembers: "We were missing Coventry, Kenny Kellett, Farrar and Rhodes, but with youngsters Bray, Harris, Busfield, Bell, Dyas and Peter Smith all standing up to be counted the team regained its best form. It was a tough encounter, but we proved too good for a determined Leigh side, who had beaten the cup favourites, St Helens, in the previous round, 21-14, to book a return trip to Wembley."

Rovers warmed up for the clash with Warrington at Wembley with a great 27-16 home victory over Salford with Busfield scoring a hat-trick. Then on the final weekend of the league programme Featherstone snatched eighth place by defeating Wakefield 19-8. In the new Club Championship end of season tournament, Rovers beat Wigan, 22-14, in the first round, but in the quarter-finals, perhaps with one eye on Wembley, went down 19-16 to Wakefield in a great match.

Peter fielded the following team in the Final, which rapidly turned into an ill-tempered contest:
H. Box, D. Dyas, M. Smith, D. Hartley, G. Bray, J. Newlove, S. Nash, L. Tonks, J. Bridges, W. Harris, A. Rhodes, J. Thompson, K. Bell. *Substitutes:* D. Busfield, R. Stone.

THE RUGBY FOOTBALL LEAGUE

Patron :

HER MAJESTY THE QUEEN

President :

The Right Hon. THE EARL OF DERBY, M.C.

CHALLENGE CUP COMPETITION

FINAL TIE

FEATHERSTONE ROVERS

v

WARRINGTON

on

SATURDAY, 11th MAY, 1974

KICK-OFF at 3.0 pm

at

THE EMPIRE STADIUM, WEMBLEY

———————

PROGRAMME OF ARRANGEMENTS

W. FALLOWFIELD, O.B.E.

Secretary

The programme of arrangements
(courtesy RFL).

Warrington outlined their intentions as early as the third minute when player-coach Alex Murphy floored Rovers centre David Hartley with a deplorable high tackle. Peter remembers the match well: "Referee Sam Shepherd should have sent Murphy off, but so early in the match, and with Murphy in his face, Sam only gave Rovers a penalty 10 yards closer to the posts. Harold Box kicked the goal before Whitehead of Warrington replied with two of his own. Box levelled the match 4-4 with another penalty before the game was marred by a vicious brawl midway through the first half. The niggling tactics of Warrington and Murphy in particular had lit the blue touchpaper and led to Philbin, Tonks, Bridges and Nicholas trading punches."

After order was restored, Warrington edged back in front with two more penalties from Whitehead. Rovers responded in the best way, John Newlove scoring the first try of the match, converted by Box, to send the holders in at half-time 9-8 ahead. Murphy, who had left the field just before half-time, returned after the break having had pain-killing injections for a rib injury. His return inspired Warrington.

In the second half Warrington scored 16 points without reply to win a truly disappointing final. But as Alex Murphy said: "Winning is winning, not how it's won". Before the Cup Final there had been a disagreement between the players and the committee. Peter recalls: "I had selected a pool of 24 players, the 15 who were actually down to play and nine others, mainly young players, who had been constantly standing in for senior players in many league matches in the run-in to the Final. By rewarding them with a trip to Wembley I thought it would instil them with the desire to want success in the future. Eventually I agreed with the players that they would share the whole pool of money offered by the committee – thereby reducing the payment to the selected team, while increasing the payment to the stand-by players, all of whom were taking three days off work."

As an end-of-season finale Rovers played in the Wills Sevens at Headingley on 11 May. Rovers beat Warrington in the first round, then Leeds to claim a place in the final against Salford. After changing ends 13-10 ahead Rovers seemed to tire a little and Salford took command to win 26-16.

The next week Peter learned there were problems with the club committee. It was clear that some of them felt their role was declining after giving Peter full control of selection and footballing matters. That group had proposed removing him as coach, but this had been prevented by the casting vote of John Jepson, Rovers' chairman. At their next meeting Jepson told Peter about the vote and the news that the committee was not prepared to offer him a contract to stay at the club he had transformed. On hearing this Peter resigned forthwith, without any plans as to his next challenge.

The 1973 Challenge Cup win with Featherstone

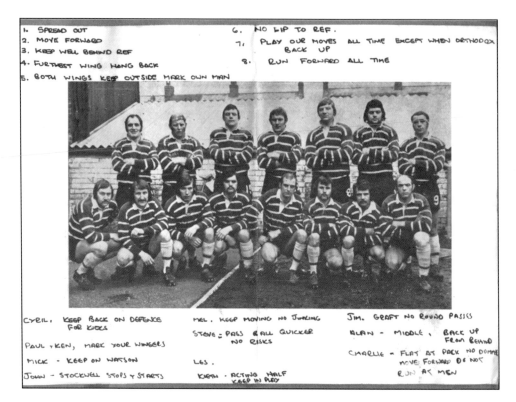

The Challenge Cup Final squad, with Peter's tactical notes for the match.

THE CHAIRMAN AND MEMBERS OF
FEATHERSTONE URBAN DISTRICT COUNCIL
request the pleasure of the company of

Mr. and Mrs. P. Fox

at a

Civic Reception

in honour of the **Featherstone Rovers Rugby League Football Club**

to be given in the LISTER BATHS HALL, FEATHERSTONE, on

MONDAY 14th MAY 1973

at 6.00 p.m. for 6.30 p.m. when dinner will be served

to be followed by a

Civic Ball

R.S.V.P. by not later than 7th May 1973:
The Clerk of the Council
Town Hall, Featherstone, WF7 5LX

Peter and Joan's invitation to the Civic Reception to celebrate the Wembley win.

9. Two years at Trinity

Having lost his job due to problems on his club's committee, Peter found himself in the same predicament as his brother Neil. A season that had promised much at Belle Vue had almost descended into farce as sections of the Wakefield Trinity committee warred openly over the future of Neil, the club's player-coach. By mid-March, Neil had had enough and terminated his coaching contract four months early. The responsibility for fielding a team for what remained of the season falling to Trinity's 'A' team coach, David Lamming.

Trinity's committee members immediately increased the urgency of their search for a successor. Some idea of what had been going on can be gained by knowing that Peter's name had been discussed as a possible replacement the previous November. Peter was unaware of Trinity's interest until he was approached by a committee member, Ron Rylance. An interview was arranged and an offer made. Having rid themselves of one brother, Trinity's committee found themselves in the odd position of welcoming another into the Belle Vue hot seat. Peter knew nothing of Neil's problems with the committee, but was soon to learn at first-hand what difficulties they were going to cause him, particularly with team selection.

Although he was not given a contract, Peter took over as coach on 10 June 1974 and took the recently retired Cyril Kellett with him to Belle Vue as his assistant. Mick McGowan was recruited to coach the intermediate side and David Lamming was retained as coach of the 'A' team and assistant to the first team. It was a coaching staff that would work well together.

Peter had very little room for manoeuvre. His assessment of the squad he inherited was hardly encouraging: "Trinity had a few very good players – Les Sheard at full-back, David Topliss at stand-off and Mick Morgan at blind-side prop – but lacked a controller of the game. Along with the centres – Geoff Wrigglesworth and Terry Crook – those five were the focal players in the side. There were some young players coming through such as the wingman David Smith, the prop Roy Bratt and a second-rower Trevor Skerrett. Overall the squad was thin and lacking class. It was obvious to Peter that "the team needed strengthening, but there was little or no money available. And like my early years at Rovers I would not have sole responsibility for team selection. Once again my team sheet would have to be approved by a selection committee before each match."

It was a big task for Peter to take on. Since winning the Championship in 1968, the once 'mighty Trin' had gone into decline. Considering the city's rugby league traditions, Trinity should have had been well supported, but the fans were disillusioned. Crowds were low, money was tight and the club was ailing.

To bolster his team Peter returned to his old club, Featherstone Rovers, and signed Les Tonks for £300 to stabilise the forwards. Next he persuaded the experienced hooker Ray Handscombe to end his dispute with Trinity and resume training. There was further good news when young forward, Trevor Skerrett, made his first-team debut at the start of the season.

The first match of the season was a drawn league fixture against Castleford. The emphasis then switched to the early-season cup competitions, which seemed to be more to the liking of the Trinity team. In the Yorkshire Cup, victories over Halifax, Featherstone Rovers and Hull booked Trinity an appearance in the Final. Either side of the semi-final against Hull were the two-legs of the preliminary round of the BBC2

Floodlit Trophy. The first of the ties was at Knowsley Road and Trinity almost sprung a shock, racing into an early 8-2 lead before the Saints took control to win 21-12. At Belle Vue in the second Trinity had left too much to do and lost on aggregate 36-30.

Trinity went into the Yorkshire Cup Final against Second Division Hull KR at the end of October as favourites. Both teams took the field determined to play enterprising rugby and all the critics agreed it was a great final, played in front of a disappointing crowd of only 5,824. Trinity took an early lead and went in at half time 7-5 ahead. After the break Rovers' captain Roger Millward turned in an outstanding display behind the powerful Rovers' pack to enable the Robins to claim the trophy with a 16-13 win.

In the league it was a different matter. The table at the start of December 1974 made difficult reading. Trinity had played 12 matches and accumulated only nine points from four wins since the start of the season. But following a heavy reverse at Castleford Wakefield translated their wonderful cup form to the league. A fine home win against Leeds was followed by a 13-13 draw at Headingley thanks to a drop goal by Ian Ellis with the last kick of the match. After a 12-12 home draw with Featherstone, Trinity probably produced their best performance under Peter so far, winning 16-6 against league champions Salford at the Willows.

Although the team was struggling at times, Peter knew that some of his players could perform at a higher level and when the chance came he advanced their cause: "One evening Alex Murphy, the England coach, rang to ask if I had anything to offer him for his team. I recommended Les Sheard, David Topliss and Mick Morgan to play against France and they got picked. Sadly only Morgan was chosen to play when that season's World Cup competition got underway in Australia."

Recognising the need for a playmaker and a midfield general Peter went after a player he had let go three years earlier. A deal was struck and the former Featherstone Rovers' scrum half Terry Hudson was signed from Hull KR for £7,500 just before the Challenge Cup register deadline.

The luck of the draw favoured Trinity in the Challenge Cup. Home advantage played its part in victories over Huyton, St Helens and Hull KR. By the start of March, Trinity were in the semi-finals. In the run up to the semi-final, Trinity's form slumped. Out of five league matches played, only one, at home to Salford, was won.

Trinity's Cup opponents were Widnes, in a match to be held at Odsal on 5 April. For Peter there was real possibility that he could make a third consecutive appearance as coach at Wembley. Standing in Trinity's way was a Widnes team that coach, Vince Karalius, had brought to the peak of physical condition. Having ended the first half all square at 5-5, neither fortune nor the referee favoured Trinity after the break. As Widnes showed signs of gaining control the referee, Billy Thompson, twice penalised Mick Morgan for offside under his own posts. Those decisions cost Trinity dearly and helped Widnes to a 13-7 victory.

A reversal of league form brought a flourish to the end of the season. Home wins over Warrington and York, a home draw with Bradford Northern and a win at York made the final league standings look much better than many critics had feared.

Trinity had finished 10th in the league, which still allowed the club entry into the new Premiership competition. Any hopes of late season glory were dispelled in the first round at Castleford, the home side winning easily 37-7.

As far as Peter was concerned, the season had shown signs of promise: "There had been some great victories and the team had reached a Yorkshire Cup Final and a

Challenge Cup semi-final. But the supporters weren't satisfied. They wanted an immediate return to their most illustrious times."

Local journalist, Frank Jeffrey, was one of those. As far as he was concerned Peter's first season in charge had not led to any overall improvement in the team's performance. Although some talent was developing in the junior ranks, the team lacked at least four class players – a winger, a centre, a prop and a second-row – if it was going to make an impact in the near future.

As he made his preparations for a second season at Belle Vue Peter offered his own candid assessment of his team's prospects: "We have a good team but not strong enough to make sure of being in the top four. There are young players coming up who will make the international grade. Our strength for the future is really exciting; but for our immediate needs, I could do with one or two players of experience."

1975-76

During the summer Peter searched for those players which might make a difference. Negotiations were opened with Bramley and by the start of the new season two experienced players, the hard-tackling Graham Idle and Alan Smith, the latter on loan, had joined Trinity. Looking to the future Peter signed two young forwards, the Rayne twins. Keith and Kevin were products of Wakefield schoolboy rugby league and had impressed Peter on and off the field. Coincidentally both were serving apprenticeships at IMI where Peter was the training manager.

An opening day victory over Castleford at Wheldon Road was sadly not a harbinger of good times to come. Over the next few weeks Trinity were knocked out of the Yorkshire Cup in the first round, the BBC2 Floodlit Trophy in the preliminary round and lost three league matches. Only the visit of Castleford to Belle Vue towards the end of September allowed Trinity to rediscover some form and secure a victory.

The following week, Bradford Northern were defeated in the first round of the Players No.6 Trophy. Castleford ended hopes of further progress in that competition in the next round.

Autumn 1975 saw a swarm of young Australians arrive in the north of England, all carrying contracts to appear as guest players. Surprisingly, for a club strapped for cash, the Trinity committee decided to help themselves to a couple. Owen Stephens, who was brought over from Parramatta, was the most successful and made his debut against Huddersfield on 5 October. He proved a very able winger scoring seven tries in eight games before an injury sustained in the win over Swinton at the end of November curtailed his visit. His injury coincided with the start of a winning streak. Further victories followed over Bradford Northern, Salford, Huddersfield and Keighley.

Over the first half of the season the side had improved its technique, especially in the way that Mick Morgan was now able to control the set pieces. That improvement was clear to everyone when a sixth successive victory, 13-5 over Featherstone Rovers on the opening day of 1976, lifted Trinity to the top of the First Division. Top spot was retained thanks to two more victories, but a limited squad could not hold on to those heights. Despite taking an early lead Trinity went out of the Challenge Cup in the first round at Featherstone. Trinity's form then deserted them and the next five matches were lost.

A brief rally in early March brought two wins, one of which was at Knowsley Road. That win, Trinity's first at St Helens for nearly 10 years, was achieved despite fielding a weakened side. Peter remembers: "in the absence of Mick Morgan, David Topliss and

Les Sheard, I made prop, George Ballantyne, captain. Despite breaking bones in his hand Ballantyne turned out for the second half and inspired his team mates to a 10-7 victory. It was a great success for a Trinity stalwart who probably never reaped the rewards to match his ability." Sadly that spirit could not be maintained and another four defeats pushed Trinity down the table.

With only a couple of matches left Trinity were scrambling to make certain of a place in the top eight and entry to the Premiership. It was not until the penultimate league match, with a relatively easy victory at Featherstone on 16 April, that qualification for the Premiership was guaranteed. Victory over Dewsbury in the last match meant Trinity would occupy seventh place.

As Peter prepared for the first round of the Premiership he might have taken a few moments to think back over the problems that the club committee's interference had caused him that season. He might have also remembered some words of his father's: "Never work for a committee, there are too many people ready to shoot you in the back". If he wasn't thinking in that way before, Peter was almost certainly thinking that way after news of a unanimous decision made by Trinity's committee reached the press.

Even though there were critical Premiership matches still to play Trinity's committee had decided to dispense with Peter's services at the end of the season. The reason given for this decision was the widening gap between the coach and the committee which had started to appear at the beginning of the season. As far as Peter was concerned the gap was present because he had "to work with a chairman, Trevor Woodward, and a president, Jim Walker, who, in my opinion, had very little knowledge of rugby league. After all this was the same committee that had already decided to allow two members of the first team – Henry Oulton and David Topliss – to leave before the season's end in order to play in Australia." Mick Morgan, on behalf of the players, made an official protest about the committee's actions.

It was the worst possible build-up for the match at Post Office Road on 2 May. Against the odds Trinity achieved a narrow 14-10 victory over league runners-up Featherstone Rovers to progress into the Premiership semi-finals. Trinity's opponents, in what was then a two-legged semi-final, were a Salford side that had finished top of the league. Fortune did not smile on Trinity at the Willows, the venue for the first leg, where a disputed penalty contributed to a 10-5 defeat. Belle Vue welcomed its best crowd of the season, more than 7,500, for the visit of Salford only to see the visitors win 14-5 on the day and 24-10 on aggregate. Defeat meant that the season and Peter's tenure as Trinity's coach were over.

Play might have ceased for the summer, but the so-called 'Fox affair' rumbled on until the club's AGM. On that night the issue of Peter's dismissal provoked a heated three-hour debate. When the talking stopped, the elections for the committee were held. It was clear that the debate influenced the outcome of the voting, for the man who was viewed as the cause of Peter's problems – the outgoing chairman Trevor Woodward – was voted off the committee. Even so, when the new committee took stock they decided not to offer Peter reinstatement, which was just as well because he had no desire to return to the club.

10. Promotion for Bramley

After taking a holiday Peter looked around for new opportunities. With nothing available on the professional front Peter accepted an offer to coach a team playing out of the Walnut Tree Inn in Sandal. The Warriors, as they were named, would be bidding for honours in Division Three of BARLA's West Yorkshire League and in the cup competitions of the Wakefield and District League.

Meanwhile, at Bramley, west Leeds's perennial strugglers, an ambitious new chairman, Doug Alton, was unhappy with his club's woeful start to the season. Knocked out of the Yorkshire Cup and the Floodlit Trophy and with a defeat and a victory from the league programme, the latter over the 11 men of Whitehaven, Alton was spurred into action. Coach Arthur Keegan was dismissed and Peter was offered the job.

Some were surprised that Peter accepted a job in the Second Division, but as he says "I could not ignore Doug Alton's cry for help. I did however make it clear that I would be looking to move on at the end of the season and that I would only accept if I had complete control of all team matters." Once agreed, all that was left for Peter to do was say farewell to the Walnut Tree Inn.

His first game in charge was at home, at Bramley's McLaren Field, on 19 September 1976. Blackpool Borough provided the opposition and the match confirmed to Peter all that he had heard. The team was unfit, under-trained and unable to defend a 12-5 half-time lead. After the break Borough took control of the game to finish 20-12 winners. At that time the club's ambitions probably stretched no further than mid-table respectability by the end of the season.

Getting the players already on the club's books fit and adding some new ones were the top priorities. Peter decided to retain the services of Bramley's assistant coach, Maurice Bamford, and he was given the job of improving the players' fitness. But it took the arrival of a new pack leader to make the most of the increased fitness levels. Peter's brother, Neil, made a winning debut, 18-8, against the league leaders, Hull, at the start of October and he rapidly made an impact on the team. For Peter, the reason why Neil could do so was clear: "Most of Neil's new team-mates had never had the opportunity to play with a player of his quality, and his experience and vision helped lift their game. Bringing Neil to Bramley meant that I had someone who would ensure that my game plan was carried out on the field as well as someone who could operate as the pivot for many of my planned moves."

Even with Neil on board, Bramley's league results in October were still patchy, losing to Swinton and York, Neil's old club, but beating Huddersfield. In the Player's No.6 Trophy a victory was secured over Dewsbury. At the start of November, Peter managed to strengthen his squad by the inclusion of three new signings - Lou Lardi, an Australian from Wakefield Trinity, Alan Maskill, a £3,000 buy from New Hunslet, and Geoff Clarkson, a £2,000 signing from York - in time for the second round of the Player's No.6 Trophy. Although Workington Town were a First Division team, Bramley almost matched them, losing narrowly 17-13 at Derwent Park. Defeat was made worse by serious injuries to Clarkson and Maskill that prevented them playing again until late January.

There were clear signs that all the hard work was starting to pay dividends at Batley on 14 November. Unlike the early days of the season, Bramley's fitness levels were now a match for anybody's in the division, which meant that they lasted for the full 80 minutes. At Batley, they scored four tries in the last quarter of the match to turn a 12-3 deficit into a 23-17 victory. The next weekend another, somewhat scrappy, victory was achieved over Huyton.

Just as things seemed to be falling into place, the elements seemed to plot against Bramley. On 28 November, Peter took his team to the Boulevard. On a rain-sodden night his players rose to the occasion and had a narrow lead, 7-5, on the hour. However, the muddy conditions had become so bad that the referee, unable to identify the players, abandoned the match. It was too much for Peter who remembers that "I was furious that Hull did not have a change of jersey to allow the referee to distinguish the two teams and allow the match to continue. Bramley were by far the better team on the day."

Further bad weather then caused all Bramley's fixtures to be cancelled until early January. Training went on, but not without some difficulties. One evening in particular Peter remembers well: "When it came to the normal time to leave for Bramley I discovered that a heavy snowfall had blocked the garage. Deciding that my car was trapped I announced to the family that I wouldn't be going training that night. My two teenage daughters, Karen and Susan, were shocked by this and cajoled me into changing my mind. I dug the car out of the garage and set off to Bramley, a 12-mile journey that normally took 20 minutes. On that night it took me nearly two hours, and when I got there only two local players – Keith Waites and Gary Wilkinson – were waiting. There was nothing to be done, but cancel the session and set off home. The return journey was even worse after my car got stuck in a snowdrift."

When the new year opened Bramley were lying in ninth place in the Second Division, 12 points behind Dewsbury, the leaders, with three or four games in hand over those clubs above them.

It might have been expected that a lack of match practice would have caused problems for Bramley, but that was not the case. Shaking off six weeks' inactivity, the team quickly got back to winning ways, overcoming Halifax 15-13 on 9 January. A late Jack Austin try, converted by Neil, brought a 15-13 win over fellow promotion hopefuls Dewsbury the following weekend, and was followed by a further two league victories – over Blackpool Borough and Doncaster. Suddenly hopes of promotion, which had been written off after the bad start, were back on the agenda.

The league programme was interrupted in mid-February for the first round of the Challenge Cup. Bramley welcomed Widnes to McLaren Field in front of an amazing crowd of more than 5,000. For most of the match the Chemics' obvious advantages in pace and power were kept in check by Bramley's tenacious defence. A try from Peter Goodchild, a goal from Neil and a Dave Sampson dropped goal had levelled the scores, 6-6, as the game went into its final minutes. But the strength and mobility of the Widnes pack, with props Jim Mills and Bill Ramsey to the fore, managed to work an opening for a converted try to bring victory, 11-6, and deny the Villagers the replay their efforts had deserved.

This setback in the Cup had no impact on Bramley's league form. Winning ways had been established and the victories kept on coming, over Halifax, Huddersfield and Whitehaven. Peter was away in France with the England team when Bramley travelled to York on 20 March. It was a great morale boost for Peter to hear that Neil was instrumental in a good Bramley performance against his old club. A 15-5 victory set a new post-war club record of 10 consecutive league victories and moved Bramley into fifth place in the table.

With the season drawing to a close there was a need to clear the backlog of fixtures that had been postponed by the bad weather. Cramming matches in meant Bramley's play became scrappier, but the victories continued to come. Finally, on Friday 15 April the Villagers' unbeaten run came to an end, after 14 matches, at the Boulevard. In a replay of the match abandoned nearly six months earlier the Airlie Birds took their revenge, winning 26-10.

For weeks there had been mounting speculation about Peter's future, but nothing definite was known. Third place and promotion to the First Division was secured with a home thrashing of Batley, 42-10, on 17 April. That victory was achieved by 12 men, Bramley's pack leader, Jimmy Fiddler, having been dismissed. Derek Parker contributed a hat-trick and John Hay a brace as the Villagers ran in 10 tries to celebrate their success.

After that things moved quickly. The following day Roy Francis resigned as coach of Bradford Northern due to ill health. While speculation mounted about his successor and Peter's future, Bramley completed their league programme on Sunday 24 April and organised a celebration evening the next night. Joy at achieving promotion was tempered by more than a little sadness as Peter said his goodbyes. The official announcement was made on Wednesday 27 April. Peter had agreed a three-year contract to coach Bradford Northern.

It was with mixed feelings that Peter said farewell after an enjoyable and rewarding seven months. Peter had particularly appreciated "working with Doug Alton, who was a very enthusiastic chairman, and Jim Bowden, a board member previously with Wakefield Trinity, and long-serving secretary Les Phillips. All three gave me tremendous support. Two other gentlemen who did a fine job off-field for the players were bagman Frank McManus and Ronnie Greenwood, the groundsman.

"Bramley had some good players on the up and up, such as John Hay, probably the best full-back in the division, Steve Bond and Jack Austin. Alongside them were experienced players such as Dave Sampson, Trevor Briggs, Barney Ward, Derek Parker, Keith Bollon and a few veterans like Peter Goodchild, Chris Forster and Tony Cheshire. All it needed was the involvement of a few good players such as Jim Fiddler and Neil for a fine team to be moulded together that deserved its promotion into the elite."

The Second Division programme might have been completed, but there was some unfinished business for the top First Division clubs. Five days later, on Sunday 1 May, Peter was back at Post Office Road to see his new club take on Featherstone Rovers. Any hopes of further progress in the Premiership were short-lived as Northern succumbed 13-2. Defeat brought to a close a remarkable season that had seen Peter coach three clubs and his first representative side.

Three players who played well for Peter:

Left: Jack Austin
Middle: Jim Fiddler
Bottom: Charlie Stone

Austin and Fiddler helped win promotion for Bramley, Stone was a member of Featherstone's 1973 Challenge Cup winning team.
(Photos: Courtesy Robert Gate)

11. England

While Peter was at Wakefield the chairman of the RFL, Brian Snape, had decided to try and improve the standing and quality of the game's professional coaches. In Peter, Brian Snape saw a coach with the sort of ideas and methods that would work in conjunction with his own aims. Although Snape stood down in June 1976 his successor as chairman, Harry Womersley, held similar views and it was through him that Peter got his chance to move up from club to representative coaching.

The opportunity came in early November 1976 when Peter was asked by the RFL to become coach of the England team for that season's European Championship. It was a major honour for a coach who had no representative experience and was at that time working for a Second Division club.

It was not an ideal introduction to coaching a national team as Peter recounts: "Although I could sit in on the selection committee meetings, I could not vote. So the squad that was announced on 18 December for the match against Wales was only partially approved by me. What made the problem worse was that the squad was picked without any thought of what role each player would perform on the field."

The man that Peter wanted as captain and leader was Chris Hesketh, the Salford captain. Unfortunately Hesketh withdrew his name for selection because of injury. The blow was somewhat softened somewhat by the contents of a letter from Chris to Peter: "Listening to you on Saturday at the Willows I realised that international rugby requires total commitment and fitness and I have never wanted to cheat in sport, particularly at the expense of an international match. I liked everything you said on Saturday and your obvious dedication to the game." Peter also wanted Steve Nash as scrum-half and playmaker. As he explains, "Nashy occupied a critical place in my plans for he knew all the set pieces and had controlled them in his days at Featherstone Rovers when he and I had enjoyed great success."

Ignoring Peter's suggestions, the selectors chose Roger Millward as scrum-half and captain. This was not what Peter had wanted: "Although Millward was playing scrum-half for his club, Hull KR, it was not the position in which he had produced many mercurial performances for club and country in previous seasons. Nothing could be done, so I had to plan around a half-back pairing composed of two natural stand-offs, Ken Gill and Roger Millward."

Being the coach of a national team that rarely comes together is very different to being in charge of a club side that trains and plays on a weekly basis. To try and overcome those inherent problems Peter took advantage of the seven weeks he had available to organise a number of sessions, explaining what was required to small groups. In those sessions Peter concentrated on developing a pattern with the half-backs and pack before bringing the whole team together in the week before the match.

Peter's emphasis on and use of planned moves as the starting points for an attack was unfamiliar to some of the players, a few of whom did not appreciate the need to remember them all. There were complaints from some journalists that Peter's insistence on set moves inhibited the style and natural flair of players like Ken Gill and Roger Millward. Some of the England squad apparently even disputed the right of a coach without international experience to tell them exactly what to do. Peter's difficulties increased further when two key forwards, Phil Lowe and Steve Norton, withdrew.

On the morning of the match against Wales, at Headingley on 29 January 1977, Peter took the team for a light training session, which was not appreciated by some of the players. The England team was:

G.A. Fairbairn (Wigan), S. Wright (Widnes), J.S. Holmes (Leeds), L.P. Dyl (Leeds), L. Jones (St Helens), K. Gill (Salford), R. Millward (Hull KR), J.B. Hogan (Wigan), J.H. Bridges (Featherstone Rovers), J. Thompson (Featherstone Rovers), J. Grayshon (Dewsbury), L. Gorley (St Helens), C.D. Laughton (Widnes). Substitutes: D. Eckersley (St Helens), M.J. Reilly (Castleford).

A very close game was predicted, but it did not turn out that way. An England team, containing plenty of talented players, gave a disappointing, mistake-ridden performance. On attack the forwards had little penetration and the backs showed little skill or flair. After a scoreless first half, a dropped ball by Jeff Grayshon was collected by Wales's Eddie Cunningham of St Helens to score the only try of the match. Exasperated by the manner of the 6-2 defeat Peter was quoted as saying: "Nearly every player had an off day. Not one of the moves we had worked on was completed because we dropped the ball before they could be set up."

Nearly eight weeks passed before the match against France took place at Carcassonne on 20 March. Peter was not the only one who knew changes had to be made and a very different England team was selected. Late withdrawals altered it even further, with the result that it was a very new-look English team that departed for France. England's line up for the match was:

G.A. Fairbairn (Wigan), G. Dunn (Hull KR), E. Hughes (Widnes), L.P. Dyl (Leeds), D.R. Smith (Leeds), K. Gill (Salford), R. Millward (Hull KR), M. Coulman (Salford), D. Ward (Leeds), V. Farrar (Featherstone Rovers), P. Lowe (Hull KR), P. Rose (Hull KR), S. Norton (Castleford). Substitutes: J.S. Holmes (Leeds), G. Nicholls (St Helens).

While there were many new faces, Peter was left was left with the same old problems: "Unfortunately those wholesale changes had not addressed my main need – for players who could make play for others and control set pieces."

At a practice session in France, Peter explained his game plan to the team and expected it to be put into effect on the field. Peter broke new ground on match day by holding a lunch time press conference. All the journalists who had travelled with the team enjoyed the novelty of the coach outlining his team's tactics in detail and describing the set piece moves he had taught his players. Such a high profile was unprecedented for a rugby league coach.

Peter had given permission for Roger Millward to have a meeting with the players without his presence and he remained unaware of what was said until after the match. It was understandable for Roger Millward, the captain, to want time with his team. Unfortunately what happened was that Millward and other senior players did not to want to follow Peter's instructions and instead used the strategies of their own clubs.

The England team played much tighter in this match, but still failed to put into practice the plans Peter had practiced with them. In the first 10 minutes of the match England got a free kick and put the ball into touch 20 yards from the French line. This was an ideal position for the first set piece. As Peter recounts "I expected that after two or three drives from England's big forwards, then another drive to concentrate the French defence near to their own posts we would have created the perfect position for a switch play. I expected Roger Millward at acting half-back to switch play to Kenny Gill, on the blind side. Gilly would then move the ball on to the full-back, George Fairbairn, who would in turn send the winger in at the corner. But, to my dismay there was no switch and no try, just another drive and then another, which the French snuffed out."

Peter could not believe what was happening. The French were a fast and rugged outfit that tackled hard and at times late. England suffered a number of injuries, the worst being to David Ward with a broken jaw. It was another disappointing display by England that allowed France to win 28-15. Two defeats meant that England finished bottom of the championship table.

After the match Peter was chatting with RFL Secretary Bill Fallowfield when Ken Gill approached and said: "Peter I want to explain the first penalty into the corner, which was ideal for your switch play move. Well before the match you gave your permission for the captain, Roger Millward, to have a chat with the players on his own. It was decided that we would not play any moves until we had hammered the French into submission, hence no switch play, which I am apologising for because I believe it would have worked." Having heard that, Bill Fallowfield said to Peter "You should tell the selectors what Gilly has told you." But, Peter couldn't see the point, it was all too late. And that was not to be the last time that Peter would suffer bad publicity for players not following his plans or ideas.

During the build-up to the French match the RFL was inviting applications for the job of Great Britain coach for the World Cup in Australia and New Zealand that summer. A shortlist of four was pulled together – Peter, Alex Murphy of Warrington, David Cox of Dewsbury and David Watkins from Salford. It was Watkins, who had no club coaching experience whatsoever, but had been player-coach of the Welsh team in the European Championship, who got the job, primarily on the basis that his team had beaten England.

Looking back, Peter reflects that "it was probably not the best time for me to be coach of England. I was with a Second Division club and although I had taken Featherstone Rovers to Wembley in successive seasons, I had not built my image up as a successful coach and so was not as well known as I needed to be with quite a few of the players selected. Not being involved in selection of the team gave me no position of authority and therefore the players felt able to make their own decisions on how to play the game and ignore my game plan. It was unfortunate for my own self esteem, but I would get the opportunity to put a lot of things right later in my career."

Half time talk against Leigh in January 1983 – Jeff Grayshon is fourth in from the left.
(Courtesy Robert Gate)

Watching the action (Photo: Sig Kasatkin, rlphotos.com)

12. Bradford Northern

Peter's move to Bradford Northern from Bramley was mainly as a result of the influence of Harry Womersley, the club's chairman of rugby, who had been instrumental in Peter being made coach of England. However, there was no guarantee of a warm welcome from the players as Peter quickly discovered: "On my first appearance at Odsal, I was approached by Mick Murphy, one of the senior players at the club, who informed me that the players were a bit upset because they believed that Barry Seabourne would become player-coach when Roy Francis left. I was grateful to Mick for the information and I immediately tried to convince Barry that he was much admired and had a key role to play in Northern's future success."

However, Barry subsequently received an offer from Keighley to become player-coach and took the job, even after Peter told him, "Play for us for the next two years and you can have the coaching job at Bradford at the end of it".

After Peter's departure from Bramley his assistant, Maurice Bamford, had wanted to take over his old job. When it became clear that the Bramley board had no intention of approaching Bamford, Peter made contact and offered him the job of assistant coach at Odsal. Bamford accepted and joined Peter in June 1977. Fitness training was assigned to former Rochdale Hornets' coach Graham Starkey, who was credited by Peter at the end of the season with making Northern one of the fittest teams in the league.

After that hectic first week Peter had the close season to make his plans. Roy Francis's 18 months in charge might have ensured Northern's top-flight survival, but he had not addressed a number of the team's weaknesses. Peter quickly let the fans know that he was as ambitious as they were for their club: "In 1971 I took my first job as a professional rugby league coach with Featherstone Rovers and was virtually unknown in top-class rugby league circles. Since that time, however, after short periods with Wakefield Trinity and Bramley and many verbal clashes with different groups inside the sport, I am probably a little better known. I have been accused of talking too much, but if it all brings colour to our great game – I intend to go on talking. When success arrives at Bradford Northern (and arrive it will), I am sure that we can maintain it over a period of time. It is a great personal challenge to me, one which I relish and no effort will be spared on my part to bring back the great days to Bradford Northern."

Peter was able to enjoy his work: "The board at Northern gave me all the support they could with the chairman, Mr Cooper, the financial director, Ken Winduss, and Harry Womersley my main backers." Northern's first target was Vince Farrar and Harry, Ken and Peter travelled over to Featherstone to meet him. But Farrar could not be talked into leaving Rovers because of family commitments in Featherstone.

At that time Jimmy Thompson, who had spent the summer with the Great Britain World Cup squad in Australia and New Zealand, was not available. Once that situation changed, Northern stepped in. Harry Womersley and Ken Winduss went to Featherstone to negotiate and were told it would take a club record fee of £10,000 to get his signature. Upon his return Womersley told Peter that Rovers' price was "like £2,000 and Stan Fearnley". Northern had allowed Fearnley to go to Halifax for £8,000 before Peter had arrived at the club. On hearing this Peter told Womersley "to get back to Featherstone and do the deal. You will never regret it". He did and Peter got a player who would, through leading the tackle count and the defensive effort by example, prove to be worth every penny.

Later in September Stuart Carlton was swapped for David Dyson of Halifax, who would provide cover as hooker, and Jack Austin was brought from Bramley, at a cost of £1,000 plus Les Sellars, to fill one of the wing positions. In October there were another couple of signings – Ian van Bellen, a veteran forward, joined from Huddersfield for £1,500 and David Barends, York's South African winger, was signed for £9,000.

Peter remembers his first meeting with Barends: "When I went to sign David at his home I went to his back door, he came out of his front door and we finally met up in the driveway at the side of his house. David had his arms raised above his head and said 'I thought you would never come for me, but now you have I am going to win something, which is the only reason I left South Africa'."

Peter's most crucial move was to convince Johnny Wolford to change position: "At the time Wolford, who I rated as the team's most creative player, was playing at loose-forward. Overcoming his initial resistance I managed to convince Johnny that his lack of pace was not a major problem and that he could successfully play at stand-off." It proved to be a master stroke as Wolford's guile at stand-off made a huge difference to Northern's play. Wolford's place as loose-forward was filled by moving the hard-working Bob Haigh from the second-row.

Even more guile would have been added to the team if Peter could have acquired the services of Steve Norton. Ever since returning from a summer spent guesting with Manly-Warringah in Australia Castleford's highly rated loose-forward, Steve Norton, had been unsettled. Castleford's reaction to his transfer request was to reluctantly place him on the list for a record fee of £25,000. Peter moved quickly: "I convinced the board to meet the asking price and thought we had a deal, but Castleford's chairman, Phil Brunt, played for time. It dragged on until January when Hull came in and matched Northern's offer and Castleford accepted immediately."

It was clear that the reason for the delay was that Castleford's chairman was not prepared to sell Norton to Bradford at any price. Hull then bought three of Peter's 1973 Featherstone cup-winning team, Vince Farrar, John Newlove and Charlie Stone, to put the club back in the big time.

After two fairly easy friendlies, the season started in earnest with the Yorkshire Cup first round on 21 August 1977. Featherstone Rovers were the opposition and beat Bradford fairly easily 20-9. That match gave no indication of what was to come. As new players were added, the team got stronger and stronger.

The next 14 matches – 11 in the league and three in the Player's No.6 Trophy, against Bramley, Workington Town and Huddersfield – were won.

Northern had reached the John Player Trophy semi-final, which was held at Swinton on 3 December. Under new coach Frank Myler, Widnes proved just as difficult to beat as they had under Vince Karalius, ending Northern's hopes 14-10.

The team appeared to lose its edge in the league, being defeated by Workington Town, Castleford and Wigan, held to a draw by Widnes and St Helens and only recording one victory, over lowly Bramley.

Maurice Bamford resigned as assistant coach in February 1978 and took over as coach at Halifax. Almost immediately he was involved in making a deal with his old club. With many of his first team's threequarters injured Peter needed a centre quickly. Maurice Bamford also needed new players to address his own team's weaknesses. Peter was able to persuade Bamford to release centre Lee Greenwood, but Bamford was unsure about taking Peter's deal of Mick Blacker and £1,000 in return. Blacker had been a great servant to Northern, but Peter could no longer guarantee him a first team place.

Eventually Maurice was convinced and Blacker proved to be a great signing for Halifax, becoming captain and a solid team leader in subsequent years.

Just before the Challenge Cup deadline, Peter signed Derek Parker from Bramley for £8,000 and Neil once again linked up with his older brother, this time on a free transfer from Huddersfield.

Bradford started their Challenge Cup campaign at the end of February with a visit from Second Division Barrow. The men from Furness mounted a stern challenge and Northern had to work hard to turn a 13-4 deficit into a 21-13 victory. Two weeks later there was an even sterner challenge as Northern travelled over the Pennines to take on Wigan. An excellent performance brought a win, 22-10, **Northern's first at Wigan for more than 25 years.**

The Cup draw gave Northern another away match, at Headingley, the following Saturday. The tie turned into a hard forward battle. After a scoreless first half, Northern scored first through a converted Dean Rastrick try to lead 5-0. Northern piled on the pressure and it appeared that the initiative was with them. However, Leeds had pace and two stunning long-distance tries turned the game in their favour. Although Jack Austin scored a try, it was too late to stop Northern losing 16-8 to the eventual Cup winners.

Although Widnes had taken the title, Northern and St Helens continued to battle over the runner-up spot. Northern's form was good and wins over Hull KR, Workington Town and Dewsbury meant that victory on the last weekend over Featherstone Rovers would be enough to secure the runner-up position. But the game was never played.

As a result of an internal dispute Featherstone Rovers' players went on strike and refused to turn out for the final match against Northern. It fell to the emergency committee of the RFL to decide what to do. As it was impossible to complete the season normally, the committee decided that league positions would be determined by a percentage of possible points won, which meant that Northern finished as runners up.

First Division top three teams

	P	W	D	L	F	A	Pts
Widnes	30	24	2	4	613	241	50
Bradford N	29	21	2	6	500	291	44 (75.86%)
St Helens	30	22	1	7	678	384	45 (75%)

In the first round of the play-offs Northern disposed of the Challenge Cup winners, Leeds, 18-10. Missing Forsyth, Fox and Alan Redfearn through injury it hardly seemed likely that Northern would be able to end a 29-year wait for victory at Knowsley Road. Victory did in fact prove beyond them, but the team was in good spirits as it returned home having restricted the Challenge Cup runners-up to a four-point winning margin in the semi-final first leg.

Northern's confidence looked misplaced when St Helens took an early lead, 8-0 at Odsal in the second leg. Working hard, Northern reduced the deficit, to finally win the match 19-12 and beat St Helens 29-26 on aggregate.

Northern's team for the Premiership Final at Swinton on 20 May was:
K. Mumby, D. Barends, P. Roe, J. Austin, D. Redfearn, J. Wolford, A. Redfearn, I. van Bellen, D. Raistrick, J. Thompson, G. Joyce, D. Trotter, R. Haigh. Substitutes: N. Fox, C. Forsyth.

November 1977 Rugby League man of the month award.

Their opponents were Widnes – a club that had already defeated them three times during the season. Peter's team started slowly and were lucky that their opponents were only 5-0 ahead after 20 minutes. The remainder of the first half was much better for Northern as first Haigh scored a try that Mumby converted and then Roe scored a try, followed by a Wolford drop goal to give Bradford a 9-5 interval lead.

Bad injuries to two of their forwards early in the second half forced the Chemics to reorganise their pack. But although Bradford's pack was having the better of the forward battle it was Widnes who put the next points on the board, an unconverted try closing the gap to 9-8. That try stung Bradford into action. Dave Redfearn scored a try that Mumby converted followed by a Barends try to give Northern an easy 17-8 victory. Northern's captain, Bob Haigh, won the man-of-the-match award, the Harry Sunderland Trophy.

Although team-strengthening had cost more than £30,000, Peter had worked hard to offset the cost. During the season there had been additional outbound player movement. Peter Astbury had moved to Halifax, Dave Stockwell to Batley, Gordon Pritchard to Barrow and John Wills to Blackpool Borough. As a result the net cost of new players was only around £15,000. There was even better news for the directors at the turnstiles. Improved performances had pushed up the average gate to 7,236, an increase of 2,567 per match over the previous season.

Peter's assessment of his first season was characteristically realistic: "We have not yet reached the pinnacle of our teamwork. Our strategy and our tactical play can still be improved. We still have to master the techniques of how, when and where we bring our set-pieces into operation to complement our approach play. Many is the time we get to the line and just fail to capitalise. Our understanding, though, is getting better, and when the players can recognise what the situation requires then we shall be very close to having a team whose potential has been realised. Set-piece moves have been introduced and will become more effective as the players practice and perfect them."

There were so many positive things to take from that first season. A major trophy, runner-up in the league and only one match lost at Odsal all season, and that only by two points. Peter felt inspired, and he knew that with the right backing from his board Bradford Northern could go far. To make that happen, Peter had reassembled his coaching team, recruiting Cyril Kellett and Mick McGowan his former aides at Wakefield, as 'A' team and colts team coaches respectively. Alan Rhodes, the former Northern full back or centre, was brought in to replace Graham Starkey as fitness trainer. They were added to a good back-up squad consisting of Ronnie Barrett, the physio, and Fred Robinson, the kit man

1978-79

A round of transfers heralded the start of the new season. The first incoming player, on a free transfer, was the veteran former international Tony Fisher from Castleford, to fill the troublesome hooker position. Three 'A' team players left – Jimmy Birts, Graham Garrod and Derek Howard – to join their former coach, Maurice Bamford, at Halifax, for £5,000 in total. For another £5,000 Francis Jarvis went to Featherstone Rovers.

All the players were part-time professionals in those days and each of them had to maintain a balance between the game and their day job. One of the young wingers on Northern's books, Les Gant, had decided that the latter took priority. Peter got in touch to try and talk him around: "Lorry driving was what Les liked best and for over a season he gave up the game. During the summer of 1978 I managed to talk to him and after making some changes with his employers, Les was able to get back involved and soon would make a place in the first team his own."

The Yorkshire Cup eventually provided a really positive start to the season, although it did not look that way when in the first round Northern trailed Leeds 15-5 halfway through the first half. The second half turned to a real thriller, a converted try in the 77th minute giving Northern victory 24-23. Drawn again at Odsal in the second round a Dave Barends hat-trick helped Northern overcome Hull KR 28-17. Rovers' Humberside neighbours, Hull FC, visited Odsal in the semi-final and were beaten 12-7.

One September evening after training Peter stood on the field and looked all around the vast Odsal bowl. As the scale of his surroundings sunk in Peter could hardly believe his good fortune: "I was coach of a club that had once had one of the best teams I had ever seen, the Northern team of the late 1940s and early 1950s. I was also coach of a club that possessed one of the most charismatic names of all rugby teams – Bradford Northern."

Peter had decided on what his strategy must be: "To take the club forward I wanted to improve the quality of Northern's squad and so I began to target players around the British test team when they became available. Such players were not cheap, but I considered them essential if Northern was to enjoy real success."

The first of a number of expensive signings was made at the start of October. Jeff Grayshon, then a second-rower, was signed from Dewsbury for a new club record fee of £14,000. This was something of a gamble, for although Grayshon's play had brought him England caps in the past he had only just returned to action after a serious knee injury. As well as being a big, powerful, pacy forward Grayshon had good hands and could use the ball well. It was a combination that would make Grayshon a feature of Peter's teams for many years to come.

Jeff Grayshon made his debut against the touring Australians at Odsal on 8 October 1978. The match provided Peter with a chance to try out his game plan – hard active defence to close down the Australians and then rely on British handling skills to bring tries when on attack. Neil Fox, by then 39, accounted for two tries, the first from an interception after just 30 seconds, and two goals. Northern still led 11-10 with 20 minutes remaining. However, the departure of Neil Fox early in the second half left the home side without any real leadership and the Australians came back to win 21-11.

Peter's blueprint for the forthcoming test series, for which he had been recently made Great Britain coach, had had its first workout.

Headingley, on 28 October 1978, was the venue for the Yorkshire Cup Final. It should have been a mismatch, First Division Northern against Second Division York, but just in case Peter arranged for Johnny Wolford to be flown back from a business trip to Singapore the day before. On the day the underdogs played above themselves. At half-time the scores were tied 5-5. At the interval Peter decided to change stand-offs, bringing Johnny Wolford off the bench in place of Ian Slater. It proved to be a key move as Northern, responding to Wolford's promptings, ran in three more tries to lead 18-5 with a few minutes to go. A late York revival, which brought a try, could not stop Bradford lifting the Yorkshire Cup for **the first time since 1965**. Their team was:
K. Mumby, D. Barends, L. Gant, D. Parker, D. Redfearn, I. Slater, A. Redfearn, J. Thompson, A. Fisher, C. Forsyth, N. Fox, D. Trotter, R. Haigh. Substitutes: J. Wolford, M. Joyce.

A few days later Peter heard that Johnny Wolford wanted to leave the club, despite such a good start at Bradford. Peter tried to change his mind "but Johnny was adamant that he wanted to join Second Division Dewsbury and he also persuaded his mate, Jack Austin, to go with him. Jackie was another player I rated highly, both at Bramley and Bradford". Their move gave Peter the chance to negotiate an exchange. In return for Wolford and Austin, Peter got centre Nigel Stephenson. Peter saw in Stephenson, someone with similar skills to Johnny Wolford and successfully converted him to take over the stand-off position. Stephenson made his debut against Leigh on 19 November and fitted into the side almost immediately.

Talent was not all brought in from outside. During the autumn two youngsters, who would go on to reach the game's highest level, made their league debuts – Henderson Gill against Barrow at the start of September and Ellery Hanley against Rochdale Hornets at the end of November.

On the pitch, perhaps there was a loss of focus on the league as Northern suffered defeats at the hands of Warrington, Castleford and Salford. But just before Christmas an opportunity to really strengthen the pack presented itself. In preparation Peter transferred Dean Rastrick to Halifax and Ian Slater and Graham Joyce to Leeds, which together brought in around £27,000. Peter was aiming to sign Len Casey, a tough skilful loose-forward who had enjoyed being part of Peter's Great Britain squad. Wanting to work more with Peter, Casey requested a move and Hull KR agreed in return for cash plus young scrum-half Paul Harkin, in a deal which was estimated to be worth a club record £23,000. Although in his early years he had acquired a reputation for being difficult to manage, Len built a good working relationship with Peter.

In the renamed John Player Trophy, Bradford won at Barrow in the first round, then at Hull and finally 16-13 at Belle Vue to knock out Wakefield Trinity in the third round.

Progressing to the later stages of both the Yorkshire Cup and the John Player Trophy had caused the postponement of a number of league matches. That would not have been a problem provided the weather did not become a factor, which of course it did.

Frost and snow blanketed the north at the start of the festive season and ushered in two desperate months. Fixture disruption was widespread, but the exposed Odsal Stadium caused Bradford Northern more problems than most. Away fixtures were a lifeline. The match against Leeds on 6 January was switched to Headingley and Northern secured a welcome 10-5 victory.

Another swap meant a visit to Widnes on 17 January, but the outcome was much less satisfactory – Widnes nilling Northern in the league for the first time in three years. By then Northern's management was looking at all ways to get matches played. Similarly the home fixture against Workington Town, scheduled for Saturday 21 January, was swapped with the away game so that Derwent Park could be used, and it produced a welcome win.

The bad weather had forced the rescheduling of the John Player Trophy semi-finals. Instead of the planned weekend the match was played the following Wednesday at Widnes, where the home side won easily 21-3.

With the arrangements for the final and semi-finals immutable, the Challenge Cup had to take priority, making further disruption of the league fixtures inevitable. Northern travelled to Swinton in the Cup on 20 February. A victory there brought a home tie, against Hull KR, on 4 March. The weather relented and enabled Northern to play at Odsal for the first time in 1979. A 14-7 victory meant another home tie the following weekend. The ambitious Airlie Birds were Northern's opponents and a hard encounter, played in high wind, ended in a draw. A replay at the Boulevard the following Wednesday saw Northern score the only two tries of the match for an impressive 8-4 win and a place in the semi-final.

Now that Odsal was no longer needed for Challenge Cup ties the weather closed in again. By this stage Northern were getting desperate to play matches. With Odsal snowbound once more, Northern searched unsuccessfully for a neutral venue before deciding to sacrifice ground advantage. Agreement was reached with Featherstone Rovers to switch the home match on 25 March to Post Office Road. Unfortunately the switch proved more beneficial to Rovers and produced an unwanted defeat for Bradford.

On the eve of the Challenge Cup semi-final Peter again turned to the transfer market to strengthen the team at the key position of hooker by signing Keith Bridges from Featherstone Rovers. The deal was estimated to have cost £24,500 – in the usual mixture of cash plus a player, Tony Smith. It was the third time in six months that Peter had upped the club's record fee to get the player he wanted. Peter had Keighley to thank for a good proportion of that outlay; they had paid £10,000 in total for Lee Greenwood, Kevin Farrell and Graham Evans.

The draw for the Challenge Cup semi-final brought Northern and their bogey team, Widnes, together. The two arch rivals met at Swinton on 31 March. It looked for a while like Northern's fortunes might change. Trailing 14-3 the omens looked bad for Bradford, but the introduction of Neil Fox changed the match and tries from Len Casey and Nigel Stephenson, plus a goal from Keith Mumby put Northern back in contention at 14-11. Try as they might though Northern could not conjure another score and Widnes managed to hold on to win.

Odsal finally became available again for league action at the start of April, but getting the ground back did not bring an end to Northern's problems. Too many matches had produced a glut of injuries. Peter struggled as best he could to field a team, but by late April the injury situation was so serious that the club was forced to postpone matches against Wigan and St Helens. The RFL was not sympathetic and fined Northern £200.

Calls for the season to be extended were initially rejected by the RFL because it would interfere with the scheduled Great Britain tour to Australia and New Zealand. Eventually there was no choice, the season had to be extended, twice, finally to 13 May, and the Premiership Final was put back to clear the backlog of fixtures. Northern needed the full extension to play 11 league matches in 29 days. At least the evenings were getting lighter, which meant for a stadium like Odsal with no floodlights that kick-off times were pushed back from 6pm to 7pm. It was only an hour, but it made Peter's dash from work to the ground less hectic.

As they entered the final week of the season, Northern's weary players still had three home league matches to complete. Victories over Huddersfield on Tuesday and Hull KR on Thursday were followed by defeat at the hands of Widnes on Saturday 12 May. A season that had looked so promising at the start was fortunate to end with Northern in eighth position and a place in the play-offs.

The Premiership might have been a competition too far, but Northern's players made clear their determination to retain the trophy, despite having acquired the bad habit of conceding early leads. In the first round, on 15 May, a 13-0 half-time deficit at Hull KR was turned into an 18-17 victory. In the semi-final at Warrington, Northern again trailed at half-time, 11-5, before a Colin Forsyth try and three Steve Ferres goals produced a 14-11 victory and a place in the final against Leeds.

The Premiership Final was held at Fartown on Sunday 27 May. Badly affected by injuries, which had denied him the services of Barends, Dave Redfearn, Roe and Stephenson, Peter was forced to play reserves and four players – Casey, Grayshon, Mumby and Alan Redfearn – who along with Barends would be departing with the Great Britain squad for Australia two days later. Northern's team was:

K. Mumby, D. Parker, E. Okulicz, L. Gant, A. Spencer, S. Ferres, A. Redfearn, J. Thompson, J.H. Bridges, C. Forsyth, D. Trotter, J. Grayshon, L. Casey. Substitutes: I. van Bellen, D. Mordue.

A Steve Ferres penalty goal opened the scoring, but a tired team could not sustain any momentum on attack. Neither could Northern's usually reliable pack get the better of the Leeds six. Even so, only five points separated the two teams at half-time. Unfortunately in the second half Bradford could not raise their game, Leeds winning easily 24-2.

Peter's second season at Odsal had shown to all concerned what he was building. Further team strengthening and greater success were, however, thrown into jeopardy by the club's financial problems. Peter had expected some problems, the club's league crowds having fallen by 1,500 on average as a result of the bad weather. Yet the report given at the club Annual General Meeting painted a far more depressing picture. In Peter's first season, 1977-78, there had been a small loss reported of £4,238, which took the club's overall deficit to £51,959. That was nothing to what the report for the second season contained – a loss of £53,721, which effectively doubled the overall deficit to £105,680. Some pointed the finger at the amount spent on transfer fees, but nearly all had been self-financing. Peter's future strategies would be bedevilled by the worsening financial situation at the club.

13. Great Britain 18 Australia 14

During his second season at Odsal, Peter had faced an additional, even greater challenge than just taking Northern to the top of the British game. Thanks to the active sponsorship of Harry Womersley, the Great Britain team manager, Peter was appointed coach in July 1978 for the visit of the Australians that autumn.

The one downside to that appointment was that Peter did not have responsibility for picking the team; that was vested in an eight-man selection committee. "The committee was chaired by Bill Oxley, the Barrow club chairman. I was invited to give the selectors an insight into my methods and ideas for preparing the players to meet the Australians. I believed then, and always have believed, that set pieces in critical areas of the field are essential to open up the opposition's defence. That means a team has to have players who can organise others and players who do what the organisers want. Just picking the best 15 players available does not necessarily make the best team. This is what I told them." Yet, before Peter finished speaking Bill Oxley interrupted him and said "Peter we know you like plans and ideas, but look we'll pick the team. You just put them out onto the field to play."

Peter reflects: "That summed it up. I was not going to get any opportunity to suggest who I wanted in the team. But, through the influence of Harry Womersley and his assistant, Dick Gemmell, who had listened to my ideas, Steve Nash was brought into the squad as scrum-half." So at least Peter had one player who had previously successfully worked with his methods. To help Peter knock the selected squad into shape it was agreed that they would assemble at Rothwell, near Leeds, three days before each test match.

The home coach is always at an initial disadvantage against a touring team, who are training together ever day. Having whitewashed the Kiwis three months earlier, the Australians arrived in Britain full of confidence. Peter's opposite number, Frank Stanton, was able to work with his squad every day if he wanted for four weeks. During that time the Kangaroos won all seven of their matches in the build-up to the first test. Peter was not so lucky and did not even have any continuity on which to build because Great Britain had not played a match since the 1977 World Cup.

Peter made clear his approach in an interview with *Open Rugby*. He was open about his intentions – to go about the job in the same manner as before: "I'm not going to train Great Britain – I'm expecting them fit and ready to play for their lives when I get them. It's the responsibility of every club coach to make sure that any of his men selected are fit when they come to me."

Despite all their time together, the tourists were not playing particularly well in the run up to the test and it was thought that Great Britain had a good chance of winning the first clash at Wigan on Saturday 21 October. However, the selectors blundered when they chose the final 15 from the squad of 22 by leaving Brian Lockwood out as sixteenth man. It was a decision that left Peter's test team devoid of a pack leader. The British team for the first test was:

G.A. Fairbairn (Wigan), S. Wright (Widnes), E. Hughes (Widnes), E. Cunningham (St Helens), J. Bevan (Warrington), R. Millward (Hull KR – captain), S. Nash (Salford), J. Thompson (Bradford N), D. Ward (Leeds), P. Rose (Hull KR), G. Nicholls (St Helens), L. Casey (Hull KR), S. Norton (Hull). Substitutes: J.S. Holmes (Leeds), P. Hogan (Barrow).

Great Britain went in at half-time level pegging at 6-6 from three penalty goals apiece. After the break things remained even until the 55th minute when the two scrum-halves, Tommy Raudonikis and Steve Nash, were sent off for fighting. It was the turning point. Nash's sending off seriously affected Great Britain and he apologised to Peter after the match for losing his temper and control. Nash's tackling had been an inspiration to the other players. Britain's forwards continually dropped the ball when looking to put the Australians under pressure. Nevertheless Britain scored the first try of the match 15 minutes from time when John Bevan pounced upon an Australian mistake to move into a 9-7 lead. It was not enough. Two Australian tries in the last 10 minutes made the score 15-9 and snatched victory away from a Great Britain side that had not really done itself justice.

The selectors deliberated for four hours over the team for the second test at Odsal on Sunday 5 November. Six changes were agreed. Eddie Cunningham would be replaced by Les Dyl of Leeds, John Bevan by John Atkinson of Leeds, Jimmy Thompson by Widnes's Jim Mills, Paul Rose by Brian Lockwood, his club colleague from Hull KR and Len Casey by Phil Lowe who also played for the east Hull side. Paul Rose would replace Phil Hogan as forward substitute. When all those positions had been changed the selectors returned to the right centre position. The committee was unanimous that Eric Hughes be dropped, but they could not agree who should replace him. To try and make progress the chairman turned to Peter and asked him if he could suggest a player for consideration: "I said 'yes' and suggested John Joyner of Castleford, a young player who I believed could go far. Joyner was chosen and went on to have a good game." So Peter's first recommendation worked out well, but he was not asked to make any more.

Along with those retaining their place this was a selection that had great experience of both playing against the Kangaroos and of playing for Australian clubs – Lockwood, Lowe, Mills, Millward and Norton had all spent considerable time playing with the leading Sydney clubs. The Great Britain team was:

G.A. Fairbairn (Wigan), S. Wright (Widnes), J. Joyner (Castleford), L.P. Dyl (Leeds), J.B. Atkinson (Leeds), R. Millward (Hull KR), S. Nash (Salford), J. Mills (Widnes), A. Fisher (Bradford N), B. Lockwood (Hull KR), G. Nicholls (St Helens), P. Lowe (Hull KR), S. Norton (Hull). Substitutes: J.S. Holmes (Leeds), P. Rose (Hull KR).

Peter had always believed that inspiration could be achieved through the spoken or written word. Knowing that if Great Britain did not win the second test his international career would be over, he needed to find ways to convince his players that no individual could win the match himself, but that by playing for each other and working together a victory could be achieved. Peter chose to read to his players a piece of poetry, *The Indispensable Man* by American poet Saxon White Kessinger, at the final team talk, which he hoped would generate the necessary inspiration.

Some time when you're feeling important,
Some time when your ego's in bloom;
Some time when your friends keep on saying
You're the most talented man in the room;
Some time when you feel that your going
Would leave an unfillable hole,
Just follow this simple instruction,
And see how it humbles your soul.

Take a bucket and fill it with water,
Put your hands in it up to your wrists
Pull them out – and the hole that's remaining
Is a measure of how you'll be missed.
You may splash all you please when you enter;
You may stir up the water galore;
But stop – and you'll find in a minute
That it looks just the same as before.
The moral of this is quite simple;
Do just the best that you can;
Be proud of yourself – but remember –
There is no Indispensable Man.

Afterwards John Atkinson was sufficiently inspired to say: "Foxy, I never thought I liked you, but after that I like you a lot".

Much would depend on the two veteran props, Jim Mills, aged 34, and Brian Lockwood, 32. When David Ward withdrew, his replacement was Tony Fisher from Bradford Northern, aged 35, who had not played test rugby for seven years. With George Nicholls in the second-row and John Atkinson and Roger Millward in the backs all over 30 it was not surprising that Peter's ageing team was dubbed by some journalists as a 'dads' army'. It certainly contrasted sharply with a Kangaroo outfit whose average age was in the mid-20s.

Age proved no barrier to Lockwood who won the man-of-the-match award for a superb job of organising the support play of the forwards. A Stuart Wright try and four George Fairbairn goals allowed Britain to reach half-time 11-4 ahead. At half-time some decisions had to be made. As Peter recounts "It was clear that Roger Millward was not going to be able to get through the second half with a calf injury so we decided to pull him off. Putting on John Holmes altered the shape of the back play and caused Australia some new problems." When play resumed, a second Wright try, converted by Fairbairn, extended the lead to 18-4. A late Australian rally ate away at the margin, but Great Britain held on to win 18-14. The veterans had done it and the series had been levelled. After the match Peter commented that "everything went according to plan".

After the match the reporters wanted to know which poem had inspired the Great Britain performance. Peter wouldn't say, so they offered him £2,000 for a copy. Peter wouldn't sell it to them, but they would eventually get back at him, as they always did.

There was only one change for the third test at Headingley on Saturday 18 November – John Bevan replacing Les Dyl. Peter and his squad of 22 players went to Rothwell, a day early, on Tuesday 13 November, to get extra preparation time. To get the most out of their stay Peter tried to create a tour party atmosphere. Unfortunately Brian Lockwood's knee ligaments did not respond to treatment and he had to drop out. The selectors brought in Vince Farrar of Hull, aged 31, to take his place.

A poor, mean-spirited attitude hampered Great Britain in the first half when the team's tackling was high and poor. To make things worse, George Fairbairn had a bad day with the boot, missing all eight kicks at goal. Having conceded two penalty goals and a converted try in the first quarter of the match Britain fought back and held the Australians until almost half-time. Then in the last two minutes of the first half Australia ran in two converted tries to lift the score from 9-0 to 19-0. It was obvious as the team trooped off at half-time that the match and the Ashes were Australia's.

It was a painful first 40 minutes as Peter remembers: "Once the match has kicked-off a coach can only get to his players at half-time to change things that are not going right on the field. When the players got into the dressing room all they could talk about was giving the Australians some pain. I sat them down and told them to forget that stupid drivel and get back to playing rugby as we had planned."

There was little that could be done with substitutions because John Holmes was already on the field, standing in for the injured John Atkinson. To their credit the team went out and gave a much better performance, containing the Australians and actually scoring two tries, through Millward and Bevan, to their opponents' one. However, the match was lost, 23-6, and so was the series. Press reaction to the one-sided decider was fierce. There was no praise for the closeness with which Great Britain had come to winning the Ashes for the first time since 1970. One journalist laid the blame at Peter's door, writing that what "Great Britain need is a coach not a poet laureate".

As the Kangaroos moved on to France, British thoughts turned to the upcoming tour of Australasia, only six months hence. Peter was certainly looking forward to that tour. "After my appointment David Oxley, the secretary of the Rugby League, had told me that if the team performed well and were competitive then I would be appointed as coach for the 1979 British tour to Australasia. I certainly thought my team had met those conditions and so did the team manger, Harry Womersley, and his assistant, Dick Gemmell, who had given me every support at the selection meetings."

Sections of the press, speculating on who would be appointed coach, described Peter merely as one of the contenders. Knowing who he wanted to work with, Harry Womersley requested that the Rugby League Council appoint Peter as tour coach, but met major opposition. When, early in the new year, it came time to choose the coach, Peter was rejected and Eric Ashton, the St Helens and England coach, was appointed by a large majority. Ashton was even granted the right to pick his own team as has every Great Britain coach since. Angry and upset by the Council's attitude, Womersley threatened to resign as team manager, but was talked out of it by Peter.

For Peter it was a bitter blow because touring down under was one of his great ambitions. Many believed that he would have been even better as a tour coach than he was for single matches. Peter always believed the media had become prejudiced against him thanks to the attitudes of certain leading figures who were resistant to change and it was that that turned the Council against him.

The Australian team that would be waiting for the British tourists to arrive would be even harder to beat than the one just departed. After preparing teams for four hard matches Peter understood: "They had fitness levels that matched those of full-time professionals, they could maintain their intensity through a full 80 minutes, they had a large pool of very talented young players and they had great defence. Getting the better of them was never going to be possible without thorough preparation and a lot of hard work." Australian power was set to rule the league world. Probably nobody on the Council realised it, but it was going to be 10 long years before another British coach would match Peter's achievement of beating the Kangaroos in a test match.

Peter may have gained a reputation for being blunt and outspoken – a combination that both created enemies and laid him open to criticism. Many also believed that he was solely interested in proving that his was the right way and that team spirit suffered as a result. That certainly was not true of what Peter was to achieve at club and county level in the future.

Coaching Great Britain

The 1978 Great Britain squad: back: J. Mills, S. Wright, J. Holmes, J. Joyner, G. Nicholls, J. Bevan, P. Rose, J. Atkinson, P. Lowe; middle: F. Robinson (kitman), T. Fisher, L. Casey, P. Hogan, V. Farrar, G. Fairbairn, M. Smith, S. Norton, B. Lockwood; front: L. Dyl, R. Barritt (physio), K. Mumby, H. Womersley (manager), R. Millward, D. Gemmell (assistant manager), S. Nash, P. Fox (coach), G. Stephens. (Courtesy Robert Gate)

Above: With John Atkinson and Les Dyl

Right: With Tony Fisher and Jim Mills

Union and League – meeting Cliff Morgan (second from right)

Speaking at a presentation at Bradford in the 1970s.

14. Championships for Bradford

The new season began on 19 August 1979 with a visit to Fartown for a first round Yorkshire Cup tie. Keith Bridges' absence allowed an 18-year-old product of local schools rugby league, Brian Noble, who would later go on to captain and coach Great Britain, to make his debut. Neil Fox kicked his last goals for Bradford before he had to leave the field injured. Neil's magnificent career effectively ended that day, but his achievements and his points-scoring records remain. A win at Fartown brought a visit by Wakefield Trinity in the next round, which produced an unexpected 30-5 home defeat. Although it was a setback Peter remained bullish, saying that "anybody who writes us off after that game is taking an awful risk".

League matches started on Sunday 2 September 1979 and by then Peter had the team focused. There was no mistake, Northern recording a 13-5 victory at Hunslet on the opening day. After that the league wins kept on coming, at home over Wakefield Trinity and a stunning 21-10 victory over St Helens at Knowsley Road, **the club's first there for 30 years**. In the John Player Trophy away victories were secured over Doncaster 48-0 and Keighley 15-9, the latter a last-gasp affair.

As the season moved into October a home victory over York and win against Hull at the Boulevard took Northern to the top of the league. But all that good work was undermined by a couple of bad results. An acrimonious match at Wilderspool made referee Fred Lindop work hard for his money. Two players were carried off, two were booked and four sent off – three of whom were Northern's front row of Jimmy Thompson, Brian Noble and Ian van Bellen – as Warrington grabbed a 10-8 win. The next league match, at Odsal, saw Northern squander a 15-8 lead and lose 17-15 to Leigh.

While league form continued to be patchy – a victory over York being offset by defeat at Castleford – Northern managed to turn in a superb second half display to beat Leigh and qualify for the semi-final of the John Player Trophy. That match was held at Headingley on 17 November and Northern's performance moved Peter to describe it "as the best display of rugby league football I have seen from a team for years". Northern's 16-3 victory over Wakefield ensured a place in the final.

Finally, after lots of fund-raising work, Odsal's new floodlights were ready. The club had been the first to install lights in 1951, but they had been damaged in a storm and the club had been unable to afford to replace them. The daytime league match against St Helens was brought forward for the official switch-on. Erected at a cost of £42,000, the new lights lit up Odsal for the first time on Tuesday 27 November. A rather disappointing crowd of 5,861 saw Northern take an early lead. Although St Helens applied a lot of pressure, Northern held on to win 13-9 and enjoy the satisfaction of both ending the Saints' seven-match unbeaten run and registering a rare league double over their Lancashire visitors.

Confidence was growing and Northern's performances were improving accordingly. The following Sunday, Northern went to Central Park and registered a win over Wigan, **the first there for 27 years**. As if shocked by that achievement the team, without the services of the suspended Jimmy Thompson, promptly slumped to a home defeat at the hands of Hull KR.

As Christmas approached Northern ran into fine form. A win at Headingley on 16 December paved the way for a visit to Salford a week later. The Red Devils were top of the league, but Northern outscored them three tries to one to claim an important victory, 14-11. After an easy home win over Blackpool Borough on Boxing Day, league action stopped for four weeks, due to the John Player Trophy Final and postponements due to bad weather.

The John Player Trophy final was held at Headingley on Saturday 5 January. Northern's opponents were Widnes and Peter, expecting the usual hard, close match fielded the following team:

K. Mumby, D. Barends, D. Redfearn, D. Parker, L. Gant, N. Stephenson, A. Redfearn, J. Thompson, J.H. Bridges, C. Forsyth, J. Grayshon, G. van Bellen, L. Casey. Substitutes: I. van Bellen, S. Ferres.

A number of Northern's players were felled as Widnes took an aggressive, over-physical approach in the first quarter. Northern survived the onslaught and their forwards quickly gained the upper hand. Against a tough Widnes defence Northern slowly put points on the board. A Keith Mumby penalty goal, a long-range Derek Parker try and a Nigel Stephenson drop-goal were the only scores, but they were enough to see Northern home 6-0. A proud Jimmy Thompson was on hand to receive the John Player Trophy and Len Casey was voted man-of-the-match.

After the match Peter approached the board: "I told them that if they would put up the money for me to buy Trevor Skerrett and Charlie Stone, both of whom were available, that I would bring both the league trophy and the Challenge Cup to Odsal. I was convinced that by the addition of those two, my team would have been a strong enough combination to win the game's main honours. It was certainly a squad that every coach would have dreamed of."

It was possible, but Northern's directors had neither the vision to back their coach nor the money to fund it. Alas, two weeks later, Len Casey, shocked the rugby league world by submitting a transfer request. Apparently certain contractual payments owed to him could not be met by the Northern board. Despite Peter's objections, Casey's request was granted. Peter wanted the board to hold out for a player trade, but the desire for hard cash was too strong. By the end of January Casey was back in the colours of Hull KR for a fee of £38,000. His 13-month stay at Odsal was over and had realised a profit of £15,000 for Northern.

By chance, the first league match after Casey's transfer was against Hull KR at Craven Park on 27 January. Casey was forced to watch both his new and old team-mates struggle to gain any advantage. It took a Nigel Stephenson drop goal, scored with the last kick of the game, to give Northern a 10-9 win and stretch their unbeaten run to four matches.

Shrugging off the loss of Casey, Northern's powerful pack were instrumental in securing another three league wins, over Hull and Castleford at Odsal and at Leigh, to stay in the title race. By the end of February, Northern were one of four teams in with a realistic chance of the Championship – the other three being Hull, Leeds and Widnes.

As the Challenge Cup deadline approached, Peter was allowed to sign Geoff Clarkson for £4,000 from Hull KR. Clarkson, who had played for Peter during his Bramley days, was in his mid-30s and hardly the sort of long-term recruit that the team needed.

There were hopes of a run in the Challenge Cup after wins over Blackpool Borough and St Helens. Having already completed a league double over Hull and being drawn at home meant that Northern were made favourites when the two sides met on 7 March. However, a combination of Hull's defence and the referee, who disallowed two Derek Parker tries, meant that the Airlie Birds scraped through 3-0, thanks to a penalty and a drop-goal. Humberside was at the centre of a resurgence of rugby league support at that time and the crowd inside Odsal was swelled by an army of Hull fans. The attendance, 20,827, was the best outside Wembley that season and nearly triple Northern's average gate.

There was no alternative to concentrating on the league and wins at Workington and Widnes showed Northern meant business. The latter win, over the league leaders, was secured by turning round a 10-1 half-time deficit into an 11-10 victory at full-time. It was Northern's **first win at Widnes for 14 years**.

Home wins over Salford and Wigan and a win at Leeds, 7-2, kept the pressure on Widnes. Defeat at Blackpool was only narrowly averted – Les Gant scoring a try in the last 90 seconds to secure a win, 15-14. Warrington were not so accommodating and ground out a 10-4 win at Odsal.

Northern had to win their last two matches – both at Odsal – to take the title. The first was against Workington Town and Northern played like champions, running in eight tries – four from Dave Redfearn and three from Les Gant – in a 32-15 victory. The final match was against Hunslet on the evening of Wednesday 16 April. There was a festive atmosphere around Odsal as Northern celebrated in style scoring nine tries in a 41-16 victory. Victory put Northern at the top of the table, one point ahead of Widnes. After a 28-year wait the Championship trophy was once again presented to a Bradford skipper, Jimmy Thompson, and then the celebrations began.

First Division top four teams

	P	W	D	L	F	A	Pts
Bradford N	30	23	0	7	448	272	46
Widnes	30	22	1	7	546	293	45
Hull	30	18	3	9	454	326	39
Salford	30	19	1	10	495	374	39

Adding the Championship to Northern's honours-board meant that Peter had now won every major trophy open to him as a Yorkshire-based coach. Peter explained the significance of the latest trophy in the club's celebration booklet: "To win the Challenge Cup requires more than a share of luck, to win the Premiership requires stamina, to win the Championship requires a team of players dedicated to the game and willing to play not only for themselves, but for each of their colleagues. We are lucky in having the right type of players at Northern and I am a lucky person to have them under my charge."

The first round of the Premiership began with a visit from St Helens. This season the Saints had no answer to Northern's power and lost 30-0 at Odsal. In the semi-final Northern overcame Leigh on aggregate over the two legs by 31-16.

Station Road, Swinton, on 17 May, was once again the venue for the Premiership final where Northern's opponents were Widnes. Peter's team was:
K. Mumby, I. MacLean, D. Redfearn, D. Parker, L. Gant, N. Stephenson, A. Redfearn, J. Thompson, J.H. Bridges, C. Forsyth, G. Clarkson, J. Grayshon, G. Hale. Substitutes: S. Ferres, G. van Bellen.

A Dave Redfearn try, converted by Keith Mumby, gave Northern an early 5-0, lead. Widnes fought back, levelling the scores and then built a 9-5 lead by half-time. Perhaps

Northern's stamina had run out because after the break the Chemics controlled the game slowly, running in three more tries without reply to finish 19-5 ahead.

Defeat in the last match was a slightly disappointing way to end a great season. But as Peter said in the souvenir brochure published to celebrate winning the Championship: "Looking back over the season I realised a great ambition and that was to have won all the major rugby league trophies in my career as a coach. I will be ever grateful to the team for achieving for me a little place in the history, not only of Bradford Northern, but also of rugby league."

Peter's work at Odsal had brought him the Serena Coach of the Month award in January. Five months later, on a glamorous night at the Wakefield Theatre Club, Peter collected the Trumanns Steel Coach of the Year award. Besides the awards there was also the satisfaction of being offered and accepting a new contract that would keep him at Odsal for the next four years.

Peter's brother Neil retired as a professional player at the end of the season. He reflected on his time with Peter in the game: "I suppose he was my first coach, being six years older than me meant that he knew a lot about the game when I started to play it. He showed me how to play the game – how to tackle and how to pass. Tackling was particularly hard because he was so much bigger than me. He used to practice his goalkicking and Don and I were roped in to fetch the ball. It paid off for both of us because Peter insisted that we could only return the ball by either a drop-kick or a punt. It's no wonder that both Don and I turned into excellent kickers.

"He always looked out for me. When Wakefield Trinity came to the house offering me terms to sign on, I made sure Peter was there before I signed. I knew he'd look after my interests - just like an agent he made sure I got a good deal.

"Towards the end of my career with Wakefield I became player-coach. I did not want to coach full-time as I had my own business. I had six betting shops to run, so full-time coaching was not possible.

"As a coach you've got to rely on preparing your players and trust them to carry out your plans. Peter was a master at doing that. Whereas I would fall out with players, Peter never did. He always understood the need to take a psychological approach. He always worked on the basis that you had to coax the best out of your players, not lay into them. This is why he was successful with his coaching.

"We'd never played in the same team, so when Peter asked me to join Bramley, it gave me a chance to work with him for the first time in my career and we had a successful time. It was the same at Odsal when I joined him. Although I was 38 I was part of a good side and club. I was lucky that by then Peter knew how to get the best out of me by using me in shorter bursts. It kept me going and I enjoyed a great last 18 months in the game".

1980-81

Over the close season Northern attempted to further strengthen the squad. During July Peter parted with cash and Colin Forsyth to recruit Graham Idle from Wakefield Trinity. He also recruited Jim Fiddler from Bramley to fill Forsyth's prop position. To cover his spending Peter managed to sell Ian van Bellen to Fulham for £5,000. A restless Henderson Gill was allowed to move to Rochdale Hornets for £9,000 at the end of August.

Above: With the 1979-80 championship-winning squad.

Trophies from 1979-80 with Bradford Northern:

Left: With the John Player Trophy
Right: With Jimmy Thompson holding the
Championship Trophy

Trumanns' 1980 coach of the year: With David Oxley (on right)

Peter received news at the start of September that Northern were considering a radical shift in their approach to team strengthening. Stories began to appear in the press linking Northern with the stand-off and captain of the Argentine Rugby Union team, Hugo Porta. Although no details of the deal were released it would have been a bold move for the 28-year-old architect. Apparently the deal fell though when Northern discovered just how old he actually was. There were also stories linking Northern with a South African back, but they similarly led to nothing. Peter followed the stories in the press, but was not involved at all. More conventionally, Peter allowed the much travelled Geoff Clarkson to join Oldham.

Nigel Stephenson took over the captaincy for the new season, which began as usual with a first round Yorkshire Cup tie. Batley were the opposition at Odsal on 17 August 1980. A victory brought a tie at Fartown the following weekend. There any hopes of a good cup run quickly faded as Huddersfield won 20-13.

There was a difficult start to the league campaign, a trip to St Helens that resulted in a 16-6 defeat. That setback was quickly forgotten as Northern won the next five matches, three at home against Oldham, Keighley and Leeds and two at Barrow and Wakefield. This unbeaten run came to an end at Hull KR, 28-14, on 12 October.

Two days later the New Zealanders visited Odsal for the fifth match of their tour. Just four days before the first test two tries, apiece from Derek Parker and David Barends and three drop goals from Alan Redfearn were enough to give Northern a 15-10 victory.

Returning to league action Northern registered another three victories over Salford, Warrington and Barrow. However, Peter was by then having to deal with a lengthening injury list. This caused selection problems and accounted for the team losing three league matches and a John Player Trophy first round tie by the start of December. The team's loss of form seemed to have scuppered the chance of retaining the Championship.

Peter's man-management skills were called upon to get the team back on track. At the start of December Jeff Grayshon, the team's pack leader, was put on the transfer list for £55,000 at his own request. Fortunately, it did not take Peter too long to persuade Grayshon to change his mind, but there was further bad news the following month when it became clear that the first team hooker, Keith Bridges, had lost his appetite for the game. Peter quickly secured a replacement in Tony Handforth of Oldham.

While all this was going on the team was very inconsistent. The festive season produced three league wins, including a double over Halifax. However, that good work was undone by three defeats — at Castleford and Widnes, and at home to Workington Town — at the start of January. Two of Peter's old clubs — Wakefield Trinity and Featherstone Rovers — unwillingly eased the pressure, providing valuable points by the start of February.

Wins were proving difficult to come by and Peter made a bid for Featherstone Rovers' captain, Mick Morgan, as the Challenge Cup approached. The bid was unsuccessful and without him so were Northern — losing 17-13 in the first round at Salford.

With four games in hand and a three point cushion at the top of the table, the Championship was Warrington's for the taking by the middle of March. All Warrington had to do was keep winning, but the fixture congestion made that difficult. On 29 March Northern travelled to Wilderspool, the day after the Wire had lost to Widnes in a Challenge Cup semi-final. It was a critical match for both clubs, but a weakened Warrington could not hold Northern.

Northern won the next three matches — beating Featherstone Rovers and Widnes at home, before completing the double over Leeds at Headingley — to take the Championship race to the last day of the regular season, 20 April. Bradford and Warrington were together at the top of the table, both having 39 points. Warrington's superior scoring difference meant that Bradford had to beat Hull at Odsal and hope that their rivals would slip up against Leigh. In front of their home crowd Northern took control and extended an 18-8 half-time lead into a 38-18 full-time victory. There were a few anxious minutes to wait before the news came through from Wilderspool — Leigh had won and the Championship trophy was staying at Odsal.

First Division top four teams

	P	W	D	L	F	A	Pts
Bradford N	30	20	1	9	447	345	41
Warrington	30	19	1	10	459	330	39
Hull KR	30	18	2	10	509	408	38
Wakefield T	30	18	2	10	544	454	38

No club had managed to win back-to-back Championships since the reintroduction of two divisions and Peter was rightly proud of his team's achievement. However, the strain of the run-in seemed to have taken its toll on the team, a lacklustre performance at home against St Helens saw Northern ejected from the first round of the Premiership, 14-12. Peter was one of three nominated for the Trumanns Steel coach of the year award but, unlike his team, did not retain the title.

As the season drew to a close, Peter entered a new era as the Championship winning team started to break up. During May Jimmy Thompson and Steve Ferres moved to newly formed Carlisle for £12,000. They were followed to Carlisle two months later by Nigel Stephenson in a deal worth £20,000. Keith Bridges, who had returned to action, and later Derek Parker submitted transfer requests, and were listed at £15,000 and £25,000 respectively, before making their peace with the club. A further blow was the injury to the highly rated centre Peter Roe that ended his career with the club.

1981-82

Peter's only significant recruit was 23-year-old loose-forward Alan Rathbone from Leigh. Although a bit on the small side for a back-row forward Alan Rathbone was a hard man on the field who had the ability to boss a game. The former Great Britain under-24 international was brought to Odsal for a fee of £16,000. Rathbone's signing drew criticism because of his reputation for being dismissed, but he would perform well under Peter's guidance. Rathbone, who would be the last major signing in Peter's first spell as a coach at Northern, went straight into a restructured team, led for the first time by Alan Redfearn. Peter had also wanted to sign Colin Maskill, but the young hooker chose to join Wakefield Trinity instead.

Ellery Hanley had just returned from three years enforced absence and was intent on resurrecting his career. His original signing was brought about by the leader of the Corpus Christi youth team recommending him to Harry Womersley. Peter and Harry went to watch him play in Wakefield. After the match Harry asked Peter what he thought. Peter replied: "He's not the cleverest or fastest of players, but I think he's awesomely strong and will develop. For now I can't pinpoint a position for him to play". On that basis a deal was offered to the 17-year-old Hanley, who signed at the start of June 1978 along with two of the Wakefield youngsters – Russell Smith, who went on to become a very fine referee, and Mark Fleming, whose size prevented him from developing into a fine loose-forward.

Hanley was handed the stand-off position and Jeff Grayshon was converted into an open-side prop forward. In their new roles, both players strengthened the team, but overall Peter was left with an even thinner squad with which to chase the top honours.

There was one factor that Peter hadn't bargained for at the start of the season – an officially sanctioned two-month period during which referees could crack down on scrummaging, in a bid to tidy them up and force offenders to abide by the rules. For a coach there was little to do except to hope that the crackdown did not produce too much team disruption nor disadvantage his own team too much. As usual the crackdown generated an outcry by spectators about disrupted matches and an excess of penalties.

Northern's small squad size did not hamper a strong run in the Yorkshire Cup. A trip to nearby Halifax on 16 August saw hooker Tony Handforth booked as Northern overwhelmed the home side in the second half to win easily 33-5. The crackdown was to cause Northern further problems at Headingley the following weekend. After a number of scrum penalties were awarded, both Tony Handforth and the Leeds hooker were dismissed either side of the break. Thanks to a superb defensive performance, a disrupted Bradford team made it through to the semi-final 11-5.

Tony Handforth returned from suspension to take his place in Northern's team for the semi-final on 2 September. Once more the purge on scrum offences saw a hooker dismissed, Hull KR's David Watkinson, and Handforth seemed certain to follow after he was booked. To try and prevent that happening Peter moved centre Gary Hale into the hooking role, only to see him dismissed for his first offence. For most of the match the advantage lay with the home side before a converted try five minutes from time gave Northern a one-point lead, which they held until the final whistle.

Northern saved their worst performance of the season so far for the Final against Castleford at the start of October. Hooker Tony Handforth was forced to pull out of the team and his place went to Brian Noble, who not only managed to stay on the field for the whole match, but also to win the scrums 16-14. A penalty goal, kicked by Ellery Hanley, opened the scoring halfway through the first half. Unfortunately Northern did not score again for 50 minutes. During that time their opponents coped much better with the atrocious conditions to build a 10-2 lead. A Derek Parker try minutes from the end raised hopes among the Northern supporters, but Castleford held on until the hooter sounded. Bradford's team was:

K. Mumby, D. Barends, G. Hale, A. Parker, L. Gant, E. Hanley, A. Redfearn (captain), J. Grayshon, B. Noble, P. Sanderson, G. van Bellen, G. Idle, A. Rathbone. Substitutes: D. Redfearn, D. Jasiewicz.

The excitement of the Yorkshire Cup campaign helped distract attention from a poor start to the league campaign. Only one of the opening four league matches was won and by mid-November Bradford were hovering on the edge of the relegation zone with only six points from nine matches.

The danger was that Northern would stay near the relegation zone as problems within the team started to break out into the open. Money and morale often go hand in hand and a dispute over the former led Keith Mumby to threaten to submit a transfer request in November. Finally, after months of waiting, an offer, at the full asking price, was received for Derek Parker from Wakefield Trinity. Peter used £18,000 from Parker's fee to sign Leeds's David Smith, a winger he had previously coached at Wakefield.

All Peter's other signings had to be made from the youth team or the local amateur game. One of those was a young prop, Mick Atherton, who signed for Northern from Manor Social Club ARL of Wakefield at the end of November. So limited were the first team squad's resources that Atherton found himself facing up to the intimidating Widnes pack on his first-team debut at Naughton Park one week later.

Fortunately, Peter's ability to turn promising youth into quality senior players continued to serve Northern well. During January and February both Ellery Hanley and Brian Noble were called up to play for the Great Britain under-24s against France.

As the February Challenge Cup transfer deadline approached Peter set his sights on Workington Town's centre, Kieron O'Loughlin. Unfortunately, when Peter approached Northern's directors he discovered that the club could not afford to enter into negotiations for a player that might cost around £30,000. Peter had no choice but to drop his interest.

Victories over Dewsbury and Workington Town in the first two rounds of the Challenge Cup brought a home quarter-final against Widnes. As usual the match was extremely close. Just when it looked like Bradford would take a narrow lead into half-time through a penalty goal and a drop-goal to a drop-goal, Widnes intercepted and scored a converted try to lead 6-3. After the break Bradford fought back to lead 8-6 until a Widnes penalty goal brought a draw. The replay took place the following Wednesday, when Widnes won 10-7.

Having lost all interest in the Cup Northern turned their attention to the league. Northern's form was impressive and nine wins in the last 10 league matches, including wins at Workington and Wigan, pushed them up the table.

Fifth place brought a visit to the fourth-placed club, Hull KR, in the first round of the Premiership on 3 May 1982. It was a match that Peter cannot forget: "A day which started with the hope of fame and fortune was to turn into one of the most miserable days in the club's history. Robin Whitfield, the referee, struggled to control a fiery encounter, peppered with confrontations and brawls. A forward from each side, John Millington and Gary van Bellen, were the first to be dismissed and they were followed by a back from each side, Steve Hartley and Dean Carroll. By the time Whitfield blew his whistle for half-time a third Bradford player, Ian Ellis, had also been dismissed."

"Fifteen minutes into the second-half, Jeff Grayshon's reaction to a referee's decision was to throw the ball to the ground. Unfortunately the ball bounced up and caught Robin Whitfield on the shoulder. Grayshon, Northern's captain, was immediately given his marching orders. Confusion followed as Grayshon trudged off the field. Grayshon claimed that he was indicating to one of the remaining nine Northern players to come over and take the captain's armband. A weary and disillusioned team took his gesture as an instruction to follow him off the field, which they did."

"Fearing serious injury if the team returned, Northern's chairman Ronnie Firth and some of the other directors rushed to the dressing room. Although Ronnie Firth accepted all responsibility he was not only the only director ordering the team to stay put. Even though I warned those present that the consequences of their actions would be severe. Firth stepped outside and announced to the assembled press and match officials that the team would be returning to Bradford immediately. Whitfield was left with no option but to abandon the match."

Two days later the Rugby League Council met to consider the extraordinary events at Craven Park. They decided to award the match to Hull KR and allowed the score, 17-8 to Rovers, to stand. Then they considered the day's events and decided that Jeff Grayshon had deliberately led his team from the field. For that Grayshon was banned from playing until the end of September. They also censured the members of Northern's team and the club chairman. Northern were also banned from next season's John Player Trophy, the Challenge Cup and the Premiership, and fined £4,000.

The severity of the sanctions imposed by the council threatened the very survival of the club. An appeal was heard in July. Although the fine was upheld the decision by Ronnie Firth to resign as chairman helped convince the council to suspend the ban on entering the three cup competitions for five years. The following month Jeff Grayshon also appealed and had his ban reduced to five matches.

While all this was going on in committee rooms, Peter tried to strengthen his team. A neck injury forced Tony Handforth to retire, but there was a more than adequate replacement already in place in Brian Noble. No wonder Peter was more than happy to let a third hooker, Keith Bridges, go to Hull for £15,000 in August. Besides that there was little movement, which meant that Peter would have to hope that there were good players coming through the colts and the 'A' team if Northern were to remain competitive.

1982-83

There was a reorganisation of the fixture list – the new season opening with league fixtures to allow the Yorkshire Cup to start at the beginning of September. Despite fielding five 'A' teamers in place of the suspended players, Northern opened the new campaign with a win over Castleford.

But after defeats by Oldham and St Helens, Bradford and Peter in particular suffered a hammer blow when on the day after the latter match, 26 August, Harry Womersley, a man instrumental in the club's reformation in 1964 and development since then, died aged only 55. The death of that true Northern hero was to signal the end of the Fox era when it came to the renewal of Peter's contract. Peter later said that "my lowest point at the club was the loss of Harry Womersley, who was always my strongest ally".

At the start of October Billy Kells joined Northern. A stand-off for Waikato and a member of the 1980 Kiwi touring team, Kells had suffered an injury blighted New Zealand season before moving to Bradford. Unfortunately for Kells, who had the potential to develop into a fine player, his bad luck with injuries persisted and after only five appearances, two as substitute, his career with Northern was over.

Just when it appeared they were on the way out of the Yorkshire Cup, trailing 14-5 to Hull KR, Northern rallied and scraped through to the second round 15-14. A second round victory over York took Northern into a semi-final at Post Office Road. There was little to choose between Northern and Featherstone Rovers as a scoreless first half showed. In the second half Northern managed to pull away to reach the final, 11-0.

For the Yorkshire Cup Final at Headingley on 2 October, Northern's opponents were Hull FC. Unfortunately Northern had to take the field without Ellery Hanley who was in dispute with the club over money. Nevertheless Northern held Hull to a one point lead at half-time. It was different in the second-half when Hull pulled away to win 18-7. The Bradford team was:

K. Mumby, D. Barends, L. Gant, A. Parker, S. Pullen, K. Whiteman, D. Carroll, B. Noble, G. van Bellen, G. Idle, D. Jasiewicz, G. Hale. Substitutes: D. Smith, P. Sanderson.

However, things were to get worse. From mid-September onwards Northern lost five consecutive league matches to take the club into the relegation zone by the end of October.

A week after Australia had humiliated Great Britain 40-4 at Hull, the tourists paid a visit to Odsal and paid Northern the compliment of fielding a near test-strength team. For the match against the Kangaroos, on 7 November 1982, Peter employed a basic, restrictive, but effective game plan. "The aim was to play the game in the Australians' 25 – so John Green, normally our 'A' team full-back, was instructed to kick downfield early in the tackle count to neutralise the Australians' fast, aggressive rush and for Northern's defensive line to get downfield quickly and then tackle hard to keep them pinned back." The plan worked for a while, restricting the Kangaroos to a 7-6 lead until two tries in the last eight minutes made the score a more definitive 13-6 in the Australians' favour.

Two of Northern's players who excelled on the night – Keith Mumby and Alan Rathbone – were called up for the second test and the man-of-the-match, Jeff Grayshon, was awarded the British captaincy. While there was no wider recognition the match did give Peter the personal satisfaction of proving that a side prepared by him could contain the team from down under and prove that they were in no way supermen.

After an easy win over Keighley in the first round, Northern made hard work of the John Player Trophy. The holders, Hull, came to Odsal in the second round and at 10-0 ahead appeared to be on their way through until two late Northern tries forced a replay. Three days later the two clubs appeared to be heading for another replay when a late Keith Mumby penalty goal gave Northern a 10-8 victory. The quarter-final draw sent Northern to Widnes four days later and another tense match ensued, the outcome of which was effectively decided by two Northern lapses. The first, in discipline, brought about the dismissal of Alan Rathbone after an hour and the second, in concentration, saw Alan Redfearn lose the ball on his own line to gift a try to Andy Gregory.

There were still difficulties to contend with off the field. With the club's accumulated debt predicted to pass £300,000 by the end of the season 12 local businessmen established an action committee during March. The committee set itself a target of £100,000 to meet the more urgent debts and tax bills.

After accounting for York, Fulham and Workington Town, Northern came up against a rejuvenated Featherstone Rovers in the Challenge Cup semi-final at Headingley on the last Saturday of March. Northern's performance appeared to be overcautious, producing too much one-man rugby, which too often Rovers' defence was able to stifle. Two moments of inspiration from Ellery Hanley, the first setting up a try for Gary van Bellen and the second a great length of the field solo effort down the touchline, gave Northern a 6-3 half-time lead. However, Rovers were too good in the second-half, winning 11-6, and ending Northern's hopes of a Wembley appearance for another year.

That semi-final must rank as one of the biggest disappointments of Peter's coaching career at Northern. For so long the club had been knocking on the Wembley door and this had been a real opportunity. And for Jeff Grayshon there was to be even more semi-final heartache in the coming years.

Poor league form meant the spectre of relegation hung over Odsal all season. No matter how hard they tried Northern's team could not find consistency. A series of wins would always give way to a series of defeats.

As usual the extra Yorkshire Cup, John Player and Challenge Cup ties produced a fixture pile-up. This time Northern's players had to turn out four times in the final week to complete their programme. Remarkably the team recorded four victories – over St Helens on the Tuesday, Workington Town the next day, Carlisle on the Friday and finally Featherstone Rovers on Sunday to pull clear of the relegation zone. It was almost enough to push Northern into the top eight, but ninth was where they finished, thereby missing out on entry to the Premiership.

1983-84

Peter had to face a number of challenges as he readied Northern for the following season. Most of them were the result of changes made to the laws of the game that had been agreed by the International Board in November 1982 and these were implemented in Great Britain at the start of the new season.

There were three main changes. The most obvious was the decision to increase the value of a try from three to four points. However, the other two would have a greater impact on play. It had been decided to bring the league's laws on scrummaging in line with the ones in use in rugby union and give both head and feed to the non-offending or non-kicking side as appropriate. Finally, it was agreed that the team in possession on the sixth tackle would, instead of contesting a scrum, just hand over the ball to their opponents.

Overnight the scrums did become much tidier, but only because most packs had realised it was hardly worth struggling for the ball as possession was virtually certain for the side with the put-in. And because kicking to touch was unlikely to offer a chance of regaining possession all teams had urgently to develop a variety of kicking options on the sixth tackle. Overall the changes led to a major change in the pattern of play.

Radical alterations to the international transfer rules in the late 1970s had already helped bring a large number of talented Kiwis into the British game. The impact of that decision was small compared to the effects of the decision, taken in October 1983, to lift the ban on signing Australian players. All of a sudden there was the opportunity to bring tried-and-tested Australians, many of them test players, into the British game.

Peter did not have the money to become involved in that signing frenzy. The only overseas international player who found his way to Odsal that autumn was Phillip Ralda, the Papua New Guinea captain, and he only stayed for a couple of matches. Having reached the veteran stage, David Barends was allowed to move to Featherstone Rovers for a small fee. Fortunately he was the only one to leave. The lack of signings, either domestic or overseas, meant that Peter embarked on the new season with probably the smallest playing squad in the First Division. That situation was compounded when Jeff Grayshon went into hospital in early October for a cartilage operation that ruled him out of action until the start of the new year.

The fixture planners gave Northern a relatively easy start to the season, a visit to newly promoted Whitehaven. The new laws did not prove to be too much of a problem as Northern ran in seven tries to win easily 45-4. The following Sunday, Northern defeated Oldham 14-8 at Odsal to register a second league victory.

In the Yorkshire Cup first round, Northern only just survived a very spirited challenge from Hull KR. Even though they were reduced to 12 men after a quarter of an hour Rovers kept striving for victory and in the end Northern only won 25-22. The draw sent Castleford to Odsal in the next round. The tie became a dour match that turned on a Northern fumble - Castleford capitalised and won 12-8.

Yet again the draw for the John Player Trophy paired Northern and Widnes – the fifth time in seven years. Even by the pair's standards it was an extremely close match at Naughton Park, which Northern led for nearly 40 minutes thanks to a Dean Carroll drop-goal. In the 68th minute Widnes dropped a goal to equalise before, in the last minute, Andy Gregory kicked a second to give Widnes victory, 2-1; the lowest score in any John Player Trophy tie.

In the league it was a different story. Northern played consistent, good rugby and led the table up to new year. After Christmas, Northern faltered losing to Widnes and drawing with Castleford at home, before losing at Hull. This loss of five points knocked Northern off the top of the league and the two Hull clubs grabbed their chance.

Money continued to be a problem. Ellery Hanley had briefly stayed away in December in a row over pay. That dispute was quickly resolved only for the matter to flare up again in March. This time the dispute was more serious and led to Northern's star player being put on the transfer list at £75,000.

The first round of the Challenge Cup brought Peter's old club Featherstone Rovers to Odsal on 12 February. At the break the score was 4-4 and the tie looked wide open. However, in the second half Northern played far more enterprisingly, moving the ball wide to easily win. Second Division Hunslet gave Northern an early fright in the next round, taking a 5-4 lead in the early stages, before two short range tries from Grayshon and Noble turned the match round and set a up a 17-7 victory.

The draw for the next round set up a meeting with arch rivals Leeds in the quarter-final. At Headingley, Northern had a 12-0 lead after 20 minutes. Leeds fought back to 12-5 before a Dean Carroll drop goal, just before half-time, made the score 13-5. In the second half the Loiners slowly reduced the deficit until finally, in the last minute, they got the drop goal they needed to level the scores and force a replay.

Once again a close match turned into a nailbiter as Northern defended a four-point lead. Then with 15 minutes remaining Leeds scored a converted try to go two points ahead. In the dying moments of the game the referee gave Northern a penalty. It was kickable, but the pressure proved too much for Dean Carroll whose attempt sailed wide. Northern's chance of a draw and a second replay had gone.

Northern finished in seventh place in the league. It was enough to them into the Premiership, but their involvement was short-lived as Hull beat them 42-12.

The end of season gave everyone chance to reflect on the changes that had occurred. The sixth tackle handover had had a huge impact, doing much to revitalise the kicking game in general play and driving the number of scrums in many matches down into single figures.

It had also greatly reduced the number of pauses within a match, further speeding up play and placing an even greater emphasis on player fitness. When taken in conjunction with the new scrum laws on head and feed its effect was to devalue many of the old forward arts.

Australian influence was becoming more obvious especially in the use of the high kick or bomb on the sixth tackle when a team was near their opponent's line. For someone like Peter who appreciated the style and skills honed in Britain it was a much-changed game.

1984-85

After three difficult seasons Northern still lacked the money to enter the transfer market in anything but a modest way, selling Graham Idle to Hunslet for £3,000 in June and buying Wayne Heron from Leeds two months later, for £2,500. Also leaving was Nigel Stephenson, who, believing he still had a couple of Second Division seasons in him, was allowed to rejoin Dewsbury.

Through the club sponsor SGS, a meeting with the Welsh rugby union international scrum-half Terry Holmes was set up. As Holmes relates in his autobiography, Peter and Barry Stamper of SGS met up with him shortly before he was due to depart with his club, Cardiff, for a tour of the Far East. In a hotel just outside Newport Peter explained how he visualised Holmes would fit into the team. Holmes agreed to think over what Bradford's deputation had said and respond after the tour. Unfortunately his response in early September was "not interested", but Holmes did promise that if he ever considered moving to rugby league it would be with Bradford Northern and Peter.

Wally Lewis, a world-class stand-off for Queensland and Australia had made a big impact on a short contract with Wakefield Trinity the previous season. On 8 July Northern made an announcement that negotiations were practically complete and that Lewis would be joining them for the new season. But no more was heard until it was learnt that Lewis had decided to stay in Australia. Peter always regarded Lewis as a fantastic player who would have transformed any team. However, he was never involved in the attempt to sign him, and therefore never had any plans to integrate him into the team.

Peter was able to secure some new blood to strengthen the team. Following the path trodden by many local clubs Peter secured two other Australians – Bret Tengdahl from Easts in Sydney and Bob Kellaway from Souths in Brisbane. He was also able to secure one of his old players, Charlie Stone, on a two year rental from Hull.

As Peter readied his team for the start of the new season one thing was very clear: "Ellery Hanley was ready physically and mentally to lead Northern's attack. Already close to the heart of the action at stand-off, I decided to harness his pace, strength and eye for an opening by allowing him a roving role. In a change to team rules I allowed Hanley to disrupt a planned move by interposing himself into it. The change worked better than I could have hoped. Ellery started running in tries on a very regular basis."

Shrugging off an opening day defeat at Hull KR, Northern recovered to register league victories over Wigan and Featherstone. In the first round of the Yorkshire Cup Hanley showed just how good his form was, running in four tries in the 30-0 defeat of Wakefield Trinity at Belle Vue. The next round brought a meeting with Leeds at Odsal at the end of September. Northern's arch rivals held a 9-4 lead at the interval. In the second-half Northern tried everything to breach the Leeds defence, but to no avail. The visitor's defence held firm to deliver a remarkable victory, 10-4.

October opened with a visit to Odsal by Hunslet. The visitors were outclassed and Northern showed no mercy. Ellery Hanley contributed 28 points, including 12 goals, to the 72-12 victory. If Hanley had been able in the last minute to successfully kick a penalty to make it 13 goals, Northern would have been able to set a new club record highest score.

In the John Player Trophy a fairly easy victory over Swinton gave Northern a home second round tie against St Helens. Although St Helens were reduced to 12 men it needed a late conversion by Steve Parrish to level the score and secure a replay. At Knowsley Road St Helens were again reduced to 12 men, but even with an extra player Northern could not take advantage and the home side won easily 24-10.

Up to the end of October, Northern had been in contention at the top of the league table. Maybe the loss of Jeff Grayshon was factor in a run of bad results that lasted until the end of January and saw the club drop to ninth in the league.

It was a bleak new year for Peter: "Since the loss of Harry Womersley I did not have either the backing nor the support a coach needs to progress in the right direction. The new members of the board were not rugby men and they, along with another board member, with whom I never could get on, decided that the club would have a change of coach. It seemed that all that I had done for the club was not enough for them to have a little more faith."

On 7 February, just before the start of the Challenge Cup, Northern's directors informed Peter that his contract, which was due to expire at the end of the season, would not be renewed. The board was quick to point out that Peter had not been sacked; he was being allowed to leave, as soon as he wished, to make way for a new coach, who could change the club's style. Fans raised petitions and called for Peter's reinstatement. The players let it be known that they did not support the board's actions.

Against this background, Northern waited patiently for the Challenge Cup campaign to begin. The first round should have seen the team travel to Southend, but the new club's financial difficulties saw the match switched to Odsal. Bad weather prevented the tie being played on 10 February. After four more postponements the match was finally played two weeks late, on 24 February. Southend Invicta proved no match for Northern, losing 50-18. The second round brought Wakefield Trinity to Odsal. This time the margin was narrower, but Northern still won, 13-2, to move into the quarter-finals.

Wigan were Northern's opponents on 10 March. With much of Odsal out of action due to construction work, the large crowd caused problems and the game was interrupted by pitch invasions. Although the home side got off to a good start, opening the scoring through a Steve Parrish penalty, Northern's pack was badly disrupted as Jasiewicz, Kellaway and Noble all had injuries. Wigan went ahead 5-2 in the second-half, but Northern struck back, Hanley making a try for Steve McGowan. It was not enough. A penalty wiped out that lead and gave Wigan a 7-6 win. By then it was obvious that there would be no change in the directors' attitude. In mid-March Peter announced he had signed with a new club, but would not say which one. In disgust Jeff Grayshon resigned the captaincy at the end of March.

Northern's season looked at one point to be about to disintegrate. Not only was Peter waiting to leave, but Brian Noble was allowed to head off to Australia on a short contract with Cronulla, leaving Northern without a recognised hooker for the closing weeks. Despite all that, Northern still managed to finish eighth in the table.

In the Premiership, Northern had to travel to Craven Park to meet Hull KR. Although obviously the underdogs Northern pushed the champions all the way, and only a late surge made the score, 42-18, look a lot easier than it had been. Defeat brought Northern's season to an end and it meant that Peter was free to leave.

Peter was able to look back with some satisfaction on the change in team rules he had made at the start of the season: "The change, which allowed Ellery Hanley to break up planned moves, worked very well. The young stand-off maintained his form throughout the season to become the first player for 23 years, and the first non-winger ever, to score more than 50 tries in a season." The good news was that 52 of Hanley's 55 tries had come when he was appearing for Northern.

The board's decision to replace Peter was almost disastrous for Northern the next season when the club just escaped relegation. Paul Fitzpatrick of *The Guardian* wrote a suitable epitaph to Peter's spell at Odsal: "The directors owe much to Fox over the years for his ability to make the best of severely limited resources and in general his record with the club has been exceptional."

15. Leeds

While working out his contract Peter "received a number of inquiries about my future availability. I had received a good offer from St Helens, but in the end the one I accepted was much closer to home." Four days after Northern's Premiership defeat, on 2 May 1985, Peter was announced as the successor to the short-lived Australian, Malcolm Clift, as coach at Headingley. Instead of the three-year contract he wanted Peter was given a gentleman's agreement that the job was his for as long as he wanted. Ray Abbey, the former Bramley scrum half, was appointed assistant coach.

After 15 years' coaching Peter had found his way to the biggest and wealthiest club in Yorkshire. "I expected that a club, which had always been in the market for quality players, would have the money to finance my team rebuilding plans," he says, but unfortunately Peter didn't realise the club's situation. The previous season's Australian influx had not only emptied the coffers, it had also left the Headingley trophy cabinet dispiritingly empty too.

Peter told the Leeds directors on joining that "Ellery Hanley wants to leave Bradford and he's a player who is going to be one of the greatest names in the game". Unfortunately Leeds did not want Ellery Hanley in the team. "Obviously young Ellery's off field antics did not gel with the Leeds directors," was Peter's conclusion. Three years later all was forgiven and Hanley was signed from the club he had joined, Wigan.

Peter's plans were dealt a blow when John Holmes, a playmaker with the kind of skills that Peter admired, announced his retirement. There were still plenty of experienced players in the squad and Peter chose one of them, David Heron, as his new captain. Also in the squad were two of Peter's former colts from his days at Wakefield – Keith and Kevin Rayne. And for one player it was a less than auspicious reunion. Colin Maskill had previously turned down the option to sign for Peter and he was not to be allowed to forget that mistake.

Leeds had used a large number of Australians the previous season and those who went home – Wally Fullerton-Smith, Eric Grothe, Neil Hunt, Gavin Jones, Rick Lulham, Trevor Paterson and Steve Bleakley – had to be replaced in the team by players who had been denied the experience they required. Only two of the Australian contingent returned – Tony Currie, a centre, and the loose-forward Terry Webb. There was also a New Zealander in the squad – the hooker Trevor Clark.

For Peter it was a frustrating time: "A scrum-half, a goalkicker and a hooker had topped my wanted list, but none were signed. The only new blood I managed to secure from Australia was Cliff Lyons on a one-year contract from North Sydney as cover for the stand-off position that John Holmes had vacated." There was a lot of speculation in the press about British signings, but only one was made. Andrew Staniland, a winger whose father had played for Leeds, was signed from Roundhay RUFC in August.

It was a much changed Leeds team that took part in the pre-season charity match at Bramley before taking the field at Crown Flatt for the opening league match against Dewsbury. Despite the unfamiliarity a victory was secured and this was followed by easy victories over Keighley, 60-12, and Dewsbury again, 48-2, to take Leeds into the semi-final of the Yorkshire Cup. But Castleford proved too strong, winning 14-10 at Headingley in a game that marked not only the end of any hopes of Yorkshire Cup success, but also the start of a truly miserable sequence.

From the start of October to the middle of December the Loiners won only one match, against Swinton, and drew two, against Halifax 18-18 and St Helens 12-12, both away. During that time five league fixtures were lost. There was also an over-physical meeting with the touring New Zealanders. Six days after watching his Yorkshire county side get the better of the Kiwis, Peter's Leeds team took on the tourists. This time things did not go so well, two Leeds players being stretchered off in a bad-tempered defeat. There was also a shock 5-2 John Player Trophy exit at the hands of Second Division Barrow.

Some of the players had to be called to account: "I told Tony Currie he could leave and go back home after Christmas because he did not appear to be fully committed to the task at Leeds. He pleaded with me to let him stay and promised his game would improve along with his effort. From then to the end of the season Currie's form and performances were excellent."

Peter went back to his old club, Bradford Northern, at the end of October to sign the 36-year-old Jeff Grayshon for £12,500; a bargain fee for a man who a few days later would enter the record books as Great Britain's oldest test representative. Grayshon's presence was invaluable in helping two promising youngsters, Roy Powell and Paul Medley, settle into the pack.

Peter's decision to move Cliff Lyons to scrum-half was a major factor in getting Leeds back to winning ways in mid-December, with a victory over Castleford at Wheldon Road. There followed another 10 consecutive victories, seven in the league, which took Leeds into the top four.

In preparation for the Challenge Cup, Carl Gibson, a promising threequarter with Batley, was signed in January 1986 for a club record £50,000. The Loiners' Challenge Cup campaign began with an easy preliminary round win at Swinton. Progress continued with victories over Halifax at Thrum Hall, and then Doncaster at Headingley. That last tie should have been played at Tattersfield, but bad weather caused Doncaster to switch it to Leeds.

Following a win over Salford at Headingley, Leeds travelled to Naughton Park for what was to become the first of four epic clashes. Widnes snatched victory through a late John Basnett try to win 20-18. A week later the two clubs met in the return league fixture. This time Leeds made no mistake, a Carl Gibson hat-trick setting up a 28-12 home triumph.

The quarter-final draw paired Leeds and Widnes for the fifth consecutive year. Jeff Grayshon and David Ward returning from injury bolstered Leeds's hopes and the decision by Peter to include teenager Paul Medley ahead of international Kevin Rayne proved inspired. Medley scored both Leeds tries to put the visitors ahead, 8-2, at the break. The second half saw Widnes regain the lead, 10-8, with only a few minutes remaining. However, in the final seconds Widnes were penalised and up stepped David Creasser, unsuccessful with his five previous attempts, to coolly strike the ball out of the cloying mud to earn Leeds a 10-10 draw and a replay.

Four days later the two sides met again at Headingley and this time the home side was made the favourite. A crowd of almost 16,000 turned out to watch the fourth meeting of the two teams in 18 days. They did not disappoint, serving up a tryless, but gripping encounter. Leeds progressed to the semi-final thanks to two Creasser penalties and a drop-goal from Cliff Lyons in a 5-0 victory. Skipper David Heron was named man-of-the-match although Jeff Grayshon, Terry Webb or David Ward could have taken the award.

Leeds United's Elland Road on Easter Saturday was the venue for the semi-final clash with Hull KR and what a pulsating match it turned out to be. Leeds appeared to have taken control of the match early on and looked certain winners after Paul Harkin was dismissed for tripping Tony Currie as he raced for the line. For Peter the dismissal was only half the penalty: "Currie had scrambled over the line to claim a try, but would have gone over under the posts if he hadn't been tripped. A penalty try wasn't awarded and the more difficult shot at goal was missed, leaving the score at 12-2 in Leeds's favour. Then, on the stroke of half-time, Rovers' David Laws dived over in the left corner, only to drop the ball before grounding it. Referee Robin Whitfield and his touch judge were both on the scene, but quite remarkably the try was allowed to stand and at 12-6 Rovers had a lifeline for the second half."

After the break Rovers retained the initiative, first levelling the scores before moving into a 24-12 lead. As the match moved into the last 20 minutes, Leeds fought back and tries by Tony Currie and then Paul Medley brought the scores level, 24-24, with a little over 10 minutes to play. In the dying minutes of this epic clash, both John Dorahy of Rovers and David Ward attempted drop-goals, but the scores remained level until the final hooter.

On reflection Peter knew that Leeds had been denied victory by those two incidents in the first half, "the trip on Currie, which should have brought a penalty try, and Laws dropping the ball as he dived over the line". Afterwards Peter was scathing of referee Whitfield who he said "had cowed out on the day costing Leeds an appearance at Wembley". Australian test forward Les Boyd, an independent judge, was also outraged by the decision, saying "British referees are diabolical. Laws clearly dropped the ball over the line. The referee clearly on the spot gave the try and no one said anything about it. The decision cost Leeds about £100,000. It's unbelievable."

The replay, the following Thursday 3 April, was again at Elland Road, and drew a crowd of 32,485, the biggest attendance at a semi-final for 24 years. A scoreless first half proved that both sides had each other's measure. But Leeds, having played a league match on the Monday against Bradford Northern which they lost 25-8 and having had two previous energy sapping battles with Widnes, ran out of steam. After the break Rovers had it all their own way to win flatteringly 17-0. For Jeff Grayshon it was his fifth defeat at this stage and he believed his chance of a Wembley appearance would never come again.

After that defeat the Loiners' performance fell away. There was the usual end of season fixture pile-up, which meant that Leeds had to play seven league matches in a little less than three weeks. By the end of that sequence they had lost five, drawn one and managed one victory, over York in the last match of the season.

Nevertheless the club finished sixth in the league. In the Premiership Leeds ended St Helens's 13-match unbeaten run in the first round, recording a 38-22 victory, their biggest ever score at Knowsley Road. In the semi-final at Thrum Hall, the Loiners led the league champions 13-10, but allowed a late Halifax try to snatch victory away and deny them a third trip to Elland Road that season.

Peter's first year at Headingley had drawn to a close. It had been a frustrating season for him: "At a time when the headlines were focusing on the big-money transfers I had only recruited two players – Gibson and Grayshon – for comparatively modest fees. We had reached three semi-finals and in each we had achieved a potentially match-winning position, but there was no silverware to show for all the effort." There was some personal satisfaction for Peter from a meeting with Tony Currie who was about to depart for Australia. He thanked Peter and said: "you've shown me where I was going wrong and now I believe I can win a green and gold jumper". This he subsequently did.

1986-87

Peter's contribution to the Leeds Supporters' Club Handbook tried to explain to the fans the difficulties under which he was operating: "I know where we need strengthening and probably so do you, the difference is we might all differ on who we should recruit, and whoever we recruit some of you might still complain. My principle is quite simple, only better players than the ones we have should be brought in. It may be my standards are higher than most so I don't rush in and recruit quickly, that would be aimless and I tell you money is not as readily available as you might think. Prices are certainly exorbitant and clubs are no longer easily tempted to part with their better players."

Peter restated to the Leeds board his need for three very good experienced recruits: "I needed a scrum-half who could dictate play for others, and I recommended Deryck Fox who was doing the job for Yorkshire and Great Britain. I also knew that he had requested a move away from Featherstone Rovers. The board, however, remained stubborn, not sharing my belief Foxy was the player we needed."

"I then recommended the signing of three rugby union players whom I believed, from what I had seen on television and read in the press, would please the supporters and be good for the team. They were Jonathan Davies, the Welsh stand-off, the All Black winger John Kirwan and Gavin Hastings, the Scottish goalkicking full-back." Joe Warham, the club's general manager, expressed his doubts about the last – he was after all a Cambridge Blue at rugby union and they never turned to rugby league. He did however offer to contact a Scottish teacher he knew to see if an approach could be made. Peter could not believe what he was hearing.

Peter's assessment of Jonathan Davies was shared by Harry Jepson, the football chairman at Leeds. Jepson had been able to establish contact with Davies shortly after he made his international debut in April 1985 and had built a good relationship with the player. Accompanied by Harry Jepson and Raymond Shuttleworth, the club chairman's son, Peter travelled to south Wales to watch Jonathan Davies play and made contact with him afterwards.

Later Davies came up to Leeds and Peter took him to Featherstone to watch Rovers' Yorkshire Cup tie with Hull KR; the first live rugby league match he had seen. Davies had doubts about his ability to make the switch which Peter tried to allay by explaining how his skills and strengths would fit into the league game. However, there was one other doubt nagging Davies and that concerned tackling. In a bid to reassure him, Peter told Jonathan: "I knew a coach at Castleford, Harry Street, who had a slight stand-off and wouldn't let him tackle, although sometimes he had to and he did. You'll be like that so you've nothing to worry about."

Unfortunately the club was worried that Davies's £100,000 price tag would break the bank and Jonathan's signature was not pursued. Jonathan was informed by the Leeds directors that the reason he had not been signed was that the coach was having second thoughts. This was completely untrue and Peter got in touch with Jonathan to make sure he knew this: "I rang Jonathan, but he was out. So I told his wife Karen the real reason and asked her to pass on the message. She then told me that Jonathan would be very disappointed to hear that Leeds were not prepared to make a commitment to him."

With a Kangaroo tour scheduled, signing top-class Australians was always going to be more difficult. Hoping for new strength in the pack, Peter allowed the injury-prone Terry Webb to leave, despite having a year of his contract still to run. Things became more difficult when Tony Currie, who should have returned, changed his mind after getting a better offer to stay in Sydney. Then Dean Bell, who Leeds had expected to return after a spell with Eastern Suburbs in Sydney, was hijacked at the last minute by Wigan's new coach, Graham Lowe.

To fill Bell's place, Peter asked Brian Noble, who was playing for Cronulla, if he had any recommendations. Noble told him that both Gene Miles and Terry Lamb were in good form and would be a success in Britain. However, both would cost quite a bit of money. A cheaper alternative was to take a relative unknown and if Leeds were prepared to do that Noble would recommend his team-mate, Andrew Ettingshausen, whom he was certain was going to be a future star. Getting agreement was made easier because Harry Jepson remembered Ettingshausen from the Australian schools' tour of Britain over a year earlier. Andrew in turn recommended his friend and centre partner at Cronulla, Mark McGaw, to Peter. McGaw, a six feet, rugged, powerful player, was also signed and both turned out to be great successes.

Leeds then signed two Australians on the recommendation of Peter Deakin who would later return home and take over as the commercial manager at Bradford Northern. Without talking to Peter, Harry Jepson signed both. One of the pair was Pete Smith, a prop who had given great service to Illawarra in the Winfield Cup, but was now at the veteran stage. The other was Bob Morris, a lightweight hooker, then playing for a country team. Neither of those forwards was to contribute much to the Leeds team. To fund some of his spending plans Peter first sold Roy Dickenson to Halifax in June and then Neil Hague, who followed him to Thrum Hall a month later for £12,000.

There was good news and bad news on the retirement front. The 34-year-old John Holmes was persuaded to restart his playing career. That good news was offset by David Ward's controversial decision in July to end his playing career and join Hunslet as coach. Further experience was lost from the pack when Jeff Grayshon, troubled by a niggling back injury, also announced his retirement. Another blow came when it was learned that Roy Powell needed a cartilage operation, which meant he was ruled out even before the season started.

Oldham's Watersheddings ground was the venue for the opening league fixture. It was a close match that the home side just won, 14-12. A home win over Featherstone Rovers, 33-12, followed by a 40-20 defeat at St Helens made it clear that this was going to be a difficult season for Leeds.

September saw the start of the Yorkshire Cup. A first round victory over Keighley brought a fixture against Castleford in the next round. There was to be no further progress as the Tigers won easily, 38-16.

With no significant cash available Peter initially had to resort to player exchanges. In mid-September he swapped Kevin Dick for Hull's scrum-half, Andy Gascoigne, and in an attempt to bolster his weakened pack, veteran prop, Trevor Skerrett, in a deal valued at £50,000. There was further bolstering at the start of October when York's second-rower,

Gary Price, fresh from impressing in the Yorkshire County side, was signed. Jeff Grayshon had also been talked around and agreed to resume playing.

October started promisingly with a big home victory, 46-10, over Salford. After that the team's performance fell away, losing at Halifax in the next match, 23-8.

Next, Leeds had a fixture on what was at that time to be the shortest ever Australian tour. The Kangaroos arrived at Headingley on 19 October 1986, for their third match. With one week to go before the first test the Kangaroos fielded nearly their full test side. They were never extended by a Leeds team containing no British test certainties. Eight tries – four in each half – without reply left the home crowd dismayed at a final 40-0 scoreline.

Bradford Northern came to Headingley for the next match and went away with a 12-4 victory. As October drew to a close Yorkshire centre Andy Mason was recruited from Bramley in return for cash and David Healey, in a deal valued at £60,000.

November followed a similar inconsistent pattern. The first two matches against Hull and Wakefield, both away, were won. Warrington came to Headingley for the first home match of the month and handed out a 54-16 thrashing. Angry at the manner of that defeat the supporters began to openly blame Peter for the team's failings and chants calling for his sacking began to be heard. A journey to Leigh the following weekend brought no relief, only a 20-8 defeat. At the end of the month the Loiners were knocked out of the John Player Trophy in the first round by Wigan.

Finally at the end of November, Phil Fox, a winger (unrelated to Peter), was signed from Leigh for £12,000. Around the same time after making only nine appearances, including two as substitute, Peter Smith's contract was cancelled.

By the start of December Leeds were lying ninth in the league. With a free weekend the club decided to hold a clear-the-air-meeting for directors, players and spectators. Peter tried to explain the difficulties the team was facing and that some players had become so demoralised they no longer enjoyed playing at Headingley. When questioned about his success at Bradford Peter replied "I was there for eight years, they were my players. Give me the tools and I will produce the goods." To those who blamed the team's ills on a breakdown of relations between the coach and his players, the captain, Dave Heron, gave Peter his full support: "There is no problem between Peter Fox and the players. If there was, I would have told him about it."

There was great pressure from all sides for the team's performance to improve and at last some progress seemed to be being made. A victory over Hull KR at home, 42-7, on Sunday 14 December drew some welcome praise. But unbeknown to Peter, his fate was to be decided at a board meeting the following Wednesday night. At that meeting it was decided that the board would terminate his position, but not until after the visit to Barrow the following Sunday. Harry Jepson was given the job of informing Peter of the decision, but after a 23-16 victory he hadn't the heart to do it.

Supposedly it was the season of goodwill to all men, but Peter cannot have felt any of that shortly after the doorbell rang on Christmas Eve. The man ringing it was Harry Jepson and he had called to tell Peter of the board's decision. The last two victories counted for nothing. The decision had been made.

The decision was distressing for Peter after taking the club to three semi-finals and almost achieving a Wembley appearance. Peter was hurt - deeply hurt - and angry. The one comforting factor was a phone call from Derek Turner the following night. Peter recalls Turner telling him: "he knew how I felt, it had happened to him in 1973". As he thought about what had happened Peter decided that, "if only two coaches had been sacked by Leeds, and all the others had left by mutual consent, I was not in bad company if the other one was Derek Turner".

Leeds had to win the next game against Wakefield to put them into the top eight. That they did and then their form dipped dramatically. The Loiners were very fortunate as only Oldham's narrow 24-22 defeat at already relegated Barrow saved them from relegation. Safety was achieved on points' difference. Both teams had 26 points from 30 matches, but Leeds's points difference was -6, whereas Oldham's was -125.

Club captain David Heron said "Leeds have made a lot of bad decisions in recent years, but the worst was not keeping Foxy there as coach. Things were starting to come right under him and he made the most out of what was a pretty bad side at the time. Leeds wanted instant success and weren't patient enough to wait and realise that Foxy was laying the foundations." Peter is still angry about what happened at Headingley: "I thought of the players Leeds had recruited even as far back as the late 1940s when I was still at school. When I was keen to become a loose forward my first hero was Leeds's Ike Owens. From those days I also remembered well Arthur Clues and Bert Cook. The best player Leeds signed during my own playing days was the great Lewis Jones. Along with the likes of Jeff Stevenson, those were the type of players I wanted to recruit for Leeds, to bring success to the club and its supporters.

"I had a great rapport with all the players at the club, but unfortunately the experience we required was just not there. I believed that by bringing in Deryck Fox along with my other recommendations to the board like Ellery Hanley, Jonathan Davies, John Kirwan and Gavin Hastings alongside Andrew Ettingshausen and Mark McGaw and the returned John Holmes would have certainly brought Leeds back into the big time. I was terribly disappointed that the Leeds directors did not support me in recruiting the class of player needed and then left me to carry the blame for Leeds's demise. What made it worse was that instead of blaming the board the fans blamed me. I was really sorry that I wasn't allowed to do the job the fans wanted."

Waiting for the next opportunity

While Leeds were struggling to stay in the First Division, Peter was coping with the shock of suddenly having no coaching. To fill some of his Sunday afternoons Peter returned to local radio, working as a summariser with Jack Wainwright for BBC Radio Leeds.

The first coaching opportunity to present itself came when Phil Lowe quit as coach of Second Division York in March. Peter was approached and it looked likely he would be on his way to Wiggington Road, but the club's offer of a two-year contract proved a stumbling block. Peter's reluctance "wasn't a matter of job security. It was all about getting a guarantee of time to put things right. I knew it would take three years. The first year would be spent getting to know the team, the second putting in improvements and the third would be when the new team would be fully in action."

Peter had a good meeting with members of the York board and was keen to do well for them. However, movement on the contract was slow. Featherstone Rovers announced at the start of May that coach Paul Daley had resigned following the club's relegation to the Second Division. Shortly afterwards, two Rovers' committee men made contact with Peter. They made Peter an offer, which he accepted. By the time York's board came back with a three-year contract Peter had done the deal with Rovers.

Coaching at Leeds – making a point from the bench. (Courtesy *Rugby League Journal*)

David Heron - a key player for Peter at Leeds (Courtesy Robert Gate)

16. More success with Featherstone

After being a free agent for five months Peter rejoined Featherstone Rovers in May 1987 as team manager on a three-year contract. After 13 years Peter was back at Post Office Road. The ground looked a bit different – there was a new main stand and new dressing rooms built to replace the old ones lost in the disastrous fire two years earlier. At heart the club hadn't changed. It was still run by a committee that had been trimmed to a more manageable size. And despite the battering it had taken during the recent miners' strike neither had the town. It remained a hotbed of the game.

Bob Ashby, Rovers' president and the club's main financial backer, while offering no money for team strengthening, implored Peter to get Rovers out of the Second Division. Peter set about bringing in his own team. Kenny Loxton, formerly a player with Huddersfield, Keighley, Halifax and Bramley, was appointed as Peter's assistant and 'A' team coach and Steve Young was given the job of organising physical training. Deryck Fox, the scrum-half Peter had tried to take to Leeds, was appointed club captain.

Peter inherited the playing squad that had suffered relegation: "There was a core of good players who I would have to rely on to secure promotion. My first pressing problem was to convince Peter Smith, priced at £60,000 and Deryck Fox, priced at £150,000, to withdraw their transfer requests and stay with the club for what would hopefully be a single season in the Second Division. Peter Smith was one of only two players who remained at Post Office Road from my previous time in charge. The other was Keith Bell and he would go on to make his 400th appearance in Rovers' colours during the season."

Rovers looked anything but favourites to bounce back to the top flight when they lost their two opening league fixtures at Barrow and York. The outlook improved a little when the team managed to beat Whitehaven 11-4 in the first home league match.

Batley made Rovers work hard to get on top in the first round of the Yorkshire Cup, but eventually, inspired by Deryck Fox, Rovers secured a 28-6 victory. York proved easier in the next round, Rovers winning 43-6. But in the semi-final, Castleford proved too strong.

The Papua New Guinea Kumuls opened their eight match tour of Britain – their first against professional opposition – at Post Office Road on Sunday 11 October. Adjusting well to the British conditions the Kumuls went in at half-time 12-8 ahead. Two tries in five minutes just after the restart put Featherstone in front 16-12. That lead was short-lived – the Kumuls running in two more tries to gain a morale-boosting 22-16 win.

Of the first eight league matches Rovers won only four. Rovers even struggled to beat an amateur team, Thatto Heath, in the preliminary round of the John Player Trophy. Victory brought a first round tie and defeat against Castleford. As Rovers struggled other clubs began to make enquiries about the availability of their best players.

Unable to get loan players from neighbouring professional clubs Peter turned to the amateur game – signing John Bastian from Milford in Leeds, Andy Bannister from Walton in Wakefield and Paul Hughes, Tim Sharp and David Sykes from the local amateur side Travellers' Saints. All were tall, well-built young men and Bastian, Hughes and Sykes were thrown straight into the first team.

While Peter was struggling to pull together a team on a shoestring, his old club Leeds, had suddenly found lots of money and embarked upon a major spending spree: "That was galling enough, but there was a certain bitter irony in the Leeds's board's decision to try and sign the one player that I had implored them to buy for 18 months, Deryck Fox. In return Leeds offered John Holmes, a player I greatly admired, and four other players." Dismissing the offer Peter retorted "If we do a swap then I will choose the players Leeds give us."

Just before Christmas, Rovers finally found their form. A festive double over Trinity gave the fans the Christmas present they wanted and that was accompanied by another eight wins by mid-February. Rovers' return to form earned the club the Second Division team of the month award for January.

An easy home win, 32-21, over York kicked off Rovers' Challenge Cup campaign. A trip to Hull KR was their reward in the next round. There they had a disastrous start conceding six points practically straight from the kick-off. Things went from bad to worse and at one stage Rovers were 25-2 down. Two tries to Peter Smith, plus one apiece for Deryck Fox and Chris Bibb, pulled Rovers back into contention, but in the end they could only turn the final score into a more respectable 35-26 defeat. However, Rovers put it behind them to finish as runners-up in the Second Division and were one of the three teams to be promoted.

Second Division top four teams

	P	W	D	L	F	A	Pts
Oldham	28	23	1	4	771	335	47
Featherstone R	28	21	2	5	712	353	44
Wakefield T	28	20	1	7	666	315	41
Springfield B	28	18	0	10	448	356	36

At the end of the regular season Rovers entered the Second Division top eight play-offs. An easy victory over Mansfield Marksmen set up a home semi-final with Wakefield Trinity. The visitors scored first and last, but in between Rovers held the advantage, amassing sufficient points to win, 20-16, and progress to meet the champions, Oldham, in the Second Division Premiership Final.

The match was at Old Trafford on 15 May as a curtain raiser to the First Division Premiership Final. Peter selected the following Rovers team:
S. Quinn, A. Bannister, D. Sykes, A. Banks, R. Marsh, G. Steadman, D. Fox (captain), G. Siddall, K. Bell, K. Harrison, P. Hughes, P. Smith, P. Lyman. Substitutes: J. Crossley, J. Bastian.

For the first half hour there was only one team in it, and that was Oldham. Four tries left Rovers trailing 22-0 just before half-time. But Rovers kept trying and just before the break managed to put six points on the board through a Graham Steadman try and a Steve Quinn touchline conversion. After the break there was a total reversal of form. Tries by Steadman and Andy Bannister, both converted by Steve Quinn, made the score 22-18. With less than 10 minutes left an Andy Sykes try, once again converted by Quinn, took Rovers into the lead. Two minutes later a Quinn penalty goal extended the lead to four points. But Oldham responded and snatched the lead and victory with a late converted try. It was a cruel end to the match and Peter sat for a long time afterwards with his head in his hands.

Nevertheless Rovers had gained promotion and would be back in the big time. Reflecting on the season Peter said: "There's a fabulous spirit, as ever, at Post Office Road. It's a spirit that money can't buy, and we'll use that spirit when we meet the big boys next season. I'm not kidding myself or anyone at Featherstone – it will be very hard to hang on in the top division next season. The top-flight clubs are spending enormous amounts of money to try and achieve success, money that Featherstone haven't got. I can't compete on those terms. Peter Fox is once again battling against the odds. I've lost none of my old confidence and guiding Rovers back to the big time ranks with any of my previous achievements, believe me."

Ultimately gaining promotion was due to a combination of several top-class performers in Deryck Fox, Peter Smith, Karl Harrison, Paul Lyman, Graham Steadman and Chris Bibb working well with a group of senior experienced professionals including Steve Quinn, Keith Bell, Gary Siddall and John Crossley. To that mix was added a group of youngsters who developed through the season such as Ian Smales, Paul Hughes, John Bastian, David Sykes, Tim Sharp and Andy Bannister. It was a perfect recipe for promotion.

1988-89

The First Division that Rovers returned to had been reduced to 14 teams. Peter's primary task was to survive and not be one of the three relegated clubs. The *Rugby Leaguer* wrote that "the forthcoming season presents Peter Fox with one of his greatest challenges ever if he can stabilise Featherstone Rovers in a 14-team First Division, on such meagre resources. Even those few who doubt his coaching ability will be forced to concede that the man is a unique motivator of players."

Rovers were up against teams like Wigan and increasingly Leeds that were paying the kind of the money that could ensure their players followed training regimes as rigorous as those used by full-time professionals.

Team strengthening was critical and Peter once again turned to Jeff Grayshon, who joined on a free transfer from Bradford Northern in July. Grayshon, who had confounded the sceptics by regaining full fitness after a breaking a leg nine months earlier was, despite his age, perfect to mentor and lead Peter's young team. Peter also sought out Trevor Clark, the Maori hooker, who had been released by Leeds. Phil Carey, a utility back with Canberra Raiders, was also signed, but he was hampered by injuries suffered in his domestic season and most of the appearances he made were for the Alliance team. Glenn Bell, a New Zealand prop, was also added to the squad.

Besides experienced players, Rovers went after the best local juniors. Their signings were not always guaranteed as Peter remembers: "We very nearly didn't get the best one whose play for Featherstone Miners Welfare was getting noticed. At the 11th hour I attended a meeting at the home of Rovers' chairman, Richard Evans. After hearing the details, Evans secured Bob Ashby's support to match an offer Hull were making and we were able to sign the 17-year-old Paul Newlove." Four months later, in November, Rovers added another local junior, Martin Pearson, to their roster.

An opening day defeat by Leeds, 32-18, caused some concern for the season ahead. However, the team rallied and won the next two league matches over Hull KR and

Oldham. Matching the stronger teams was always difficult and a visit to Naughton Park showed a difference in class that Widnes exploited to score 16 points in the last eight minutes to run out 58-2 winners.

The early season cup competitions did not go well. After a victory over Second Division Doncaster, Featherstone were knocked out of the Yorkshire Cup in the second round, defeated by Hull 18-0 on 27 September. A crop of injuries meant that Paul Newlove, after only five 'A' team matches, was brought into the team for the Hull game, making his debut on the wing. In the John Player Trophy, a preliminary round victory over Hunslet, 46-2, set up a meeting with Widnes, which the Chemics won 37-12.

Success on the field was all down to making the most of very limited resources. Players had to be prepared to play out of position and tactics had to be tailored to fit the team on the field. Even if they were not always consistent, Rovers were always capable of surprising the best of the top teams.

Against other potential strugglers Rovers did well. A home victory over Halifax was particularly welcome. On a very windy night at the Boulevard, Rovers played superbly to build a 6-2 lead over Hull at the break and then defend through the second half with a masterly defensive display based on kicking early in the tackle count. A league double over Salford followed to leave Rovers in mid-table as Christmas loomed.

By the middle of the year it was clear that a number of players would be on their way. At 35 years of age, First Division rugby was proving too much for Steve Quinn and he announced his retirement at Christmas. At the end of January, Peter allowed the highly rated Paul Lyman, who had never quite fulfilled his promise with his home-town club to move to Hull KR, in return for £55,000 and the former test second-rower Chris Burton. There were some who questioned Peter's judgement in swapping a young second-rower in return for a 33-year-old replacement, but Burton, who had impressed Peter as a member of the Yorkshire team, was to prove a shrewd acquisition.

In the Challenge Cup, Rovers opened with a victory over Whitehaven. In the second round Graham Steadman scored nine of his team's points in the 10-4 win at Wakefield to earn a trip to Knowsley Road. Rovers managed to hold Saints in the first half but after the break the home side proved too strong.

As the season drew to a close the team if anything got better. Another double was achieved, this time over Halifax. When Rovers travelled to Knowsley Road in mid-March there can have been little thought of completing a double. Although Rovers had managed a narrow victory, 13-12, over Saints earlier in the season, the away match was an entirely different prospect. That was not how it turned out. St Helens were below par and allowed Rovers to establish a 21-0 lead by half-time. Although the second half was closer, Rovers held on to win 31-10 and complete a very rare double over the Saints.

A further double was achieved over Hull, which along with victories over Bradford and Warrington made the season end on a high note. Rovers had finished in sixth position. It was a marvellously unexpected achievement.

The first round of the Premiership took Rovers to Headingley. There, with only three minutes remaining, Featherstone substitute Glenn Booth scored the decisive try to claim victory over Peter's old club, 15-12. There was then a two week before the semi-final in at the start of May. While waiting for that match Peter visited a tailor in Headingley and by chance got talking to a lady supporter. She told him how angry she and her family had been about the unfair way Leeds had treated him. A couple of days later he received a letter from her and he family. In it she said "we wish to congratulate you and your boys, especially good old Jeff, on your smashing win over our lads. [No sour grapes there.] We wish you good luck in your forthcoming big game and in the future". Unfortunately luck was not enough to see Rovers victorious in a heat wave at the Boulevard, where Hull proved too strong, demolishing Rovers 23-0.

In a demanding season, Alan Banks and Deryck Fox had played in every match, while Chris Bibb had missed only one.

Peter was the only British nominee for Greenall's Coach of the Year award, but sadly was not chosen. But there can be no finer accolade for Peter's work at the end of the season than that provided by Peter Smith, a player who was appreciating his second spell of Peter's coaching: "It's been fascinating to have seen the man at work against the odds. He was a great coach when I first came to the club in 1972 – now I think he's even better.

"Peter's more experienced of course, but it's his vast knowledge of the game and players, which makes him, for me, a coach without equal. We owe much of our success to his ability to get the best out of the players at his disposal. He's a unique motivator. We have the oldest pack in the league – but Peter judges his players on their ability and that's all any player wants."

1989-90

As he came towards the end of his contract, it was believed that Graham Steadman had been unofficially approached by Castleford. Apparently having secured the player's agreement Castleford officially approached Rovers and asked for an indication of the fee that would be required. Rovers asked for £185,000, Castleford offered £100,000, with the result that Steadman's future had to be resolved by a tribunal on 7 June. After listening to both cases the tribunal set the fee at £145,000, plus a further £25,000 if the player gained international honours, paid in three instalments. Steadman was duly capped in April 1990 and Castleford had to pay out £170,000 in total. But as far as Peter was concerned "getting the money from Castleford was no compensation for losing such an important player as Steadman".

Prop Karl Harrison, who had been keen to leave Rovers, was sold to Hull in August for £57,500 giving Peter money to use for team building. The first £50,000 of that fee was spent within days on bringing Gary Price, a second-row forward he had previously signed, from Leeds. Peter then used up his overseas quota by signing three New Zealanders – Glenn Bell, Trevor Clark and Iva Ropati.

Things started well in the league with an opening-day 22-20 win at Castleford, which was made all the sweeter by the presence of Graham Steadman in the home team. The sweet taste soon departed because the next two league matches, against the newly promoted Sheffield Eagles and the reigning champions Widnes, were lost.

After that the team refocused on the Yorkshire Cup. In the first round Rovers met Keighley and rewrote parts of the club record book. The match result, 86-18, set a new club record score. It also enabled Mark Knapper, on only his third appearance in the first team, to break Peter's brother Don's record of 12 goals in a match set back in 1965 and to also set a new record for total points of 30. Chris Bibb also equalled the record number of tries in a match, which was six, held by Mike Smith.

Doncaster made Rovers work harder in the second round and actually went in at the break leading 14-12. After a half-time pep talk Rovers fought back to win 37-22.

The Yorkshire Cup semi-final draw brought Castleford to Post Office Road where a capacity crowd watched the home side emerge pleased with an 18-18 draw. Ten days later at Wheldon Road, Rovers looked to be on the way out, trailing 26-16 as the match moved into its final quarter. Rovers rallied and thanks to a try and Mark Knapper's touchline conversion four minutes from time secured a win, 28-26.

On 5 November, Bradford Northern provided the opposition in the Yorkshire Cup Final at Headingley. It was an uninspiring match whose first half had to be suspended for five minutes due to trouble on the terraces. Rovers took an early lead through two Deryck Fox penalty goals before referee Robin Whitfield awarded Northern a penalty try for obstruction. Northern moved into a 6-4 lead, which they never lost, eventually winning 20-14. The Rovers team was:

C. Bibb, B. Drummond, I. Ropati, P. Newlove, A. Banks, I. Smales, D. Fox (captain), J. Grayshon, T. Clark, G. Bell, G. Price, G. Booth, P. Smith. Substitutes: A. Dakin, A. Fisher.

Two days after the Yorkshire Cup Final a below strength Rovers tried hard, but finished on the wrong end of a drubbing from the touring Kiwis 44-20.

While the cup run was going on, the league results were a matter for growing concern. After the opening day victory Rovers did not win again for three months. By mid-December alarm bells were ringing. Rovers had lost at home to all three of the newly promoted clubs – Barrow, Leigh and Sheffield Eagles – and were firmly entrenched in the bottom three. The prospect of relegation was becoming a reality.

The team had suffered some major disruption due to the loss of a crucial figure. The need for an operation to repair a shoulder injury incurred at Wigan in mid-November caused Peter Smith to announce his retirement at the start of December, bringing an end to a career that had seen him make more than 400 appearances for the club.

To get the team back to winning ways Peter paid out some of the Steadman windfall on three players – £30,000 on Keighley's centre Terry Manning in October, a further £20,000 for Keighley's Gary Rose, a second-row forward, in December and the same amount again for Doncaster's hooker, Mark Gibbon, in February.

The John Player Trophy had been renamed the Regal Trophy and its first round paired Rovers with Trafford Borough, previously Chorley Borough. The newcomers proved no threat, Rovers winning 36-18. Accounting for Hunslet 34-4 in the second round saw Rovers restrict their opponents to less than 18 points for the first time that season. The cup run ended in the next round, Second Division Halifax knocking Rovers out 23-10.

The season and survival hung on the outcome of the Christmas league programme. First up was Wakefield Trinity at Post Office Road on Boxing Day. A performance more akin to those in the Yorkshire Cup ties gained a win, 15-8. The experience of the return match at Belle Vue was not so positive, Trinity turning the tables to win 22-14. Sheffield's homeless Eagles provided the final leg of the festive programme – they were using Belle Vue as a temporary home. Just when hope seemed to be slipping away Rovers' spirit asserted itself. In the last 10 minutes of that match Rovers scored three tries to turn an eight-point deficit into a precious 30-20 victory. It came with a cost – Gary Price suffering a broken arm.

In the new year the team's performance improved. Although defeated in the first round of the Challenge Cup at Warrington, 20-12, Rovers went to Wilderspool in the league and recorded **their first win there for 12 years**. A crucial league double over the Wire had been achieved. Another league double followed over Castleford. Through hard work and effort the club hauled itself out of the relegation zone.

Just when it appeared that Rovers were out of trouble, three league defeats dragged them back down into the mire, but a surprisingly easy home victory over third-placed Bradford Northern in the penultimate league match lifted the club up to 10th, its highest position all season.

The outcome of the final match against Leeds became irrelevant once Wigan's defeat of Leigh condemned the last to relegation. It was testimony to the man's fitness that Jeff Grayshon, aged 41, had played in every match.

1990-91

There was plenty of press speculation about Featherstone's attempts at team strengthening. Apparently Rovers, keen to land a big name, made a serious bid for Wally Lewis – by now at the veteran stage. The deal, allegedly worth £250,000, collapsed when Lewis decided instead to join a new team on Australia's Gold Coast.

However, Oldham's young prop Leo Casey was signed in July for £100,000. The following month, in a bid to provide greater pace on attack, Peter tracked down the Leeds winger Ikram Butt in Australia and agreed terms for a move that would cost £30,000. Further pace would be added to the threequarter line in November when Owen Simpson was signed from Keighley for £50,000. Simpson, in particular, would prove a great buy as he built a good wing partnership with his centre, Paul Newlove.

Money was also made available to sign two forwards from New Zealand – Brendan Tuuta, on a short-term contract, and Clarry Iti, Rovers' first rugby union signing for 20 years. Local talent was not neglected and 19-year-old goalkicker, Martin Pearson, was given his chance, initially on the wing, and took it well. It was a young side but as Peter acknowledged "Grayshon puts the average up a bit". Jeff Grayshon put in a major contribution on the field in every match, especially when the opposition made derogatory remarks about his age.

The Yorkshire Cup had returned to the first two weeks of the season and thanks to a decisive victory over Bramley, Tuuta was in time to make his debut in the home second round tie against Hull KR on 9 September. A good first half saw Rovers turn around 18-3 ahead. However, in the second half the Robins clawed their way back to win 31-22.

League matches began with another encounter with Hull KR. It was a bad tempered match that ended in a 14-14 draw. The first League victory came at the start of October when Sheffield Eagles were defeated at Post Office Road. Further success came in the next match, at Headingley, where Rovers beat Leeds 18-16. A third victory, at home over Rochdale Hornets, completed a very successful October.

November was a much crueller month with only one victory, but a very satisfying one for Peter in one respect: "Hull's departing Australian coach, Brian Smith, had taken the opportunity to share his opinions with the British public and one of his prime targets was the age of my team. Smith publicly ridiculed my team because it included veterans such as Grayshon, Clark and Burton. When Hull, the league leaders, arrived at Post Office Road at the end of November there was a lot more than just league points at stake and Rovers rose to the occasion. With Grayshon to the fore we beat Hull 14-6 to leave Smith with a lot of egg on his face."

The Regal Trophy occupied the early part of December. Rovers had an easy away win over Barrow, running in 10 tries in a 54-16 rout. St Helens arrived at Post Office Road in the second round and showed their class, winning 33-16.

Back-to-back wins over Trinity around Christmas along with wins over Rochdale Hornets and Oldham improved Rovers' league position. However, interest in the Challenge Cup ended almost immediately when Sheffield Eagles reversed the earlier league result to win 19-12.

Loose-forward Brendan Tuuta's physical style and deft handling had been making a great impression. Loath to lose Tuuta when it came time for him to return to Western Suburbs in Sydney early in the new year, Rovers approached the Magpies, agreed a deal and the young Kiwi accepted a two-year contract.

With the Challenge Cup out of the way Rovers' team had to face up to a tough run in to the end of the league season. A trip to the Boulevard saw Rovers lose 40-22 in a match described as a 12-try thriller. The next home match saw a more sedate victory achieved over Warrington.

Away to St Helens the following week it was back to the high- scoring matches of earlier in the season. St Helens ran away with the first half, building up what should have been an unassailable 38-4 lead by the break. After the restart Rovers, against all expectations, took control and closed the gap to just six points, 44-38. When Rovers were unable to strike the final decisive blow, Saints found the resources to score two late tries to win a 16-try thriller, 54-38.

Widnes were given a real scare at Post Office Road – Rovers pushing the visitors all the way only to lose 27-22. Wigan, the only club above Widnes in the table, provided the next opposition. Again Rovers played above themselves only to lose 24-16. Leeds were the visitors for the last home match of the season. Although Rovers needed points to finish in the top eight one journalist described the defences as being almost non-existent. It was a poor Rovers performance and they lost 52-20.

A broken finger had sidelined Jeff Grayshon before the end of the league campaign. Without him Rovers went to meet Bradford at Odsal in the last match of the season, the outcome of which would determine whether they took part in the play-offs. A hat-trick of tries from Ian Smales and two from Paul Newlove helped turn a 12-4 deficit into a 34-18 victory and secure eighth place in the First Division. Nonetheless, this was felt by some associated with Rovers to be disappointing in view of the money spent.

As usual in the first round of the Premiership the club that finished eighth had to travel to the club that finished top. For Rovers that meant a trip to Central Park to meet high-flying Wigan. Showing little respect for their humble opponents the Riversiders decided to rest 11 of their probable first-choice squad in preparation for the Challenge Cup Final six days hence. It was an unwise decision as Rovers, inspired by Deryck Fox, ran in six tries to grab a shock 31-26 win at Central Park; their first there since 1965.

It proved impossible for the team to repeat that performance in the semi-final at Naughton Park two weeks later. Widnes did not make Wigan's mistake, quickly taking a 16-0 lead. Rovers responded to close to 28-12 at half-time, before Widnes went ahead 42-12 after the break. Rovers never gave up and three late tries made the final score 42-28. The season had been tough for Rovers. But it had ended on a high note with an unexpected win at Odsal to secure a top eight place. And there was the win at Wigan in the Premiership. There was something for Rovers to build on for the future.

1991-92

Once the previous season had ended, Rovers' committee took a look at the playing squad and decided that Jeff Grayshon would be released. It was not a decision based on performance. Collectively the committee still believed that Grayshon could perform well on the field. It was his age, 42, that disturbed them and the image that gave of the club. Peter was incensed and publicly criticised the committee. Peter told the committee that Grayshon was "instrumental in our tactical strategies and a guardian for our younger players. I also made sure the committee knew that if he wasn't re-signed when I returned from holiday, I would resign." Coach and club were on a collision course.

It was this point that a former colleague, Ron Hird, arranged for Peter to meet the Bradford Northern chairman, Chris Caisley. Peter told Caisley he was expecting to resign as coach of Rovers, but added the rider that he would not talk to Caisley "until my resignation was accepted".

Despite the internal frictions Rovers made a great start to the new season. League matches were restored to the two opening weekends and Rovers recorded victories over Halifax and Swinton. Those wins were followed up by an easy first round Yorkshire Cup win over newcomers Scarborough Pirates and then a third league victory over Warrington.

An early exit from the Yorkshire Cup looked likely when Hull took a 14-2 lead in a midweek second round tie at the Boulevard. Undaunted Rovers fought back to snatch an unlikely 16-16 draw. The following weekend Rovers overcame Bradford Northern in the league.

After that the fixture list became more congested with a midweek cup replay against Hull at Post Office Road. Once again it was a close match, with the final result, a 21-18 home win, determined by Deryck Fox's goalkicking. Results went against Rovers after that – Wigan demolishing them 52-10 in the league the following week before an 18-10 defeat at the hands of Castleford in a midweek Yorkshire Cup semi-final.

Still angry over the decision to release Jeff Grayshon, Peter informed Rovers' committee of his decision to resign on Saturday 12 October. The decision was so sudden that Rovers' secretary, Terry Jones, had to call in at Peter's home the next day to collect the letter, on his way to Post Office Road for the match against Hull. Both Rovers' players and spectators were left dumbfounded by Peter's decision. Featherstone Rovers were handily placed, in seventh position of the First Division, when Peter resigned.

Jeff Grayshon, the player at the centre of the dispute that ensured Peter's departure from Featherstone, looks at his time with Peter: "I didn't know Peter before I joined Bradford Northern, but I soon got used to his ways. There was always a sighting of him at training on Tuesday evening – that was given over to fitness training – but on Thursdays and Saturday mornings he'd be there and we'd work through moves. You had to do what he told you. If you didn't he'd tell you straight. That was especially true if you were his captain and he expected you to be his voice on the field.

"His man management skills were second to none so, although he never had all the best players, he got the best out of all the ones he had. Everyone in the team had a job and was told what it was by Peter. He'd tailor his requirements depending on the opposition. His strength was that not only did he know the abilities of his own players he knew the abilities of the opposition as well.

"I was told by Peter that if I wanted to play for Great Britain again I'd have to switch to open-side prop. It was a mark of the respect that I had for the man that I agreed. He then put the time in to teach me the scrummaging skills – how to push and strike for the ball – that a prop needs. Having moved into the front row he used me as a playmaker. I became the pivot in the run around moves we used a lot. Having been turned into a ball-handling prop Peter's prediction came true and I was recalled to the Great Britain team.

"Peter was my coach for nearly 15 years and only one of his promises never came true. He always said he'd get me to Wembley, but despite getting close three times he never did. Perhaps I was his jinx?"

17. Unbeaten for Yorkshire

Just as Peter's tenure as coach at Bradford Northern was drawing to a close the RFL announced, in April 1985, a sponsorship deal to introduce an annual challenge match between Lancashire and Yorkshire, initially for three years. The match would be known as the War of the Roses, with player qualification based strictly on place of birth. The hope was that the contest would match the intensity of Australia's State of Origin matches and provide a representative stage on which emerging talent could blossom.

The match offered the chance to coach a representative team once more and Peter let his interest be known, after which he got the job, and recalls: "When initially offered the Yorkshire job I said I had no wish to coach a side selected by others, quoting my experience in 1977 and 1978 with England and Great Britain respectively. Once I was given sole responsibility for picking the team I accepted and held the job from September 1985 onwards." Although the match was scheduled shortly after the start of the season, ahead of the selection of the test team for what was then the usual autumn test series, it was not a trial match. When asked before the first Roses match about its relation to Great Britain's plans Peter's answer was clear: "I'm not involved in those plans, so all that really concerns me is how well Yorkshire perform on the day."

Yorkshire 26 Lancashire 10
11 September 1985 at Wigan

Preparing the Lancashire team for the first meeting of the two counties for three years was Alex Murphy, Leigh's coach. He had plenty of experience to draw on and had twice coached Lancashire to the County Championship in the 1970s. Murphy's Lancashire team, although hit by a number of withdrawals, was rated as favourites by the pundits.

Several of Peter's selected team became unavailable before the match. Ellery Hanley, Lee Crooks and Kevin Ward dropped out and with Jeff Grayshon and Garry Schofield previously discounted things were not going Yorkshire's way. Ellery's position at stand-off was given to John Joyner, who was selected as skipper, with Gary Hyde replacing Joyner in the centre. David Hobbs was switched from prop to replace Kevin Ward in the second-row. With Crooks also out Peter picked new props – 21-year-old Brendan Hill, and a veteran, Mick Morgan, verging on 37 years old. When Mike Smith of Hull KR cried off Peter drafted in Andy Mason of Second Division Bramley to fill his centre berth. Yorkshire's makeshift side, including three Second Division players, was not thought to be strong enough to get the better of a strong Lancashire team.

Some good fortune turned two speculative kicks into tries – credited to Gary Hyde and Andy Mason – and these, plus a Deryck Fox penalty, enabled Yorkshire to lead 10-6 at the break. That lead was short-lived as Lancashire levelled the scores early in the second half.

But Mick Morgan's inclusion proved inspirational for Yorkshire. His ball-handling skills were decisive in setting up two close-range scores for David Hobbs and David Heron, which along with Andy Mason's try and two goals from Deryck Fox, sealed the win for the white rose county.

The inaugural match drew 6,743 supporters to Central Park, the best attendance for a Roses match since 1968 and raised hopes for a successful future for the new venture. The Yorkshire team was:

A. Kay (Hunslet), C. Gibson (Batley), G. Hyde (Castleford), A. Mason (Bramley), D. Laws (Hull KR), J. Joyner (Castleford – captain), D. Fox (Featherstone R), B. Hill (Leeds), D. Watkinson (Hull KR), M. Morgan (Oldham), D. Hobbs (Oldham), C. Burton (Hull KR), D. Heron (Leeds). Substitutes: P. Lyman (Featherstone), A. Dannatt (Hull).

Mick Morgan has many good memories of being coached by Peter: "I'd been on Trinity's books for nine years when Peter took over as coach in 1974. He was totally different from any coach I'd had before. By comparison the ones I'd known were just glorified trainers. He was way ahead of his time.

"At Trinity the training sessions changed practically overnight and some players struggled to adjust. We'd never had game plans or set moves under previous coaches. Suddenly we were expected to learn moves and to spend time at training practicing them. Peter also brought him with defensive patterns and we had to learn them as well.

"Peter was the first coach I had who really coached me. He taught me skills, moves and how to think about the game. He also got me to change position – from running loose-forward to ball-handling blind side prop – and added another 10 years to my career.

"That change of position was responsible for providing one of the highlights of my career. I was playing for Oldham in 1985-86 when I was granted a 20 year testimonial. Only a week or so after the season had started Peter brought his Leeds team over to Watersheddings and they got the better of us. The following night the phone rang and when I was told it was Peter, I assumed he was phoning to say he couldn't speak at my testimonial dinner. That wasn't the reason. He told me he'd lost both his first choice props for the inaugural War of the Roses match in two days time and after watching me on Sunday would I be able to play? I said yes right away and Tuesday night I went to Castleford for a squad session. There was little time to get the team organised so he gave me the job of coaching the forwards saying 'you know how I want you to play' while he coached the backs. His plans all came together and we recorded a wonderful victory over Lancashire the next day."

Yorkshire 18 New Zealand 8
23 October 1985 at Bradford

For the first time since 1967, and the first time against New Zealand since 1965, Yorkshire was allocated a fixture against a touring team. Unfortunately the match was scheduled four days after the first test and thus was not as helpful to the British selectors as it might have been.

Some players who had been unavailable for the Roses match were available for this match, but others weren't. Peter rang Andy Goodway, who had retired from representative rugby, and wasn't in anyway, but he talked with Andy's wife. After listening to Peter's reasons for wanting Andy to play, his wife said she'd talk to him and try to get him to change his mind. She obviously succeeded because Andy rang back to say he would like to join the Yorkshire squad.

With Ellery Hanley back in action following his move to Wigan, Garry Schofield back home after a summer spell with Balmain and Jeff Grayshon back in harness at Odsal, Peter was able to pick from strength. Peter also took the opportunity to give Brian Noble, also recently returned from a summer stint in Sydney, a chance to return to the representative stage for the first time since the 1984 Australasian tour. On paper the team selected looked much stronger.

The Kiwis' inexperienced second string made a slow start and Peter's team took full advantage to lead 12-2 at the break. Although the Kiwis put up a better performance in the second half, Yorkshire held onto their advantage to win 18-8 and inflict a second defeat on the tourists.

Peter was very satisfied with the win: "It was a well-earned victory by three tries – to Andy Goodway, Ellery Hanley and Carl Gibson – to our opponents' one. Deryck Fox deservedly picked up his second man-of-the-match award in as many months for making two of Yorkshire's tries and kicking two goals. Yorkshire's young players – Gibson, Mason and Creasser did exceptionally well. The half-backs, Hanley and Fox, constantly created space for their colleagues and, behind an experienced pack of forwards, commanded the game for Yorkshire."

There were mixed fortunes for Peter's props. The good fortune went Jeff Grayshon's way – he did enough to earn a recall to the British team for the second test and enter the record books as Britain's oldest international. Trevor Skerrett fared worse, suffering a broken jaw in a tackle. The injury incensed Peter and led to an angry confrontation with the Kiwis' bench. The Yorkshire team was:

K. Mumby (Bradford N.), C. Gibson (Batley), D. Creasser (Leeds), G. Schofield (Hull), A. Mason (Bramley), E. Hanley (Wigan), D. Fox (Featherstone), J. Grayshon (Bradford N), B. Noble (Bradford N), T. Skerrett (Hull), L. Crooks (Hull), A. Goodway (Wigan), D. Heron (Leeds). Substitutes: G. Steadman (York), P. Lyman (Featherstone).

Yorkshire 26 Lancashire 14
17 September 1986 at Leeds

Peter was reappointed in July 1986 for the second War of the Roses match, this time on what was then his home club ground, at Headingley. *Open Rugby* took the opportunity to interview Peter and he explained his approach to the Yorkshire job and the match in some detail: "I pick what I believe are the best players available to make a team up. In other words, I consider who will complement each other in skills. You can't just pick the best 13 players and put them onto the field. When you are a coach you have to devise a plan of campaign. You're bringing lots of players from club teams who are under different influences, different coaches who maybe play a different style of game. You've got to combine those different styles and bring them together and say 'right, what systems are we going to play against the opposition? Let's have a plan.'

"So I talk to the lads, get them together, knowing that I have a plan in mind. They'll have their say, we'll go out and practise and that's the system, and I'll expect every lad to fulfil his potential; that means he plays as well as he can.

"I look for certain qualities in players to see if they can fit into the overall system. Certain players are responsible for controlling the game, and it doesn't have to be the captain. I might have three captains on the field, but only one of them tosses the coin at the start. They have all got responsibilities – it doesn't just boil down to one player.

"The Australians prove their players in top-class opposition against each other – and that's the very reason why we should play Lancashire versus Yorkshire. We need to have the best players playing against the best players, therefore you get the cream."

Injuries to key players can always disrupt the team selected, but fortunately with players eager for the chance to represent their country there were always others willing to come forward and grab the opportunity. Peter lost two of the key members of his pack when Lee Crooks and Andy Goodway were forced to withdraw, but in Gary Price, of Second Division York, and Hull KR's Andy Kelly he found more than adequate replacements.

Psychologically, Yorkshire struck a major blow on three minutes when Deryck Fox and Paul Lyman worked a planned move from a tap penalty that brought the latter a try. Two more tries from Hanley and Marchant plus three goals from David Hobbs took Yorkshire into an 18-8 lead at the break. Although the second half was much tighter, a second try from Hanley and two more Hobbs's goals ensured a Yorkshire victory. The Yorkshire team was:

I. Wilkinson (Leeds), C. Gibson (Leeds), A. Marchant (Castleford), E. Hanley (Wigan), H. Gill (Wigan), J. Joyner (Castleford – captain), D. Fox (Featherstone), A. Kelly (Hull KR), B. Noble (Bradford N), D. Hobbs (Oldham), P. Smith (Featherstone), G. Price (York), P. Lyman (Featherstone). Substitutes: A. Mason (Bramley), P. Medley (Leeds).

Peter wanted to make more of his team's success. But unlike the previous season's Kiwi tour, there was no place on the Kangaroos' itinerary for a match against Yorkshire. Peter thought it was a ridiculous decision and said so, explaining that: "We talk about increased competition in this country at the top, but they don't want our international players exposed against this opposition regularly. Maybe Great Britain wouldn't like Peter Fox to do with Yorkshire what Great Britain haven't been able to do."

Yorkshire 16 Lancashire 10
16 September 1987 at Wigan

With three victories under his belt, Peter's retention of the Yorkshire coaching position had become almost a formality.

There was a better attendance for the rematch of Lancashire and Yorkshire at Central Park. Once again Yorkshire struck the opening blow through a try by Ellery Hanley after 15 minutes, which David Hobbs converted. Although Lancashire fought back Yorkshire were able to go in at half-time 6-4 ahead.

After the break Yorkshire applied the early pressure. Tony Marchant was on hand to pounce upon the loose ball after a Deryck Fox grubber kick rebounded off John Woods' legs and grab an opportunist try. Deryck Fox converted. A Henderson Gill try, scored while Lancashire were a man short, enabled the white rose county to move further ahead, 16-4.

Again Yorkshire's forwards were superb. Kevin Ward leading the pack, for the only time he was available to play for his county, propping his club hooker, Kevin Beardmore, with Hobbs, Crooks, Burton and Goodway giving everything they had.

Yorkshire's lead was jeopardised when Chris Burton was sent to the sin bin with 10 minutes remaining. A Lancashire try reduced the margin to only six points and sensing victory Lancashire threw everything at the Yorkshire line. Yorkshire's defence was superb in those closing minutes and managed to hold on to the lead until the hooter sounded. The Yorkshire team was:

I. Wilkinson (Halifax), C. Gibson (Leeds), A. Marchant (Castleford), A. Mason (Wakefield T), H. Gill (Wigan), E. Hanley (Wigan – captain), D. Fox (Featherstone), K. Ward (Castleford), K. Beardmore (Castleford), D. Hobbs (Bradford N), L. Crooks (Leeds), C. Burton (Hull KR), A. Goodway (Wigan). Substitutes: J. Joyner (Castleford), P. Dixon (Halifax).

Yorkshire 28 Papua New Guinea 4
27 October 1987 at Leeds

Since getting their opening victory over Peter's Featherstone team, the Kumuls had found things getting harder, a draw with Lancashire being their best result in the next four fixtures. Unfortunately their opponents had worked out how to deal with a touring team that lacked players of the size and power to match the locals.

Three days after Great Britain had overwhelmed them at Wigan a tired, but strong, Kumuls side took on a much changed Yorkshire team at Headingley. This was a match that gave Peter the opportunity to give other players, who had not previously had the chance, such as Paul Eastwood, Karl Fairbank, Seamus McCallion and Roy Powell, to show their ability at a higher level.

A terribly wet night kept the crowd down and made play very difficult for both teams. A low-scoring first half ended with the scores level at 4-4, Yorkshire's points coming from a Karl Fairbank try.

As the Kumuls tired after the break, Yorkshire moved up a gear and overpowered them. Carl Gibson helped himself to a hat-trick of tries, Tony Marchant and David Creasser grabbed one apiece, and David Hobbs managed to kick two goals in atrocious conditions to record what turned into an easy victory. Yorkshire's team was:

K. Mumby (Bradford N), P. Eastwood (Hull), A. Marchant (Castleford), C. Gibson (Leeds), A. Mason (Wakefield T), J. Joyner (Castleford - captain), D. Fox (Featherstone), D. Hobbs (Bradford N), S. McCallion (Halifax), R. Powell (Leeds), C. Burton (Hull KR), K. Fairbank (Bradford N), P. Dixon (Halifax). Substitutes: D. Creasser (Leeds), D. Heron (Leeds).

Yorkshire 24 Lancashire 14
21 September 1988 at Leeds

After three defeats at the hands of Yorkshire, Lancashire decided that a change of coach was essential and appointed Doug Laughton, of Widnes, to succeed Alex Murphy. Laughton's appointment gave Peter added motivation. Peter recalled those England matches in the 1970s when after addressing the team, Doug had asked him "What gives you the right to tell us how to play when you've never played international rugby yourself?" "Well I'd never played county rugby before, but as Yorkshire county coach I'd won five out of five and I was determined to show Dougie Laughton what coaching at county level was all about."

Laughton responded to the challenge by choosing a side, blighted as always by withdrawals through injury, that contained eight Widnes players. Laughton was relying on the Widnes group to provide the cohesion his side needed to overcome Peter's Yorkshire combination that seemed to thrive on a mix of experience and loyalty.

Yorkshire's squad were all seasoned performers with only one newcomer, Castleford's in form full-back, David Roockley. John Joyner was named as 16th man and taken along simply to boost the team's morale. Peter once again gave the captaincy to Ellery Hanley "because I knew that responsibility would ensure his commitment to the team plan and not just to himself". This was somewhat of a gamble because this would be Ellery's first match back in Britain after playing throughout the summer for Balmain in Australia. The match went exactly to Peter's plan.

The travel didn't faze Yorkshire's skipper one bit because he scored the first try, which Hobbs converted, after only three minutes to put Yorkshire in the ascendant. A try from Henderson Gill and a Hobbs penalty goal put Yorkshire ahead, 12-0, at the break.

An early strike from Lancashire in the second half was countered by a Marchant try, converted by Hobbs, to keep Yorkshire's advantage. As the match went into the last quarter two Lancashire tries briefly threatened the home side's advantage before a Garry Schofield interception try and a Hobbs conversion made the outcome clear.

Once more the public had shown that interest in the fixture was growing – Headingley hosting the best attendance at a Roses match in Yorkshire for 22 years. The Yorkshire side was:

D. Roockley (Castleford), H. Gill (Wigan), G. Schofield (Leeds), A. Marchant (Castleford), C. Gibson (Leeds), E. Hanley (Wigan – captain), D. Fox (Featherstone), D. Hobbs (Bradford N), K. Beardmore (Castleford), K. Skerrett (Bradford N), P. Dixon (Halifax), R. Powell (Leeds), A. Goodway (Wigan). Substitutes: G. Steadman (Featherstone), D. Heron (Leeds).

Yorkshire 56 Lancashire 12
20 September 1989 at Wigan

Doug Laughton was given a second chance to end Peter's four-match winning streak. Although neither Ellery Hanley nor John Joyner was available for selection due to injury, Peter was still able to put out a strong side for what was described in the press as a test trial for the upcoming Kiwi tour. There was a further injury blow when Kevin Ward was a late withdrawal: "I was always prepared to give younger players the opportunity to shine provided they had the right credentials to succeed. If they were playing well for their club and showed dedication to the county cause, then it meant they would be focused on their responsibilities to Yorkshire's team plan," said Peter. Having a settled and very accomplished back division gave Peter the opportunity to give three such youngsters, two from Featherstone Rovers – Chris Bibb and Paul Newlove – and Sheffield Eagles' Daryl Powell, the chance to show what they could do in representative football.

Almost from the kick off Yorkshire took control, opening the scoring through a Schofield try after only two minutes. That try set the scene for a rout as Yorkshire's pack quickly took control providing a platform behind which Steadman and Fox could work. Having seized the initiative from a surprisingly uncommitted Lancastrian team, Yorkshire ran in a further five tries – from Newlove, Steadman, Fox, and Goodway with two – plus four goals from Hobbs, to lead 32-0 at the interval. Unfortunately, the half ended on a sad note when Garry Schofield had to be helped off with a suspected broken ankle.

Immediately after the break there was a brief Lancashire revival. Despite the loss of Schofield, Fox managed to restore the white rose's rhythm once more. Another four tries – from Medley, Newlove, Steadman and Hobbs – plus four Steadman goals gave Yorkshire an easy 56-12 victory over the old enemy.

That evening Central Park hosted the biggest attendance for a Roses match for 23 years, 10,182, but the abject failure of the Lancashire team cast doubts about the fixture's long-term future. Unless the match was competitive there was no way crowds would continue to turn out on that scale to watch the biggest score and the highest winning margin in Roses' history.

Even though it had been one-sided, the match did enable some players to press their claims for higher honours. Paul Newlove's play had impressed Great Britain's management, who picked him as one of the substitutes for the first test the following month. That appearance would make him Great Britain's youngest ever international. After being ignored by the selectors for three years, Deryck Fox got back onto the British subs bench for the second and third tests.

C. Bibb (Featherstone R), C. Gibson (Leeds), G. Schofield (Leeds), D. Powell (Sheffield E), P. Newlove (Featherstone), G. Steadman (Castleford), D. Fox (Featherstone), K. Skerrett (Bradford N), K. Beardmore (Castleford), P. Dixon (Leeds), D. Hobbs (Bradford N – captain), R. Powell (Leeds), A. Goodway (Wigan). Substitutes: A. Mason (Wakefield T), P. Medley (Bradford N).

Both the World Club Challenge and the War of the Roses were suspended in 1990, apparently because of fears of fixture congestion at the start of that season's Australian tour. That decision threw the War of the Roses' future into further doubt.

Yorkshire 17 Lancashire 12
18 September 1991 at Leeds

The War of the Roses was revived in 1991. Peter was once again made Yorkshire's coach and there was the added incentive of a clash with a new Lancashire coach. Ray Ashton, Second Division Workington Town's young player-coach, had been given the task.

After five consecutive encounters there was a new duel at half-back, caused by Lancashire's Andy Gregory's decision to retire from representative football. Bobby Goulding was called up to do battle with Yorkshire's ever-present scum half, Deryck Fox. Peter initially brought in two newcomers – Lee Jackson and Anthony Sullivan – but both were already blooded at the highest level having been on the 1990 tour down under. A third newcomer, Ian Smales, was added when Daryl Powell was forced to withdraw at the last minute.

This match turned into Yorkshire's toughest test so far. Lancashire came out looking for the win and finished the first quarter ahead, before Yorkshire fought back to level the scores at half time, 8-8. A burst of scoring immediately after the restart left the scores tied at 12-12; although Lancashire led the try count by three to two. Yorkshire's two coming from Deryck Fox and Chris Bibb.

At the start of the final quarter, a try from Featherstone's Ian Smales gave Yorkshire the lead once more. With 13 minutes remaining Deryck Fox dropped a goal to clinch victory for Yorkshire and bring to an end his magnificent performances at scrum-half for his county.

C. Bibb (Featherstone R), C. Gibson (Leeds), I. Smales (Featherstone), A. Mason (Wakefield T), A. Sullivan (St Helens), G. Schofield (Leeds), D. Fox (Featherstone), K. Skerrett (Wigan), L. Jackson (Hull), L. Crooks (Castleford), P. Dixon (Leeds), K. Fairbank (Bradford N.), E. Hanley (Leeds – captain). Substitutes: G. Steadman (Castleford), R. Powell (Leeds).

Although the Kumuls were once again touring Great Britain and their itinerary was purely made up of meetings with representative teams there was no place for Yorkshire. It marked the end of the Yorkshire county team and Peter's representative coaching career.

Unfortunately, a six-year period, in which Peter had recorded six consecutive victories over Lancashire, could not be continued. Lancashire, despite employing three coaches – Alex Murphy, on three occasions, Doug Laughton, twice, and Ray Ashton, for the last one, – had failed too often to produce any credibility. For whatever reason, the Roses challenge had never inspired the leading players to the west of the Pennines in the way it had those to the east. As a result the fixture was cancelled.

Probably the best appreciation of Peter's contribution to Yorkshire's success can be found in the comments of two of his players in the 1991 Wars of the Roses programme. The first was from John Joyner: "He praises his players to the heavens and very rarely criticises them. That makes them feel 10 feet tall and gives them both a sense of confidence in themselves and a loyalty towards him. If his side loses, he's man enough to take the brunt of the criticism."

The second came from Mick Morgan: "He's a coach in the true sense of the word ... Peter is a great tactician who thinks carefully about how to win each game and he also explores his players' minds. He's one of the game's great thinkers and motivators ... And he keeps things simple, using basic moves which aren't too complex, ideal with just two or three sessions available with his squad prior to a county game."

Another member of the Yorkshire squad, Garry Schofield, had this to say about Peter's approach to his players a couple of years later: "He sits you down in the changing room and calmly and rationally put his views over – and you want to work for him. Even if things are going wrong at half-time he doesn't fall back on ranting and raving. Some coaches, like Alex Murphy, wind players up by shouting and bawling, but Peter is just the opposite." Over a remarkable seven years Peter had proved the doubters wrong. A county team could work – provided there was a coach capable of infusing his teams with ideas, pride and passion. But as the Yorkshire team faded from the game's fixture lists, Peter was about to resume his career at Bradford Northern.

18. Another spell at Odsal

Chris Caisley had taken over as the chairman of Bradford Northern in 1989. Since then there had been some successes in cup competitions, but Northern had failed to build upon them. In the league a fourth place in 1989-90 had turned into seventh the following season. Mid-table mediocrity was not why Chris Caisley had taken the job. He wanted to bring success back to the club and match the standards being set by Wigan both on and off the field.

With only one win from the first six matches of the new season, Northern were second from bottom of the First Division and eight points adrift of the club immediately above. Things were not just getting worse, they were getting desperate and Chris Caisley knew something had to be done immediately. Peter's sudden availability made him the obvious answer. The need for change was explained to David Hobbs, who had been operating as player-coach for a year and a half, and he agreed to stay on with Northern if the new man was Peter. Hobbs told Peter: "I wouldn't have stood down for anybody else". Peter agreed terms and the legal processes were set in motion that would take him back to Odsal as team manager-coach on a three-and-a-half year contract.

Chris Caisley sang Peter's praises as he announced his return to Odsal: "I rate Peter very highly and there is nobody in rugby league with as much knowledge as him. I believe he will relish the move back to Bradford and he will have total control. Peter is regarded as a messiah by Bradford supporters and I am sure that now we have been able to secure a contract with him the fans will rally round and be delighted."

There was at least some good news to lighten the Odsal gloom; Northern had qualified for the Yorkshire Cup Final. Peter's negotiations were nearly complete and he was able to watch his new team take on Castleford at Elland Road on Saturday 20 October. Northern put up a good performance in the first half but after the break Castleford went on to win easily 28-6. It was clear to Peter that Northern's play lacked vision and the teamwork was poor.

Peter's first task was to get the club out of relegation zone: "To make sure the team was fit for the challenge ahead I brought Steve Young with me as physical conditioner, but kept the two coaching assistants that were already at Odsal – Francis Jarvis and John Simpson." It was not an easy task because Odsal had the worst training facilities of any club in the top flight.

Already at Odsal were a small group of players who had served Peter during his years as Yorkshire coach: David Hobbs, Tony Marchant and Paul Medley. In addition there were good experienced players such as Jon Hamer and up-and-coming youngsters like Steve McGowan. There were also three talented former rugby union men in Darrell Shelford, Brett Iti, who were both New Zealanders and Neil Summers, who had played union for Headingley, in the squad.

Peter's first match in charge was against Castleford at Odsal on 3 November. Castleford won 18-12 and a further defeat the following weekend at Warrington saw Northern bottom of the league.

Performances in the Regal Trophy showed signs of promise. A first round visit from amateurs Leigh East provided a gentle warm up, with four tries from Henderson Gill helping Northern to run up a record score, 76-0. Then a try and eight goals from David

Hobbs underpinned an easy home victory over Second Division Sheffield Eagles. Little by little Peter was instilling confidence and pattern into the team's play.

However, a quarter-final at Knowsley Road proved too big a hurdle. A poor first-half performance saw the Saints move into a 20-2 lead at the break: "In the dressing room at half-time I called for greater effort or a big defeat was on the cards. The team responded and matched Saints in the second half to restrict the final score to 30-12."

Just how much that second-half performance had done for the team's confidence became clear the following Wednesday when Widnes, the league leaders, came to Odsal. Northern showed no respect for the Chemics' league position, taking them on up-front to set up a 36-14 victory. Another home win over Warrington showed that Peter's changes were beginning to make a difference.

The festive season started promisingly with a 16-10 home win over Warrington on 22 December. On Boxing Day, Halifax came to Odsal. A six point home victory did more than lift spirits as it took Northern out of the bottom two in the table.

On New Year's Day, Northern travelled to Thrum Hall for the return match. Referee Ronnie Campbell's decision to rule out a Darrell Shelford try, that many thought perfectly legal, caused uproar. To make matters worse Campbell then penalised Northern for dissent. Peter could not contain himself: "I marched onto the pitch to make my views known to Campbell. When ordered off the playing area I left and Northern went on to win the match 26-18, but that was not the end of the matter. A police officer accused me of being abusive to fans behind my dugout and that led to an investigation. In the end the police did not follow up their investigation. A police inspector interviewed John Hamer, one of the team members who served in the same force in Halifax, and he told him that I was not the type of person to do what the officer at the game had accused me of. The charge was duly dropped. Once the police decided to take no further action I was summoned to headquarters and subsequently received a six-match touchline ban."

Northern lost the next three matches to Hull and Wigan at Odsal and at Castleford to fall back into the relegation zone and make the situation even more fraught. Some respite came with the start of the Challenge Cup campaign. A first round victory, 52-4, over the Pirates at Scarborough brought a journey to Barrow. An easy victory, 30-13, took Northern into the quarter-final.

The draw set up another visit to Halifax. After only 13 minutes Tony Marchant was dismissed and Northern's chances looked poor. But instead of exploiting the extra space available Halifax chose to try and play down the middle. Northern's pack dealt with the assault and thanks to a late David Hobbs penalty the visitors went in at half time 2-0 ahead. Still Halifax persisted in playing down the middle while Northern managed to create the space for Gerald Cordle to score a try. Although pressure brought a belated try for Halifax, two more David Hobbs penalties gave Northern a 12-4 victory.

Northern should have been buoyed up after the Cup victory when they returned to league action. It didn't look that way when a poor display led to defeat against Salford at the Willows. Peter turned to the transfer market. An unwanted and out-of-contract Roy Powell was recruited from Leeds at the end of February 1992 for £80,000 and made his debut against Featherstone Rovers at Odsal. Adding Powell to the pack stiffened the defence and helped the side to three successive victories – over Rovers, Swinton and Widnes.

The Cup semi-final was fixed for 28 March at Burnden Park, the home of Bolton Wanderers FC. Facing Wigan with five regulars out injured was an impossible task and

Northern's opponents showed no mercy. It was almost embarrassing at times as Wigan equalled the previous record semi-final score of 35-0 by half-time. Northern did fight back and tries by Shelford and Gill at least showed spirit. But only two tries against Wigan's 13 and a final score of 71-10 showed just how superior the Lancastrians were on the day.

Losing in a semi-final always is a big blow to a team. Losing by such a huge margin makes that blow even more severe. Peter had just seven days to lift his team for a crucial home league meeting with Wakefield Trinity. It was a very close match decided by a David Hobbs drop-goal. After the debacle at Bolton, the next match, a visit to Wigan, offered little hope of salvation. That proved to be the case, the home side winning easily 50-8.

Northern's fate hung on Easter, the last weekend of the regular season. Good Friday brought Swinton to Odsal and Northern ran riot to beat their already doomed opponents 60-0. There could be no real celebration because two league points and an improved points' difference on their own were not enough to guarantee survival.

The outcome of three matches on Easter Monday would decide Northern's fate. Northern's task was simple, beat Hull KR at Craven Park by the biggest margin possible. If both Hull and Featherstone lost, there was a chance of survival.

Grabbing what chances came their way Northern scored two tries to go in at the break 10-0 ahead. As Northern's fans began to allow themselves to hope for victory and survival the Robins had other ideas, narrowing the gap to four points through a converted try. A late breakaway try by Neil Summers re-established a two score gap and restored Northern's hopes. It was not a game for faint hearts for in the final minutes the Robins scored another converted try to reduce the gap to a mere two points. Northern's defence just managed to hold out to register a crucial win, 14-12.

Meanwhile Featherstone Rovers were not strong enough to get the better of Trinity at Belle Vue and Hull lost at Castleford. Those results meant that all three clubs finished on 22 points. As Peter's old club, Rovers, had the worst points difference they joined Swinton for the drop. Having the best points difference of the three teams, Northern finished 11th.

It had been an exciting and at times perilous season. Unfortunately the fans hadn't always really enjoyed it. Crowds had fallen and the average attendance was 500 fewer than the previous season making money tighter and life even harder for Peter.

1992-93

During the 1992 close season Peter began to assemble the team he wanted: "To get the team working in the way I wanted I made David Hobbs captain. I also took the opportunity to have a word with the former Northern stalwart, Nigel Stephenson, and asked him if he wanted to get back into the game. He did and I appointed him as assistant coach, working with John Simpson."

Dave Heron, thought by many to be too old at 34, was signed from Leeds in July 1992. In August, Peter returned to Featherstone Rovers to sign Trevor Clark, now just the wrong side of 30, for a second time. That same month the RFL Tribunal on transfer fees decided that Leigh had to pay Bradford £20,000 for John Pendlebury, giving Peter some money to spend.

Peter had hoped that the much-travelled Australian Bob Grogan, who had previously played for Northern at the end of the 1990-91 season, would be able to solve his stand-off problem, but an injury ruled him out. Although he had a few weeks left to serve of a three-month ban for testing positive for traces of cannabis, Dave Watson was signed in August 1992 from Halifax for £25,000. Watson, a Kiwi, was lined up to take over the full-back berth. Brimah Kebbie, a speedy winger, was signed from Huddersfield that same month. Brian McDermott, then a loose-forward, was signed from Eastmoor ARLC in September.

Most of these new signings turned out for the opening match, a Yorkshire Cup preliminary round match against Castleford. Brimah Kebbie looked in great form as he ran in two tries in the 16-10 victory. After that match, the league fixtures began with a trip to the Boulevard. Although Kebbie again scored two tries Northern lost 24-14. The following weekend Odsal hosted its first league match of the season and Kebbie again contributed two tries to the victory over Leigh.

Deryck Fox had returned from the 1992 British tour unhappy about returning to Second Division rugby at Featherstone. Although he was still under contract, Fox immediately submitted a transfer request and refused to resume training at Post Office Road. His availability interested a lot of clubs, but Bradford was slow to move. One evening Deryck Fox rang Peter to tell him that some of the Hull directors were outside his house waiting for his decision on a move to Humberside. Deryck wanted to know if there was a chance he could join Northern. Peter takes up the story: "I immediately rang Chris Caisley to let him know what was happening and he promised to ring back once he had checked with his fellow directors. It didn't take him long to ring back and confirm they would raise the money. I phoned Deryck to tell him we would be making an offer and he was signed in September 1992 for a club record £140,000 fee."

Reputedly Northern's directors were £20,000 short of raising the fee and Peter offered to lend Caisley the money. There was no need because supporters' contributions made up the difference.

Fox was selected as the substitute back for his debut, a Yorkshire Cup first round tie against Bramley on 13 September. He didn't stay on the bench long. An injury to Neil Summers meant he was on the field after only four minutes. Kebbie ran in another two tries in what was a straightforward introduction for Fox to his new team, Northern winning 34-22. Unfortunately Kebbie's wonderful start for his new club was soon brought to an end by an injury that would keep him out of the first team for most of the season.

A victory at Widnes indicated that Northern could be in the hunt for honours. But having been beaten by them for the previous three seasons, Sheffield Eagles sprung a surprise by turning the tables and knocking Northern out of the Yorkshire Cup in the second round at Odsal.

Being dumped out of the Yorkshire Cup seemed to concentrate Northern's attention on the league. Few teams could have relished facing Northern in this mood as they overran Leeds and Salford at Odsal, won 22-4 at Warrington and then easily beat Hull KR at Odsal.

A visit to Knowsley Road at the start of November gave a good measure of the club's progress against a home side that was unbeaten in the league. Not only did Northern outplay Saints to win 35-18, but victory took the club to the top of the table. Peter, keen to manage expectations, gave his view on the club's elevated position: "At the start of the season I would have settled for a top eight spot. Now we seem to be looking for a place inside the top four. That would be a considerable improvement on last season. I don't believe we're genuine Championship contenders yet, but we are getting better each week and that is our aim."

Peter's squad was stretched and with little talent immediately available in the reserves he turned to veterans. Keith Mumby was brought back to Odsal on loan from Sheffield Eagles and veteran Mick Taylor was recruited from London Crusaders.

A few weeks after he had taken over as chief executive of the RFL Maurice Lindsay was convinced by Fred Lindop, the controller of referees, that the game would be improved if the offside line at the play-the-ball was moved further back. Between them they agreed to double the distance from five to 10 metres. Although it generated some controversy there was sufficient general agreement to bring in the new distance on the weekend of 23 November 1992 in the middle of the season that had begun under the old rule.

Suddenly there was a lot of extra room around the play-the-ball just waiting for the team in possession to exploit it, either by organised moves or quick transfer of the ball to the wide men. Very rapidly the new law forced changes in the defensive alignment. As defenders struggled to get back 10 metres an attacking side, through quick play-the-balls, which were also being officially endorsed and encouraged, could build up momentum and go nearly the length of the field in six tackles. A new style of play had to be accommodated in mid-season.

If, as his critics alleged, Peter's was an aging defence-focused team then the rest of the season could have been very difficult. If the change was designed to favour young, mobile teams, then Northern's veterans were predicted to be in for a torrid time.

The visit of St Helens to Odsal on 22 November gave Peter a chance to see how his team would cope. Although a Saints team seeking revenge had the better of the match, winning 16-4, Northern coped well with the new rule.

Steve McGowan's six tries helped Northern overwhelm Barrow in the first round of the Regal Trophy, and brought a trip to Wilderspool in mid-December for the second round. This match saw Northern turn in a very gutsy performance to draw 12-12. The replay turned into a bitter affair that Northern narrowly won 9-6. With Odsal frostbound, Northern hired Valley Parade for the quarter-final. In those unfamiliar surroundings Deryck Fox's 13 points paved the way for a deceptively easy victory over Widnes, 21-10.

Receiving a home draw in the semi-final, Northern once again hired Valley Parade. They raced into an 18-0 lead and eventually won 19-12 as Castleford fought back.

The Regal Trophy Final, against Wigan, was held at Elland Road on Saturday 23 January. It gave Northern the chance to lay some of the ghosts that still haunted the club after the previous season's thrashing at Bolton. Peter gambled on Deryck Fox's fitness, playing him after administering painkilling injections for a groin injury. Northern's team was:

D. Watson, A. Marchant, S. McGowan, A. Anderson, R. Simpson, N. Summers, D. Fox, D. Hobbs, B. Noble, R. Powell, P. Medley, K. Fairbank, D. Heron. Substitutes: K. Mumby, T. Clark.

It was quickly clear that the injections hadn't worked and Fox was a shadow of his usual self, even though he bravely stayed on the field for 70 minutes. Despite that handicap Northern mounted a strong challenge in the first half, but only had a penalty goal by Hobbs to show for it at the break when they went in 6-2 down. After the restart Wigan got the upper hand, but a try on 78 minutes by Steve McGowan, converted by Keith Mumby made the final score a respectable 15-8.

After that match Deryck Fox had to go for surgery on his groin problem, which would keep him out of action for two months. His absence did not affect Northern's performance in the first round of the Challenge Cup too much. Third Division Workington Town were eventually beaten 28-18. A home league victory over Hull was followed by an 18-point defeat at Wigan.

Round two of the Challenge Cup took Northern to Belle Vue. Some of referee Robin Whitfield's decisions seemed to favour Peter's team and stirred up plenty of controversy. In particular Whitfield's decision to award Tony Marchant a penalty try gave Northern a lead that they were just able to defend until the final hooter to win 20-18. After a surprisingly bad performance against Salford, Northern produced a wonderful win, 42-4, at Oldham to book a semi-final spot.

There were four league matches to be played before the semi-final. Paul Medley showed his strike power as he ran in four tries in the first of those, a victory over Wakefield Trinity at Odsal. Northern then lost at Sheffield, but got back to winning ways at Odsal, beating Wigan 23-16. Finally Warrington came to Odsal and surprisingly defeated the home side 21-8.

Deryck Fox returned to action for the Challenge Cup semi-final at Elland Road on 27 March. Peter laid his plans: "Having Fox back in the team meant that I could employ a game plan based on kicking early in the tackle count in a bid to push Wigan back. It worked well and the first half finished scoreless." Enjoying a bit of good fortune Wigan scored a converted try and then added a penalty after the break. On the hour a Roger Simpson try converted by David Hobbs closed the gap to just three points. Try as they might though, Northern could not narrow the gap any further before Wigan scored another converted try to win 15-6.

There was the usual scramble in April to complete the league programme. Things started well with home victories over Widnes, Sheffield Eagles and finally Halifax on Good Friday. The Boxing Day fixture at Thrum Hall had been postponed until Easter Monday and produced another victory, 33-14. By now fatigue was kicking in and the final two away matches, a trip to Hull KR, rearranged from March, and one to Headingley were both lost.

Defeat at the hands of Leeds meant that Northern finished third in the First Division on 30 points, just ahead of Widnes and Leeds on points difference. It was the club's highest finish for six years. In the Premiership, Northern put up a below-par performance in the first round, losing to Castleford 19-6.

Once again Peter was the only British nomination for coach of the year and once again his achievements were unable to sway the panel of judges.

1993-94

At the time it struck Peter as strange that Northern's directors were so keen for him to go full-time: "Why was such a move necessary when the players were to remain part-time? However, I let myself be persuaded and in the close season I left my job at IMI and agreed a two-year contract to work full-time as Northern's team manager. On reflection, this turned out not to be a good decision. I was happy in my job and going full-time in rugby league was not the best decision I made. It also gave the board more power over me."

Tony Anderson, the Australian centre, was allowed to join Huddersfield in May. After appointing Deryck Fox as his captain, Peter made moves to strengthen the team at the start of July. Neil Holding was his first capture, brought from St Helens as cover for the half-back positions and as an assistant for 'A' team coach, Nigel Stephenson.

At Peter's prompting, Northern's board responded to their big-spending rivals – Leeds and Wigan – by finding the money to enable him to compete in a rapidly rising market. This was not easily done as Northern's average crowds were barely more than a third of those at Central Park. The club's first target was identified in a surprising way. While at Wembley for the Cup Final 1993 Peter had been asked by Eric Ashton, the coach of St Helens, to join him and some of his directors at their table for a chat. The topic of conversation quickly moved on to Paul Newlove, who was coming to the end of his five-year contract at Featherstone, and Eric wanted Peter to tell his board just how good he was. After half an hour of doing so Eric said to his directors: "I told you so and we couldn't have a better recommendation than that". It was on the way back from Wembley that Peter realised what had to be done: "It struck me, why should I be helping Saints to sign my star player at Rovers. I immediately told my board of Saints' objective and got them to make the move for Newlove. I got Newey and his father to my house and we agreed a deal. Newey signed for Northern before the fee with Rovers was agreed." It was obvious why there had been no agreement over the fee – Rovers wanted £750,000, while Northern offered £150,000.

The third player to be acquired was the veteran former test second-row or prop, Paul Dixon, from Leeds. Both transfers went to the RFL Tribunal, which at the end of July fixed the fees at £70,000 for Dixon and a record-breaking £245,000 for Newlove. Another signing involved less expenditure: Phil Hepworth, the captain of that summer's BARLA Young Lions tour to Australasia, was signed in mid-August from local amateurs Dudley Hill.

There were some radical changes to the season's fixture list. For the first time in more than 80 years there was no Yorkshire Cup competition – the clubs had voted for it to be dropped as part of a major restructuring. The other changes were that the First Division was extended to 16 clubs and its members were to be seeded into the later rounds of the Regal Trophy and the Challenge Cup for the first time.

Paul Newlove scored a try on his debut for Northern at Odsal in the opening league match of the season against Widnes on Sunday 29 August. Northern had a great start to the season, that home victory being followed by one at Oldham. Defeat had looked likely at the Watersheddings, but a fantastic last-minute try by Dave Watson, who ran the length of the field, beating man after man, snatched both points. That never-say-die spirit and the capability to play for the full 80 minutes were to be features of Northern's play all season.

Sheffield Eagles were the next to arrive at Odsal and with a lead of 14 points and only 15 minutes left it looked like an away win. When a lack of substitutes and ill discipline combined to reduce the Eagles to 11 men, Northern pounced and by the hooter had grabbed an unexpected 36-26 victory. Five victories from the first five matches put Northern on top of the table by the end of September. The first league defeat, suffered at Hull KR, did not come until the start of October.

Northern met the touring Kiwis on Wednesday 6 October. Peter fielded three New Zealanders – Trevor Clark, Darrall Shelford and Dave Watson – against the tourists. In driving rain, Deryck Fox played magnificently, setting up Cordle's try, kicking four goals and a drop-goal to push Northern into a 14-2 lead. The Kiwis pulled back to 14-10, before Northern's sound defence choked a Kiwi second-string team that lacked the possession to create further openings in the last 15 minutes. It was the tourists' first defeat and they did not like it. A mass brawl, which erupted in the last few minutes and led to Quentin Pongia and Northern's Paul Medley being sent off marred the end of a fine victory for Northern.

Four days later Warrington came to Odsal. By then there were so many injuries that Peter was forced to play Keith Mumby at loose-forward. Although rated as the best defensive team in the league, the visitors had to no answer to Northern's attack. A superb performance brought an emphatic 47-16 victory.

To support the first test match at Wembley there were no league fixtures over the weekend of 16 and 17 October. A weekend off was a boost for Northern because it meant that the loss to the Kiwis of Dave Watson and of Karl Fairbank and Paul Newlove to Great Britain would be less of a problem.

One week later Northern travelled to Leigh, one of the favourites for relegation, and put more than 40 points on the board to register an emphatic victory.

A request from the New Zealand touring team for Dave Watson to play for them against St Helens was refused, but, under international rules, he had to be released for the second test match. There was no suspension of fixtures for this game, which was played on Saturday 30 October, so the following day Watson and his two team mates who had played for Great Britain - Karl Fairbank, Northern's pack leader, and Paul Newlove - turned out to assist in putting over 40 points on board against Salford.

That victory consolidated Northern's position at the top of the league table. However, on a visit to St Helens on 7 November, the day after Fairbank, Newlove and Watson had played in the third test, a Deryck Fox penalty and drop-goal never threatened the home side, who won 54-3 to bring Northern's expectations back down to earth.

Because of the new seeding arrangements and a wider entry from outside the non-professional ranks, Northern did not have to enter the Regal Trophy until the second round. A mid-November trip to Barrow produced no problems in a 28-8 win.

Thick fog descended on Odsal just as the match against Wigan was getting underway on the evening of Friday 19 November. Ten minutes later, by which time Northern had gone ahead 4-2, the match had to be abandoned.

With Odsal frostbound Northern switched the match against Leeds, on Sunday 28 November, to Valley Parade. As usual, it was a close game that was only settled in Northern's favour by a Roy Powell try in the closing minutes.

A league victory over Castleford followed before the weather once again ruled Odsal out of action in mid-December. With no room to manoeuvre the RFL ordered Northern to switch the Regal Trophy third round tie against Halifax to Headingley. Fortunately the weather relented, Odsal was somehow got ready and the match went ahead on Thursday 16 December. Halifax produced a huge effort and it took a Karl Fairbank try three minutes from time to make the match safe at 16-8.

Three days later Northern travelled to face Second Division high-fliers London Crusaders in the fourth round. Northern fell behind and it was not until Paul Newlove scored a spectacular 75-yard try that the visitors got back into the game. Northern went on to end the Crusaders' unbeaten home run, winning 22-10.

Halifax provided the traditionally tough Boxing Day opposition. A Steve McGowan hat-trick helped Northern to a 26-18 home win. Having been defeated by Northern at Wheldon Road a month earlier Castleford arrived at Odsal on New Year's Day for the Regal Trophy semi-final knowing they were underdogs. If anything, that knowledge increased the Tigers' determination as they overturned their league form to win easily 23-10. Four days later Northern lost again, this time in the league, 20-4 to Hull.

Around this time Wakefield Trinity's board were looking to strengthen their team and made an approach for David Hobbs. Peter recalls: "It was a good move for a player nearing the veteran stage who had served Northern with distinction. I discussed the situation with David and finally agreed to let him go on a free transfer in February."

The next match, on Sunday 9 January, saw Northern embark on a run of eight wins. After completing league doubles over Oldham and Widnes, Northern travelled to the Don Valley Stadium. Sheffield Eagles played some attractive rugby to go 18-0 up, but Northern dug deep scoring tries either side of half time. When the 80 minutes were up the scores were tied 28-28, but Northern wanted victory and a drive down field set up Deryck Fox to put over a winning drop-goal and once again snatch victory from the Eagles. Having completed the double over the Eagles, Northern then did the same to Wakefield.

As a result of the new entry and seeding rules Northern did not enter the Challenge Cup until the fourth round. An end of January trip to Barrow opened the campaign and an easy 58-30 win was the result. A victory at Featherstone at the start of February continued Northern's winning run.

The fifth round of the Challenge Cup in the middle of the month took Northern on a longer journey to the northwest, to Workington, where a Town pack short of three regular forwards could not prevent a 32-0 away victory. Another break in Cup action saw Northern defeat Hull KR.

Showing that he was still as astute as ever when it came to recognising player potential Peter swooped in February for a centre, Carl Hall, who had scored 18 tries in 19 matches since arriving at Doncaster from New Zealand at the start of the season.

Headingley welcomed a big crowd, more than 22,000, for the Challenge Cup quarter-final at the end of February. It was an intense match that could have gone either way. Unfortunately for Peter, the Loiners turned a couple of openings into long-range tries that swung the match. A 33-10 scoreline made the defeat look worse than it was, but hopes of a Wembley appearance had gone for another year.

All the earlier good work was threatened by a drop in form after a league double was completed over fellow title contenders Warrington. It started with a visit from bottom-of-the-table Leigh on 13 March, which instead of providing an easy win turned into an unexpected defeat, 24-14. In hindsight, that match struck a near fatal blow to Northern's title ambitions.

A weakened team managed to recover some ground by gaining a valuable victory at Salford. But some of that ground was immediately lost through a defeat at Halifax on Good Friday. After falling behind, Northern rallied against Hull at Odsal on Easter Monday. Gerald Cordle ran in four tries, but Deryck Fox's normal accuracy had deserted him. Two of his conversion attempts bounced off the uprights and only one was successful. That narrow defeat, 32-30, dealt another severe blow to Northern's hopes.

Lying joint second on 38 points with Wigan, but having played a game more, it appeared that Northern's hopes of catching Warrington - two points ahead of both with three matches to play - were fading. Northern were also at a disadvantage because so many tough matches in so short a time favoured the clubs with the bigger squads.

Northern kept their title prospects alive by beating Castleford at Odsal on Friday night. They then had four days to prepare for two of the most difficult league matches of the season. The abandoned match against Wigan was rescheduled for Odsal on Tuesday 12 April. In front of the season's best crowd, more than double the average, Northern secured a crucial 10-6 victory. Three days later, Northern travelled to Central Park, but could not repeat the feat, losing 41-14.

The following Tuesday, St Helens provided the opposition at Odsal for the penultimate league fixture. Northern won to take the chase for the title to the final weekend. An incredibly competitive season hung on the outcome of three matches. For Peter what happened next was wrong: "Instead of all three matches being played on the same day at the same time, it was agreed to suit television that the matches would be spread over three days. The schedulers decided that Warrington would meet Sheffield Eagles on Friday evening, our match against Leeds was controversially rescheduled from Sunday to the evening of Saturday 23 April, while Wigan would meet Oldham on Sunday."

After an early scare Warrington won to increase the pressure on Northern. Before Bradford's match even kicked off there was further controversy when Leeds, preparing for Wembley in a week's time, announced a weakened side; an act for which they were later fined. A Leeds team containing half-a-dozen teenagers was no match for the visiting side who ran in nine tries – three from Paul Newlove – and Deryck Fox kicked eight goals to win 52-10.

Northern's slim hopes of glory rested on the outcome of Sunday's match. But Wigan never faltered, thrashing Oldham at the Watersheddings. The top three clubs, Bradford Northern, Warrington and Wigan had all won so each had ended up with 23 victories and 46 points. Points difference was all that separated the three clubs and Wigan's was vastly superior to the other two. Northern had to settle for the runners-up position.

In the Premiership first round Northern ran in seven tries – three from Paul Newlove – and Deryck Fox kicked seven goals to demolish a dispirited Leeds, losers at Wembley, 42-16. The semi-final was a repeat of the Regal Trophy match and for a while Northern looked Old Trafford-bound. However, having established a 10 point lead, Northern promptly allowed Castleford back into the game. The Tigers grabbed their opportunity and went away from a dismal, damp Odsal with the spoils, 24-16.

Northern's fortunes under Peter's leadership had shown an amazing turnaround. As Peter proudly pointed out: "In 1991-92 I had been instrumental in saving the club from relegation. The following season I took Northern to third place in the league and now we have gone one better – runners up, only on points difference."

Considering how successful the season had been, the relationship between Peter and the board was not as good as it might have been. Peter had for a few years been involved in after-dinner speaking and found his services were wanted at quite a number of sportsmen's dinners in the north of England. Unexpectedly this caused a problem with Northern's directors once he became a full-time coach, as Peter recalls. "One Friday evening I left an 'A' team match at half-time to attend a function. The directors objected to this and forbade me to honour a future booking for a function in Bradford even though it was being sponsored by one of Northern's vice-presidents. I appealed to Chris Caisley, who gave his permission after it was pointed out that it was John Hamer's benefit dinner. At this time the directors were insistent that I should attend all 'A' team matches and submit a written report on the matches and the performance of all the players. And all that despite having two coaches – Nigel Stephenson and Neil Holding – who were equally qualified to write the reports. It was though by making me full-time they were going to insist that all my time must be spent at Odsal." It quickly became clear to Peter that he would probably have been better been off not retiring from IMI, where he had been very happy in his job as safety and training officer.

1994-95

In May the French international centre, David Fraisse, was recruited from Sheffield Eagles. During his first season in England, Fraisse had looked a stylish attacking centre and there were high hopes of his partnership with Paul Newlove. Unfortunately those hopes would never be fully realised.

Chris Caisley, Northern's chairman, went to Australia for two weeks in June knowing clearly what Peter wanted: "I wanted two players: Paul Sironen and Paul Harrogan. They were the sort of big, fast forwards who could drive the ball in and were essential to make ground around the play-the-ball under the 10 metre rule. Caisley failed to deliver either of them, but managed to sign Robbie Paul, a 17-year-old half-back on a recommendation from the former Kiwi coach Graham Lowe, and Eugene Bourneville, a second-row forward. Neither player fitted the bill for the season ahead, although Robbie was clearly one for the future."

In July, Jason Donohue, a Great Britain under-21 scrum-half from Leigh, and David Myers, formerly with Widnes, joined Northern. Huddersfield's new coach, George Fairbairn, showed an interest in some of Northern's squad – eventually signing Brimah Kebbie for £16,000 in July, Darrall Shelford the following month and finally the veteran Mick Taylor at the start of September. Although now a veteran, Keith Mumby was still in demand and moved on to Ryedale-York.

Another great servant, Brian Noble, was allowed to leave to assist David Hobbs at Wakefield. Shortly after Noble's move Trevor Clark was injured and Peter found himself short of experienced hookers. As Peter recalls: "This was no longer a problem in the scrums for they were effectively uncontested. Where it was a problem was around the play-the-ball where the hooker's job as acting half-back had become crucial under the 10 metre rule." Over the next few months Peter would have to experiment with Phil Hepworth and Phil Russell in that position.

Deryck Fox retained the captaincy and under his leadership Northern had a wonderful start to the season. Beginning in Sheffield on the opening Sunday, 23 August, Northern won their first eight league matches – beating Sheffield Eagles, Oldham, Wakefield Trinity, Warrington, Widnes, Featherstone Rovers, Workington Town and Hull.

The last of those matches at the Boulevard, on 2 October, turned into a memorable occasion. As Peter explains "I'd always had a good relationship with the fans and the clubs over on Humberside and on that Sunday the Hull club chose to present me with a plaque in recognition of my 40 years' service to the game. It was a great moment made even better when we went home with a 12-6 victory under our belts."

All good things must come to an end and they did at Wilderspool on the first Friday in October, Warrington winning comfortably 25-2. Two more defeats at the hands of St Helens and Castleford threatened to undermine the earlier good work. Changes were made and Northern got back to winning ways, completing the double over Sheffield Eagles at Odsal at the start of November. By then Peter's contract had been extended by three years.

Having been left off the tourists' itinerary in 1990, Northern welcomed the Kangaroos back to Odsal on Sunday 13 November. With the third test only a week away the Kangaroos showed Northern plenty of respect by fielding 12 of their likely test squad. Although Northern lay second in the table, any hopes of a close match were scuppered when the home side was forced by injury to field a weakened side. Northern conceded eight tries in a 40-0 defeat. The result only confirmed Peter's view that "under international rules, which allowed for four substitutes to be used without restriction, a match against a touring side was too great a challenge for most clubs. I firmly believed then - and still do - that matches against counties were the way for future tours to go."

A number of changes had to be made to the team in November. The first was the result of a typically astute piece of business. Peter allowed Steve McGowan and Daio Powell to move on to Wakefield Trinity in exchange for their Great Britain under-21 centre or full back Gary Christie. Three days after signing Christie contributed two tries in a 34-0 demolition of his old club at Odsal. At the end of the month Karl Fairbank was ruled out of action for three months with a detached retina. His injury provided Brian McDermott with his chance in the first team.

Oldham denied Northern a double before the win against Wakefield. Then Northern welcomed French visitors, St Esteve from Perpignan, to Odsal for the second round of the Regal Trophy on Thursday 7 December. Even though Peter took the opportunity to rest a number of first-teamers the French proved no match for the home team and Northern ran in seven tries in a comfortable victory. A league double over Widnes set up the third round Regal Trophy tie at Whitehaven. Northern led 26-0 at the break and coasted through the second half to win comfortably 34-14.

A very cold Boxing Day saw the regular clash with Halifax at Thrum Hall, which ended with honours even 16-16. Victory over Salford at Odsal on New Years Day started 1995 on a high note.

With the festive period out of the way, the Regal Trophy restarted on 8 January. Northern travelled to Widnes as clear favourites to beat a club in turmoil off the field and without a league win in three months. But that counted for nothing on the day as Widnes rose to the occasion. They raced into a 20-0 lead in as many minutes and although Northern managed to staunch the flow of points the gap could not be closed. And they went out of the competition, losing 23-10.

Needing more cover for the pack, an experienced second-row, Paul Round, was signed from Halifax at the start of January. Sadly he suffered a broken jaw in a reserve match, which limited his contribution to just two substitute appearances in the first team. An easy midweek league victory over Doncaster obscured the problems to come. It was clear that the pack was not as strong as in previous years.

In mid-January a David Myers hat-trick plus tries from Dixon and Watson were not enough to beat Leeds's eight tries in a 36-18 defeat. A far better defensive performance allowed Northern to threaten Wigan but, thanks to a controversial try, the match ended in a 14-10 defeat. That was followed by a further defeat against Workington.

Paul Newlove returned from England duty in Cardiff nursing a broken jaw and was forced to sit out the Challenge Cup fourth round clash at Headingley on 12 February. That match marked the start of a very painful period for Northern. Just when it appeared that they had gained the upper hand in a very physical game a late home try reduced the visitors' lead to 12-8 at the interval. Another home try immediately after the break levelled the scores. Northern's discipline faltered and Leeds grabbed the opportunity to win the match 31-14.

For Peter the stress of that match continued long after the hooter had sounded. As he explains: "Dave Watson's name had been drawn out to be tested for drugs and he was required to provide a urine sample after the match. The sampling officers on this occasion were in the dressing rooms before the players had returned from the pitch and were in the process of being escorted out by Jon Hamer when I entered. Having no identification and being unwilling to give their names the officers were asked to wait until I had addressed the players. When I had finished Watson provided a sample and everyone thought that was that."

A couple of days later David Myers, who had twice been sin-binned during the match, was cited for deliberately colliding with referee John Connolly. To make matters worse the sampling officers announced that there had been a problem with Dave Watson's test. They also accused Peter of obstructing and abusing them.

At the end of the home match against Featherstone Rovers on the evening of Wednesday 15 February, Peter was verbally abused by two or three away supporters as he was leaving the dugout. Annoyed by the language and frustrated by his side's 24-16 defeat Peter did what show-jumper Harvey Smith had famously once done to his sport's officials and waved a 'V' sign at those berating him, which got him into trouble with the club's directors.

The following weekend Hull came to Odsal and lost. The sampling officers were once again waiting after the match. This time they wanted to repeat the test on Dave Watson and in addition carry out a test on whichever other player was drawn. This time David Myers' name came out of the hat. Neither player provided a urine sample, claiming that there were misunderstandings over timings.

When the RFL's Disciplinary Committee met a couple of weeks later Myers was fined £250 and banned until the end of the season for colliding with Connolly. Further hearings were arranged in mid-March at which first Myers and then Watson were fined £2,000 and suspended for four months for refusing to provide samples. Threats of charges against Peter for allegedly obstructing the sampling officers were not pursued after it was shown by Arnie Horsfall, our assistant physio, and other members of the backroom staff that the accusations were completely false. To make matters worse Watson failed to turn up for a meeting with the Northern board and as a result was transfer listed at £150,000. Against Peter's advice Northern's board subsequently cancelled the contracts of both Myers and Watson.

Meanwhile Northern's directors had summoned Peter to a board meeting and asked him to bring a solicitor to discuss his gesture to the Featherstone Rovers' fans. The directors showed Peter letters of complaint from several supporters who thought that the gesture had been directed at them. On the advice of his solicitor and with the agreement of the directors Peter issued a public apology and in his defence stated: "I have never knowingly in my 40 years' service to our game ever been guilty of bringing the game into disrepute. I may have caused a shadow to be cast on my own reputation with the gesture. I have made a public apology which my board of directors have accepted. I sincerely hope I can put the sad episode behind me." In addition Peter was fined £500 by the directors, half that amount suspended for 12 months, for his actions.

After the meeting Peter received a telephone call from a lady supporter, telling him that she had written to the Directors to complain about the nasty abuse he had suffered from a section of the club's own supporters and how disappointed she was by the action that had been taken against him. The call stirred Peter in action: "I went to see our secretary Gary Tasker to ask him if he had received this letter. Gary admitted that he had and showed me the letter in question and two others also in my favour. He asked me not to tell the board as it would probably put him in an awkward position. I had no intention of compromising him, but the board's action in not telling me about these letters soured my relationship with them for the next few months."

Purely by chance, while the controversy raged, Northern had no matches. When the team finally got back onto the field after a three week break it was to visit St Helens. The lack of matches showed as Northern struggled and lost 36-27. March ended with a visit from Leeds that brought another defeat.

A meeting with Doncaster on 2 April provided Northern with a chance to get the season back on track. Paul Newlove proved he had recovered from a broken jaw by running in a hat-trick in a 13-try 74-18 demolition. That morale boost only lasted one week. Northern travelled to Central Park where a Gary Christie hat-trick could not turn the tide for the visitors in a heavy defeat to Wigan.

Easter brought fresh hope with victories, at home over Halifax on Good Friday and at Salford on Easter Monday. In the final league match Northern, secure in the top eight, conceded eight tries in a defeat at Castleford. Northern finished seventh in division one. It had been a difficult season that had failed to live up to its early success with the result that the average crowd had fallen by more than 1,000.

Seventh place meant that Northern had to travel to Headingley for the first round of the Premiership on 5 May. On a sunny Friday evening Northern matched the home side and approached the hour mark on level pegging at 26-26. Unfortunately Northern gave away an interception try after which Leeds pulled away to get the best of a 14-try festival by nine tries to five, 50-30. Peter didn't realise it at the time, but that match would be the last of his long and illustrious coaching career.

Ever since the publication by the RFL in August of a major discussion document, *Framing the Future*, which outlined what the RFL and rugby league hoped to achieve in the medium term, the season had been alive with discussions about the game's prospects. Keying into those discussions Chris Caisley and Gary Tasker, Bradford's company secretary, had launched a five-year marketing led plan that floated the idea of changing the club's name at the start of April. Those discussions rapidly turned acrimonious after a meeting of club chairmen, held on Saturday 8 April 1995, agreed to the formation of an elite Super League financed by Rupert Murdoch's Newscorp. One of the central tenets of that new competition was that the season would move to summer, starting in 1996.

Fortunately for a debt-strapped Bradford Northern the club was guaranteed a place in Super League but, for a while in the middle of April, the club explored the possibility of merging with Halifax. This made many people nervous, not least the coaches as one of them, either Peter or Halifax's Steve Simms, would be out of a job. Following much disquiet over this and other club merger proposals the plans were scrapped and a new version adopted by club chairmen on 30 April. That plan guaranteed a place in Super League for the top 10 finishers in the First Division. Even under the revised plan Bradford Northern had a place in Super League.

Faced with the uncertainty, Peter made sure the supporters knew what was happening: "I have had to place on the back burner for the past two months progress to sign three, or maybe four quality players shortly out of contract wanting to join me at the club because the business finance won't allow me to move." There were also some problems with Northern's existing squad as they faced up to the last, truncated, winter season. Under pressure from Caisley, if he wanted to claim his Super League loyalty bonus, Northern's star player, Paul Newlove, was convinced to extend his contract. A couple of weeks later Peter found himself in difficulty. Some cynics suggested that Peter's contract had only been maintained until Newlove had signed.

As a result of Murdoch's financial involvement in the game mergers were also being considered in Sydney. A possible merger between St George and Sidney City Roosters meant that the former's head coach, Brian Smith, was more than happy to have a meeting with Chris Caisley while he was in town in May. News of what Caisley was up to was relayed back to Peter by Mike Ford, the former Castleford scrum-half then playing for South Queensland Crushers. According to the press Smith initially turned down the Northern job, but then reconsidered.

Having secured Smith's services Caisley returned to Bradford and arranged a meeting with Peter. The major problem was Peter's contract still had more than two years to run. Buying out that contract as cheaply as possible was Caisley's main aim when he arrived at the meeting. It was an awkward meeting during which Peter recalls that Caisley never once looked up from the table. Knowing what had happened behind his back and knowing what he had achieved for Bradford Peter told Caisley: "All you had to do was tell me what you wanted and I'll leave whenever you want." The negotiations did not take long.

A deal was struck that provided Peter with a reduced salary for the next couple of years provided he did not take another coaching job. The announcement said the club had felt it was time for a change and the termination of Peter's contract had been by mutual consent. Peter now says that "It was a great disappointment to me to be dismissed after what I had achieved for Bradford Northern."

While declining to discuss his departure Peter told reporters that he felt his "future still lay in the game. I am certainly available. Rugby league is all I know and I have thoroughly enjoyed most of my time in the game."

Brian Smith's appointment as coach was announced in early June 1995, although he would not be free of his contractual obligations to St George for another five months. The club he would be joining would also be different following the announcement that same month of the end of Bradford Northern and the birth of Bradford Bulls.

Left: Deryck Fox playing for
Featherstone Rovers, with Graham
Steadman in the background.
(Courtesy Robert Gate)

Below, right: Graham Idle.
(Courtesy Robert Gate)

Below left: Paul Newlove, who started
his career with Peter at Featherstone,
and went on to play for Great Britain.
(Photo: David Williams, rlphotos.com)

144

19. Impact Sports

Peter was caught in a trap: "The clause in my contract stipulated that if I considered another job my compensation, which was only a fraction of my salary, would be forfeited. Effectively that provision inserted by Caisley and his board prevented me from coaching in Super League." Only offers that would have provided a full-time job to replace the loss of his income from Bradford would have been worthwhile. As none were forthcoming Peter's coaching career was effectively over.

Almost immediately after Peter was dismissed, rugby union decided to go open and allow players to play professionally. Peter was approached by two of Wakefield Rugby Union club's more prominent players – Brian Barley and Martin Shuttleworth – with a proposal to form an agency, representing players in both rugby codes. Agreement was reached and the Impact Sports Consulting Group was born. With Peter as its head agent the new group received approval from the RFL.

One of the repercussions for Northern of Peter's dismissal was that Paul Newlove demanded a transfer. When the subsequent arrival of Matthew Elliott and later Brian Smith did nothing to convince Paul Newlove to stay, a transfer was inevitable. Peter, acting as Paul's agent, contacted St Helens coach Eric Hughes to let him know that Paul was going to become available. As a result St Helens made an approach that finally led to Newlove joining them at the end of November 1995 for £250,000 plus three players. Peter also assisted Paul Newlove in his attempts to get the loyalty bonus he rightly believed he was owed from Super League.

Those deals meant that Impact Sports became noticed and provided some much-needed early income. Other deals soon followed. Brian Barley left after a couple of years to concentrate on his career in insurance leaving the business in the hands of Martin and Peter. It was a total change for Peter who "enjoyed dealing with the players and advising them on their careers. But I did not enjoy the money-haggling side of the job." It was ironic that "as a coach I never was involved with agents, always insisting that I dealt directly with the players."

Radio 5Live

Peter restarted his broadcasting career while still working as a club coach. He worked initially as a summariser and commentator with Harry Gration. Commentator Dave Woods was also starting out on radio and after he moved to Radio 5Live in 1994 he started to work with Peter when Harry Gration left to join the RFL. The two began to work together and quite quickly became a regular partnership.

After leaving Bradford Northern in 1995 Peter was part of the Radio 5Live team that covered the Rugby League World Cup. The BBC's Head of Sport, Bob Shennan, wrote to Peter afterwards complimenting him on his commentaries and describing Peter and Dave Woods as a formidable team. It was enjoyable work that took Peter all over the country and to France.

However, Peter was surprised in January 1999 to receive a letter from the BBC informing him that due to the corporation scaling down its rugby league commentary teams his services were no longer required. Dave Woods was angry about the decision, but it could not be changed. After 10 years it was the end of Peter's radio career.

Dave Woods enjoyed working with Peter: "After Harry Gration left Radio 5Live I took over his job as rugby league commentator and teamed up with Peter, his old partner. We'd met before when I was working for Radio Leeds and he was coach at Bradford. Working together proved easy – we got on well and he was a great co-commentator. He had some great insights on the game and the listeners liked his passion and commitment.

"We travelled a lot together and he was a great companion. We covered Super League's opening match in Paris and went back there a number of times. We also covered quite a number of matches in London. He used to keep me enthralled on journeys with tales of players he'd known, things he'd done and people he'd met.

"I remember particularly one match day at Charlety where there was a long line of steps leading up to the commentary position. On that day it was decided that there'd be a race between the commentary team and the touchline team. I was the commentary team's representative up against David Oates for the touchline team. John Kear, who was the other member of the touchline team, gave some words of advice to Oatesy. Peter was my coach and he made sure I was prepared. It might only have been for fun, but Peter employed all his powers of motivation to make sure I was going to get to the top of those steps before anyone else. [Peter recalls that a small bet was involved!]

"When I heard that the BBC intended to dispense with his services by letter I couldn't believe it. After all the years he'd worked for them, it seemed so wrong. As no one else was going to do it I went over to his house to tell him before the letter arrived."

Wakefield Trinity Wildcats

Unexpectedly Peter received an approach from Ted Richardson, the majority shareholder at Wakefield Trinity Wildcats. This was a time of acute financial crisis and boardroom turmoil at Belle Vue, with the debt ridden club running under the protection of a creditors' voluntary agreement. As a result a number of leading players had left the club.

Richardson was trying to put together a new board of directors and bring new money into the club. Peter agreed to invest in the club and take on the job of director of football in late 2001. Taking on that role meant that Peter had to give up his agency work and he sold his interests in Impact Sports to Martin Shuttleworth.

Shortly after Peter took on the job, unpaid, the charismatic John Harbin resigned as coach. On Peter's recommendation, Featherstone Rovers' coach, Peter Roe, was brought in on 1 November as Harbin's successor on a 12-month contract. By the end of the month Roe had brought Shane McNally from Australia to work as his assistant.

New blood was a necessity. Over the close season a number of British signings were made, Paul Broadbent being the first at the start of November and he was followed by Ian Knott, who was formerly with Warrington, Kris Tassell of Salford and David Wrench, who had been released by Leeds. From contacts made on a trip to Australia Roe recruited two more players – Troy Slattery and Nathan Wood.

Right from the start the young Wildcats side were the pundits' favourite for relegation and they certainly struggled in Super League. In a bid to make the team more competitive two backs with Super League experience were signed at the start of April – Martin Moana from Doncaster Dragons and Phil Hassan, who was returning to league after a spell in rugby union.

Peter found his new job difficult: "From the start there was some tension between me and Peter Roe. He considered me to be out of touch with the modern game and didn't want me involved with the team's tactics or its members. I did however manage to get involved personally with some of the players."

The severe financial position continued to cause problems and the Wildcats' squad was further weakened when two of the best players – Nathan Wood and Ben Westwood – had to be transferred to Warrington in June.

Further problems came in the middle of July. Despite a spirited performance by the team against Bradford on 12 July, Peter Roe was told by the board in midweek that he would not be offered a new deal for the following season. Roe resigned immediately and his assistant, Shane McNally, took over the task of trying to lift Trinity off the bottom of Super League. Peter offered his resignation, but the chairman, Ted Richardson, refused to accept it.

There was further trouble when as a result of breaching the salary cap in 2000 the RFL deducted two league points from Wakefield. A tough few weeks were in prospect when Adrian Vowles was recruited from Leeds as a player and assistant coach. It was a risky move to try and partner a new player-coach with a stand-in coach, but surprisingly it worked. Between them McNally and Vowles managed to rally the side. The outcome was in the balance until the final Sunday, 22 September, when an easy home victory over Warrington, combined with Castleford's defeat of Salford, ensured Super League survival.

As the season drew to a close it was clear Peter was not enjoying his time at the Wildcats. Peter recalls: "In the close season of 2002 to 2003 the directors wanted to make Vowles player-coach over McNally. I advised them it would not be a good move, as Vowles was in the veteran stage of his career and it would devalue his services to the team. They agreed not to reverse McNally's position and it worked well for the team the following season. I resigned from my position which I felt was a figurehead. I was not convinced that was my position. Having no involvement with the players or team tactics did not enthral me, and it was those areas that had been my strength throughout my whole involvement in rugby league."

There was one major highlight of that time to look back on. It came right at the end of the season when Peter was awarded the Order of Merit at the Rugby League Writers Association dinner for his services to the game. There was something particularly apt that an organisation, some of whose members had maintained a love-hate relationship with Peter over the years, should recognise his contribution to the game.

Since retiring from rugby league, Peter's main leisure activity is golf, although he still does some after dinner speaking, and watches rugby league on television, occasionally going to matches at Featherstone or Wakefield. He is a member of the Batley Past Players' association, and enjoys their reunions. In 2007 he went to watch Batley play Doncaster when there was a Batley players' reunion, and had a good time meeting old team mates to talk about past times.

Three rugby league brothers

Peter, Neil and Don at Peter's Golden Wedding celebration in 2007.
(Photo: Peter Barnes)

20. Players, strategies and tactics

It was not easy for Peter to select his greatest team, as he explains: "In a career like mine that stretched over 50 years as a professional player, coach, agent and director of football it is difficult to choose 17 players. Playing styles have changed so much that what made one player great in one era would have been of limited use in another.

"When it came to the substitutes I wanted players who were the equal of those selected in the first XIII so that when they were put on the team would be just as strong. One player I was particularly sad to leave out was the loose-forward Harry Street. Still the 17 listed below are the ones I would choose."

Full-back: Keith Mumby - the best tackling full-back ever.
Winger: Billy Boston - never a better winger in any game.
Centre: Lewis Jones - skilful and could only be better playing alongside a powerful partner like my brother Neil.
Centre: Neil Fox - the world record points scorer – what more needs to be said.
Winger: Mick Sullivan- speedy, tough tackling and brave.
Stand-off: Alex Murphy - possesses all the qualities necessary and would be an ideal backup player.
Scrum-half: Don Fox - Don had all the attributes and instincts of a great scrum-half.
Prop: Jeff Grayshon - a great forward and a great pack leader.
Hooker: Tommy Harris - a great player in the loose in his day, who would have excelled in the modern game.
Prop: Brian Edgar - a big, strong, solid forward.
Second-row: Dick Huddart - such a big, strong fearless player would have been devastating in today's game.
Second-row: Derek Turner - a fearsome tackler who never took a backward step.
Loose-forward: Johnny Whiteley - a good handler of the ball with great speed who could make play.
Substitute: Paul Newlove - a great try scorer from anywhere on the field.
Substitute: Ellery Hanley - strong and quick, aggressive and powerful, and versatile enough to play anywhere on the field.
Substitute: Jimmy Thompson - strong, powerful and above all a great tackler.
Substitute: Steve Norton - very talented and a great playmaker.

As well as the team listed above, Peter added: "I would like to thank all the players who gave me great loyalty and the teams I have coached for the success they have brought. And also to a lot of committee and board members who have given me the opportunity to create successful teams. In particular I would like to thank John Jepson and his Featherstone Rovers' committee for giving me the opportunity to start my wonderful and exciting career as a coach in rugby league."

Over his many years in the game Peter kept notes. Sometimes the notes were the background to a game plan for a particular match. Sometimes ideas for a team talk. On other occasions they were general thoughts about the game and how it should be played. What follows is a selection of pieces from that notebook.

What makes a great team?

Position	Personal and physical qualities	Main Attributes
Full back	Must be fast and courageous	Tackling, speed, catching, positional sense
Winger	Fast, skilful and brave	Speed, catching, evasive qualities
Centre	Skilful, tough and speedy	Speed, handling, tackling, positional sense
Stand-off	Quick, skilful and tough	Speed, handling, tackling, kicking, evasive qualities
Scrum-half	Skilful, tough, courageous, a clear thinker with a good temperament	Guile, handling, kicking, tackling
Prop	Big, strong, mobile, aggressive N.B. aggressive not stupid	Physical strength, scrum technique, tackling
Hooker	Quick, tough, skilful with good hands	Scrum technique, handling, speed, tackling
Second-row	Big, strong, fast and fearless	Tackling, speed, strength, handling
Loose-forward	Tough and talented	Handling, speed, tackling
Captain	Must be a thinker and close enough to the action – always on top of his own job – and respected by his team mates.	

What does a team require?

Attributes	FB	RW	C	C	LW	SO	SH	PF	H	PF	SR	SR	LF	Tot	Rank
Speed	9	10	8	8	10	8	8	6	8	7	8	8	8	106	2
Strength	5	5	8	8	5	6	7	10	7	9	8	8	8	94	5
Tackling	10	7	9	9	7	7	8	9	9	9	10	10	9	113	1
Handling ability	8	7	8	8	7	9	10	6	8	6	7	7	9	100	3
Evasive qualities	7	9	8	8	9	9	8	5	7	6	7	7	7	97	4
Kicking ability	7	6	6	6	6	7	8	5	7	5	5	5	7	80	9
Positional sense	10	7	8	8	7	8	7	5	6	5	6	6	8	91	6
Guile and strategy	5	7	7	7	7	8	9	5	7	5	5	5	7	84	8
Special techniques	5	5	5	5	5	5	8	8	8	7	5	5	7	78	10
Temperament	5	5	5	5	5	7	9	9	10	7	7	7	8	89	7
Tot	71	68	72	72	68	74	82	68	77	66	68	68	78		
Rank	6	7	5	5	7	4	1	7	3	8	6	6	2		

From the above it can be seen that tackling is the most important attribute in any team and that scrum half is the most important position, which should be clear from every team that Peter built.

Some of the key points of Peter's approach to the game are outlined below:

Principles of success
- My knowledge of the game, the players in it and the way they play
- A belief in my tactics, methods and strategies

- I have always got players to play the way I want
- I must have players I can trust and rely upon in the critical positions and the responsible positions
- I always do what I believe is right for the benefit of the team regardless of individuals
- I trust my players and get them to trust in me

Discipline

Rugby league is a game of discipline and if we discipline ourselves off the field we train ourselves and particularly our minds to obey the rules and principles necessary to achieve the results we all want.

A well disciplined side can overcome a more talented outfit and a talented outfit, well disciplined, will win the most important matches in the highest class.

Discipline breeds respect, loyalty and gives everyone a feeling of pride because it is transmitted both ways. Rules are mutually agreed.

The Team manager is the figurehead of the whole party.
- It is his duty to see that everyone is given all the encouragement that it is possible to give to accomplish the success required – both personal and material requisites.
- He will be given the proper and correct respect of all his subordinates and it will be shown in public that he is the focal point, the judge of our actions and the guiding light of a group of dedicated athletes.
- We also hope that privately he will become one of us and a great friend.

The Coach is responsible for:
- the motivation of the team;
- the training and coaching and general fitness of players;
- improving the ability of each player as an individual and to improve collectively the ability and performance of the team;
- the discipline of the team during training and match day travelling.

He must build and maintain a happy team spirit, be fair and just, firm but sympathetic, tactful and watchful. He must teach the players to maintain a sense of the true values of the game. A coach must know his players and above all have an ambition to succeed, with the dedication necessary to achieve that success.

The Players must:
- train, keep fit and be prepared to play at short notice;
- uphold the laws of the game;
- obey the rules laid down;
- be prepared to change their own style to effect a result which benefits the whole team;
- conduct themselves in a manner which can only bring credit and prestige to both themselves and their clubs, at all times.

Specific policy of play
- Ball must always be kept moving in the easiest direction, in a controlled manner i.e. using the full width of the field and not turned back until all space is used up or the wingman has the ball. Reason: least covered ground by defence

- In attack and defence we always move forward again all across the field.
- Switching of play is the best method of creating space, but not by any static passing.
- The full-back linking as an attacking force is imperative, either by making the extra man or as a dummy runner.

It is my belief that tap penalties are the least appropriate time for moves because of the set defence. Consequently any fancy piece of play is a large risk

General policy of play
- Play in the opponents half
- Kickers are nominated and must position themselves
- Do not kick aimlessly
- Up and unders put to the goalposts
- Use grubber kicks close to the line not little kick overs
- Long passes are not just to miss out a man, but to give a distinct overlap
- Back passing must be limited – the turn pass is more effective and allows a dummy to be given
- Changes of direction must be on the move and supported
- Use double depth on attack not a flat line
- Direction of back-up play must be learned, the direction of running must be known

Sixth tackle strategy
- Up and under to posts
- Grubber – away from the full back, but not near defending wing
- Touch kick
- Drop goal
- Ball passed to wing. Wingers go for the corner or kick to posts and chase. If tackled the winger can be taken into touch
- It is imperative not to be tackled on the sixth tackle

Defence
- Long kick downfield
- Long touch finder
- Short touch finder
- Keep ball near to the touch-line particularly if near own try line
- If kicking is not possible try to run clear down the touch-line
- Push through and chase if full back has retreated, but watch for a man acting as sweeper
- It is critical that rules must be applied and followed most notably in the crucial areas
- The general application of rotation tackling is a must
- A sweeper is required in our own half
- Tackling going forward is a must

Appendix: Statistics and Records

Playing career for professional clubs:

	P	T	G	Pts
Featherstone Rovers:				
1953-54	8	0	1	2
1954-55	4	0	0	0
1955-56	18	1	14	31
1956-57	4	0	0	0
Total:	**34**	**1**	**15**	**33**
Batley:				
1957-57	27	3	6	21
1957-58	12	3	0	9
1958-59	3	0	0	0
1959-60	30	3	11	31
1960-61	31	2	26	58
1961-62	29	0	9	18
1962-63	16	1	18	39
Total:	**148**	**12**	**70**	**246**
Hull KR:				
1962-63	15	1	0	3
1963-64	13	2	1	8
Total:	**28**	**3**	**1**	**11**
Hunslet:				
1963-64	2	0	0	0
Batley:				
1964-65	28	1	32	67
1965-66	4	0	1	2
Total:	**32**	**1**	**33**	**69**
Wakefield Trinity:				
1966-67	1	0	0	0
Overall totals	**245**	**17**	**119**	**289**

Representative game:

1963-64: Hull XIII versus Australians

Coaching career: Representative teams

Great Britain
Great Britain 9 Australia 15 21 October 1978 at Central Park
Great Britain 18 Australia 14 5 November 1978 at Odsal
Great Britain 6 Australia 23 18 November 1978 at Headingley

England
England 2 Wales 6 29 January 1977 at Headingley
France 28 England 15 20 March 1977 at Carcassonne

Yorkshire
Yorkshire 26 Lancashire 10 11 September 1985 at Wigan
Yorkshire 18 New Zealand 8 23 October 1985 at Bradford
Yorkshire 26 Lancashire 14 17 September 1986 at Leeds
Yorkshire 16 Lancashire 10 16 September 1987 at Wigan
Yorkshire 28 Papua New Guinea 4 27 October 1987 at Leeds
Yorkshire 24 Lancashire 14 21 September 1988 at Leeds
Yorkshire 56 Lancashire 12 20 September 1989 at Wigan
Yorkshire 17 Lancashire 12 18 September 1991 at Leeds

N.B. For both Great Britain and England, the teams were chosen by a selection committee, not Peter Fox. For Yorkshire, Peter Fox as coach selected the team.

Professional clubs: Championship and trophies

Featherstone Rovers January 1971 to May 1974
1972-73: Challenge Cup winners, Runners up in Championship table
1973-74: Challenge Cup runners up
1973-74: Captain Morgan Trophy runners up

Wakefield Trinity: June 1974 to May 1976
1974-75: Challenge Cup semi-finalists, Yorkshire Cup runners up
1975-76: Premiership semi-finalists

Bramley: September 1976 to April 1977
1976-77: Promoted from Second Division (finished third)

Bradford Northern: April 1977 to May 1985
1977-78: First Division runners up, Premiership winners,
        Player's No.6 Trophy semi-finalists
1978-79: Yorkshire Cup winners, Premiership runners up, Challenge Cup semi-finalists
        John Player Trophy semi-finalists
1979-80: First Division Champions, John Player Trophy winners, Premiership runners up
1980-81: First Division Champions
1981-82: Yorkshire Cup runners up
1982-83: Yorkshire Cup runners up, Challenge Cup semi-finalists

Leeds: May 1985 to December 1986

1985-86: Challenge Cup semi-finalists, Premiership semi-finalists

Featherstone Rovers May 1987 to October 1991

1987-88: Second Division runners up, Second Division Premiership runners up
1988-89: Premiership semi-finalists
1989-90: Yorkshire Cup runners up
1990-91: Premiership semi-finalists

Bradford Northern: October 1991 to June 1995

1991-92: Challenge Cup semi-finalists
1992-93: Regal Trophy runners up, Challenge Cup semi-finalists
1993-94: Regal Trophy semi-finalists, Premiership semi-finalists

League results coaching professional clubs

	P	W	D	L	F	A	Pts	Place
Featherstone Rovers January 1971 to May 1974								
1970-71*	34	14	1	19	572	635	29	20 (One division)
1971-72	34	23	1	10	632	372	47	7 (One division)
1972-73	34	27	0	7	768	436	54	2 (One division)
1973-74	30	14	2	14	443	397	30	8 (First Division)
Wakefield Trinity: June 1974 to May 1976								
1974-75	30	12	5	13	440	419	29	10 (First Division)
1975-76	30	17	0	13	496	410	34	7 (First Division)
Bramley: September 1976 to April 1977								
1976-77	26	19	0	7	464	377	38	3 (Second Division)
Bradford Northern: April 1977 to May 1985								
1977-78	29	21	2	6	500	291	44	2 (First Division)
1978-79	30	16	0	14	523	416	32	8 (First Division)
1979-80	30	23	0	7	448	272	46	1 (First Division)
1980-81	30	20	1	9	447	345	41	1 (First Division)
1981-82	30	20	1	9	425	332	41	5 (First Division)
1982-83	30	14	2	14	381	314	30	9 (First Division)
1983-84	30	17	2	11	519	379	36	7 (First Division)
1984-85	30	16	1	13	600	500	33	8 (First Division)
Leeds: May 1985 to December 1986								
1985-86	30	15	3	12	554	518	33	6 (First Division)
1986-87**	30	13	0	17	554	679	26	12 (First Division)
Featherstone Rovers May 1987 to October 1991								
1987-88	28	23	1	4	712	353	44	2 (Second Division)
1988-89	26	13	1	12	482	545	27	6 (First Division)
1989-90	26	10	0	16	479	652	20	10 (First Division)

1990-91	26	12	1	13	533	592	25	8 (First Division)
1991-92#	26	11	0	15	449	570	22	13 (First Division)

Bradford Northern: October 1991 to June 1995

1991-92##	26	11	0	13	476	513	22	11 (First Division)
1992-93	26	15	0	11	553	434	30	3 (First Division)
1993-94	26	23	0	7	784	555	46	2 (First Division)
1994-95	30	17	1	12	811	650	35	7 (First Division)

* Peter was appointed in January 1971
** Peter was dismissed on 24 December 1986. Leeds had won 6 league games at that time.
\# Peter left the club on 12 October 1991. Featherstone had won 3 out of 5 league games at that time.
\#\# Peter was appointed in October 1991. Bradford had won 1 out 6 league games at that time.

Success rate for teams coached by Peter Fox:

League matches

For seasons when Peter was coaching a club for a complete season (including Bramley in 1976-77), his success rate was 62 per cent, with 795 points from a possible 1282. His teams played 641 games, winning 387, drawing 24 and losing 234, scoring 11,994 points and conceding 9,559.

On the same basis, Peter's teams finished in the top half of the table in 19 seasons out of 22. His teams finished in the top four places eight times. No team that he managed for a whole season was relegated.

League Championships and Cups:

First Division:
Champions: 2   Runners up: 2 (includes once when there was one division)

Challenge Cup:
Winners: 1   Runners up: 1   Semi-finalists: 6

Premiership:
Winners: 1   Runners up: 2   Semi-finalists: 5

Players No.6 / John Player Trophy / Regal Trophy:
Winners: 1   Runners up: 1   Semi-finalists: 3

Yorkshire Cup:
Winners: 1   Runners up: 4

Captain Morgan Trophy:
Runners up: 1

Second Division:
Runners up: 1   Promoted: 1

Division Two Premiership:
Runners up: 1

Awards

Man of Steel coach of the year
(Sponsored by Trumanns 1977 to 1983, Greenall Whitley 1984 to 1989 and then Stones Bitter)

Coach of the year 1980
Nominated: 1981, 1989, 1993.

Greenall Whitley – Sunday People Awards

November 1977: Man of the Month

Rugby League Writers' Association

Order of Merit 2002 for Services to Rugby League

Bibliography

	Leeds Rugby League Supporters Club Yearbook 1986-87
Ron Bailey	*Don Fox*
Ron Bailey	*Featherstone Rovers: 100 Greats*
Ron Bailey	*Featherstone Rovers: 50 of the Finest Matches*
Maurice Bamford	*Memoirs of a Blood and Thunder Coach*
Tim Butcher	*Rugby League 2001-2002*
Tim Butcher	*Rugby League 2002-2003*
Chris Carrington	*Bradford Northern RLFC: Rugby League Champions 1979-80*
Brian F. Cartwright	*A 'ton' full of memories*
Jonathan Davies	*Code Breaker*
Paul Fitzpatrick (ed)	*Rugby League Review 1982-83 to 1986*
Raymond Fletcher and David Howes	*The Shopacheck Rugby League Yearbook 1980-81*
Raymond Fletcher and David Howes	*Rothmans Rugby League Yearbook 1981-82 to 1995-96*
Robert Gate	*The Struggle for the Ashes*
Robert Gate	*Neil Fox: Rugby League's Greatest Points Scorer*
Roy Hinchcliffe	*Featherstone Rovers Yearbook 1988-89*
Roy Hinchcliffe	*Featherstone Rovers Yearbook 1989-90*
Phil Hodgson	*Odsal Odysseys: The History of Bradford Rugby League*
Terry Holmes	*My Life in Rugby*
Donald Hunt	*Rovers Reflections: Featherstone Rovers Past and Present*
Donald Hunt	*Rovers through the Eighties*
Donald Hunt	*Rovers through the 90s*
Graham Morris	*Grand Final: 100 Years of Rugby League Championship Finals*
Tony Pocock (ed)	*The Official Rugby League Yearbook 1988-89 to 1993-94*
Philip Rothery	*Bramley RLFC Handbook 1977-78*
Nigel Williams	*Bradford Northern: The History 1863-1989*
Colin Wilson	*Northern Review: The official souvenir book of the Bradford Northern 1993-94 season*
Jack Winstanley and Malcolm Ryding	*John Player Rugby League Yearbook 1973-74 to 1976-77*

Programmes

The War of the Roses 1985 to 1991

Magazines and Newspapers

Open Rugby
Rugby League World
Yorkshire Post
Batley News
Castleford & Pontefract Express
Hull Daily Mail

A Two Horse Town

50 years in broadcasting

Keith Macklin

The fascinating autobiography of one of the north's leading broadcasters in the post war period. Published in 2007, available post free for £14.00 (hardback) from London League Publications Ltd, PO Box 10441 London E14 8WR. Credit card orders via www.llpshop.co.uk or by phone: 0845-230-1895. The book can be ordered from any bookshop at £14.95.

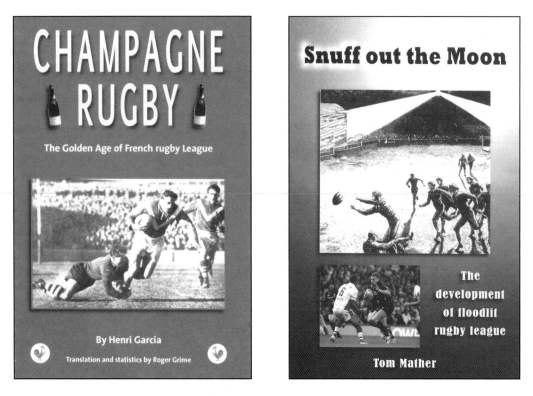

Champagne Rugby covers the 1950s was the Golden Age of French Rugby League. After being banned by the collaborative Vichy regime during the Second World War, the sport quickly rebuilt and in 1951 a French rugby league team toured Australia for the first time. Playing flowing, attacking rugby, they shocked the Australians with a decisive victory in the test series. Their famous full-back, Puig Aubert, broke the points scoring record for a tourist.

In 1955, France again defeated the Australians, and in 1960, with a squad hit by injuries, drew the test series. This book is the story of those famous tours and also gives a French viewpoint on the game's origins. First published in 1960, and produced here for the first time in English, it is a wonderful record of three great French teams. The author, Henri Garcia, was the rugby league correspondent of *L'Equipe*, and covered all three tours for that newspaper. All rugby league fans will enjoy this fascinating book.

Published at £12.95, available direct from London League Publications for £12.00.

Snuff out the Moon outlines the development of floodlit rugby league, from the early days of floodlit rugby in the 1870s to today.

This book, based on extensive original research, examines the developments in electricity that brought about those early matches and explains how they were organised. It then brings the story up to date and looks at the development of the use of floodlights in modern rugby league from the 1930s through the 1950s and the 1955 ITV Television Trophy to the use of floodlights today. The book also considers the relationship between rugby league and big business, and the issue of television coverage of the game.

Published at £11.95, available direct from London League Publications for £11.00.

Order from London League Publications Ltd, PO Box 10441, London E14 8WR;
credit card orders via our website: www.llpshop.co.uk or by phone on 0845-230-1895.
The books can be ordered from any bookshop at full price.